Lecture Notes in Computer Science 10582

Commenced Publication in 1973
Founding and Former Series Editors:
Gerhard Goos, Juris Hartmanis, and Jan van Leeuwen

More information about this series at http://www.springer.com/series/7409

Jian Chang · Jian Jun Zhang
Nadia Magnenat Thalmann · Shi-Min Hu
Ruofeng Tong · Wencheng Wang (Eds.)

Next Generation Computer Animation Techniques

Third International Workshop, AniNex 2017
Bournemouth, UK, June 22–23, 2017
Revised Selected Papers

 Springer

Editors
Jian Chang (iD)
Bournemouth University
Bournemouth
UK

Jian Jun Zhang (iD)
Bournemouth University
Bournemouth
UK

Nadia Magnenat Thalmann (iD)
University of Geneva
Geneva
Switzerland

and

Nanyang Technological University
Singapore
Singapore

Shi-Min Hu
Tsinghua University
Beijing
China

Ruofeng Tong
Zhejiang University
Hangzhou
China

Wencheng Wang
Institute of Software
Chinese Academy of Sciences
Beijing
China

ISSN 0302-9743   ISSN 1611-3349 (electronic)
Lecture Notes in Computer Science
ISBN 978-3-319-69486-3   ISBN 978-3-319-69487-0 (eBook)
https://doi.org/10.1007/978-3-319-69487-0

Library of Congress Control Number: 2017957544

LNCS Sublibrary: SL6 – Image Processing, Computer Vision, Pattern Recognition, and Graphics

Printed on acid-free paper

This Springer imprint is published by Springer Nature
The registered company is Springer International Publishing AG
The registered company address is: Gewerbestrasse 11, 6330 Cham, Switzerland

Preface

The Third AniNex workshop was held during June 22–23, 2017, at Bournemouth University, UK. The main theme is on the development and exploitation of next-generation computer animation and computer graphics techniques. The workshop is supported by the People Programme (Marie Curie Actions) of the European Union's Seventh Framework Programme FP7/2007-2013/ under REA grant agreement number 612627. The workshop was held jointly with the 11th International Conference on E-Learning and Games (Edutainment 2017).

The workshop has been devoted to "user-centered computer animation techniques for next-generation digital creation and modeling." It has reflected the current challenges in digital creation and modeling, with emphasis on two main cores: "dynamics and interaction of virtual objects" and "virtual character modeling and animation," where many novel methods and techniques have been developed, and other elements such as rendering and geometric modeling, virtual reality, and augmented reality applications are also incorporated. The focus on user-centered experience has distinguished this book from pure theoretical text books, providing case studies and practical reports on developing easy-to-use tools/algorithms in computer graphics. The use of image-based synthesis of geometry and graphical content, novel meshless simulation, machine-learning algorithms, and data-driven approaches is inevitable and has become an embedded part of the computer animation production pipelines.

The topics are structured according to four main themes:

- Simulation and Rendering for Computer Animation
- Character Modeling and Dynamics
- User-Centered Design and Modeling
- Computer Animation Systems and Virtual Reality Based Applications

We recognize the contribution and continuous support of the consortium of AniNex, the EU FP7-funded International Research Staff Exchange Scheme under REA grant agreement number 612627. The consortium includes Bournemouth University, University of Geneva, Tsinghua University, Zhejiang University, and the Institute of Software, Chinese Academy of Sciences. We deeply thank the International Program Committee for their tremendous support and all reviewers for their diligent work. We are grateful for Shujie Deng and other colleagues and students for their kind assistance and support during the workshop.

August 2017

Jian Chang
Jian Jun Zhang
Nadia Magnenat Thalmann
Shi-Min Hu
Ruofeng Tong
Wencheng Wang

Organization

Workshop Chair

Jian Chang   Bournemouth University, UK

Workshop Co-chairs

Nadia Magnenat   University of Geneva, Switzerland
  Thalmann   Nanyang Technological University, Singapore
Jian Jun Zhang   Bournemouth University, UK

Workshop Steering Committee

Shi-Min Hu   Tsinghua University, China
Ruofeng Tong   Zhejiang University, China
Wencheng Wang   Institute of Software, Chinese Academy of Sciences, China
Feng Tian   Bournemouth University, UK

Program Committee

Ehtzaz Chaudhry   Bournemouth University, UK
Hui Chen   Institute of Software, Chinese Academy of Sciences, China
Shihui Guo   Xiamen University, China
Sheng Li   Peking University, China
Jing Li   Institute of Software, Chinese Academy of Sciences, China
Youquan Liu   Changan University, China
Cuixia Ma   Institute of Software, Chinese Academy of Sciences, China
Junjun Pan   Beihang University, China
Sheng-Feng Qin   Northumbria University, UK
Bin Sheng   Shanghai Jiaotong University, China
Wen Tang   Bournemouth University, UK
Min Tang   Zhejiang University, China
Zhao Tang   Southwest Jiaotong University, China
Neil Vaughan   Bournemouth University, UK
Meili Wang   Northwest A&F University, China
Xiaosong Yang   Bournemouth University, UK
Lihua You   Bournemouth University, UK

Contents

Computer Animation Systems and Virtual Reality Based Applications

Simulation and Rendering for Computer Animation

Recent Progress of Computational Fluid Dynamics Modeling of Animal and Human Swimming for Computer Animation

Tom Matko[1(✉)], Jian Chang[2], and Zhidong Xiao[2]

[1] Centre for Digital Entertainment, Bournemouth University, Poole, UK
i7604556@bournemouth.ac.uk
[2] National Centre for Computer Animation, Bournemouth University, Poole, UK
{jchang,zxiao}@bournemouth.ac.uk

Abstract. A literature review is conducted on the Computational Fluid Dynamics (CFD) modeling of swimming. The scope is animated films and games, sports science, animal biological research, bio-inspired submersible vehicle design and robotic design. There are CFD swimming studies on animals (eel, clownfish, turtle, manta, frog, whale, dolphin, shark, trout, sunfish, boxfish, octopus, squid, jellyfish, lamprey) and humans (crawl, butterfly, backstroke, breaststroke, dolphin kick, glide). A benefit is the ability to visualize the physics-based effects of a swimmer's motion, using key-frame or motion capture animation. Physics-based animation can also be used as a training tool for sports scientists in swimming, water polo and diving. Surface swimming is complex and considers the water surface shape, splashes, bubbles, foam, bubble coalescence, vortex shedding, solid-fluid coupling and body deformation. Only the Navier-Stokes fluid flow equations can capture these features. Two-way solid-fluid coupling between the swimmer and the water is modeled to be able to propel the swimmer forwards in the water. Swimmers are often modeled using articulated rigid bodies, thus avoiding the complexity of deformable body modeling. There is interesting potential research, including the effects of hydrodynamic flow conditions on a swimmer, and the use of motion capture data. The predominant approach for swimming uses grid-based fluid methods for better accuracy. Emerging particle and hybrid-based fluid methods are being increasingly used in swimming for better 3D fluid visualization of the motion of the water surface, droplets, bubbles and foam.

Keywords: Computational Fluid Dynamics · Fluid simulation · Physics-based · Animation · Swimming · Animal · Human · Splashes · Bubbles · Solid-fluid coupling · Articulated rigid body · Particle-based fluid method · Hybrid-based fluid method

© Springer International Publishing AG 2017
J. Chang et al. (Eds.): AniNex 2017, LNCS 10582, pp. 3–17, 2017.
https://doi.org/10.1007/978-3-319-69487-0_1

1   Introduction

The focus of this review is the Computational Fluid Dynamics (CFD) modeling of animal and human swimming [1]. Computer animation research has created many virtual creatures from the natural history of animals (mammals, fish, invertebrates, amphibians and birds) and humans. A fish interacts with water with almost neutral buoyancy, and experiences hydrodynamic forces on its body [2]. In competitive swimming there is a need to understand the hydrodynamic forces on the swimmer [3]. Hydrodynamic modeling has traditionally been carried out by engineers using CFD.

Fluid force methods have traditionally been easier to use for animators than physics-based fluid simulation [2–7]. However, a more precise method requires the use of the full Navier-Stokes (NS) equations of fluid flow [1]. The NS equations can predict vortex shedding, waves, splashes and bubbles [1, 8]. Animal swimming motion differs significantly between an ideal fluid and the NS equations [9].

There are different modeling approaches for solid-fluid coupling between the swimmer and water. One method is to have the swimmer one-way coupled to the fluid, and only the swimmer influences the hydrodynamics. Another method is to only have the water influence the swimmers motion. The correct solution however is two way solid-fluid coupling, that enables forward propulsion of the swimmer [1, 9].

CFD is well established in engineering, but less commonly used for swimming. Swimming is complex as there is a deforming moving object that is two-way coupled to the fluid [10, 11]. Swimmers are therefore often modeled using articulated rigid bodies to avoid deformable body modeling [9]. A benefit of the CFD modeling of swimming is non-interference of the physical flow field [11, 12]. It is an ideal method to improve the performance of competitive human swimming [13]. Experimental validation is not included in this review, because fluid simulation for computer animation is often primarily used for visual effectiveness and computational economy.

2   Applications

A number of applications benefit from the bio-inspired fluid simulation of animal swimming: film animation, computer games, animal biology, submersible vehicle design and robotics [9]. There are computer animation studies for bio-inspired animal swimming and for human swimming. The applications for human swimming are sports science and animated films and games. Table 1 gives a summary of the research studies on swimming fluid simulation.

It is a benefit to animators, if kinematic animation or motion capture data of a human or animal swimmer can be used in a fluid simulation [15]. Biological studies focus on a single animal species and use computationally expensive CFD models for better accuracy [24]. Biological CFD studies are often validated by laboratory data.

Biomimetics is a rapidly growing field that incorporates features found in nature into engineering design [41, 47]. Marine vehicle design is able to reduce drag by studying the streamlined shapes of marine mammals [39]. Cetacean flippers (whales, dolphins and porpoises) have a similar shape to engineering hydrofoils [38]. The octopus inspires the design of underwater robots, used in search-and-rescue operations, undersea ship-wrecks and marine exploration [46]. Propulsion technology in submersible vehicles benefits from jellyfish swimming [14, 45]. Squid inspire the shape of modern submarines and ships [43]. The box fish inspires car design [24]. Fluid simulation can also be used for animal conservation (e.g. turtle, [22]).

Table 1. Swimming fluid simulation studies

Animation	Biology	Sport	Engineering
Animals	[9] (eel, fish, turtle)	**Free stroke**	**Submersibles**
[9] (eel, fish, turtle, ray, frog)	[21] (frog)	[10, 26]	[9] (eel, fish, turtle)
[1] (squid)	[11] (dolphin, shark)	(dolphin-kick)	[38] (whale, dolphin)
[14] (jellyfish)	[22] (turtle)	[12, 13, 27]	[39] (dolphin)
Humans	[23] (sunfish)	(dolphin-kick)	[40] (trout)
[8] (crawl, butterfly, dolphin-kick)	[24] (boxfish)	[28] (crawl)	[23] (sunfish)
[15] (crawl, backstroke, breaststroke, butterfly)	[14] (jellyfish)	[29] (dolphin-kick)	[41] (sunfish)
[16] (dolphin-kick)	[25] (lamprey)	**Prone glide**	[42] (sunfish)
[17] (crawl)		[18–20]	[24] (boxfish)
[18] (glide)		[30–37]	[43] (squid)
[19] (glide)			[14] (jellyfish)
[20] (glide)			[44] (jellyfish)
			[45] (jellyfish)
			[46] (octopus)
			[47] (anguilliform)
			Robotics
			[21] (frog)
			[48] (jellyfish)
			[8] (human)

Hydrodynamics is even more complex around a flexible and articulated body of a human swimmer [28] than for a rigid ship hull. A swimmer's speed depends on drag and propulsion [12]. Sports scientists aim to (i) maximize propulsion by moving arms and legs during free swimming, (ii) minimize hydrodynamic drag by gliding [16, 31]. Many human motions can be studied such as swimming, water polo and diving [8].

3 Swimming Hydrodynamics

In a human swimming race there are submerged strokes: 'glide' and 'dolphin kick', and free swimming strokes: 'crawl', 'breaststroke', 'backstroke' and 'butterfly' [17]. CFD studies of human surface swimming [8, 15, 17–20] are more prevalent than animal surface swimming for computer animation. A human surface swimmer interacts with the air-water surface forming droplets from splashes, bubbles by air-entrainment, and foam by rising bubbles interfering with the water surface [17]. Bubble coalescence occurs when bubbles make contact with each other and grow bigger. Bubbles rise to the surface (density of air is lower than water), with an increasing bubble size (effect of water depth on hydrostatic water pressure).

Underwater motion control in calm water during swimming is straightforward, since buoyancy approximately cancels out gravity. However, during large flow currents a swimmer can become unbalanced [8]. A trout in a natural flowing river is modeled for both submerged and surface swimming [40]. Boxfish vary in shape from triangular to square, and maintain straight swimming trajectories even when the flow direction changes [24]. A flow current can alter the flow field and swimming vortex structure, which rotates a swimming jellyfish [49].

4   Swimming Biomechanics

4.1   Animals

There is an amazing variety of locomotion in animal swimming (Fig. 1, [9]), that includes thrust from a tail, moving an elongated body by a sinusoidal waveform, paddle-like motions of flippers, kicking with legs, bird-like flapping of fins, in a CFD study of articulated rigid bodies [9]. A manta ray swims by the slow flapping strokes of its wing-like fins. Sea turtles are underwater flyers, moving themselves forwards with a flapping of their two front flippers. Their smaller rear flippers act mostly for balance [9]. Frogs are self propelled by the classic frog kick on the water [21].

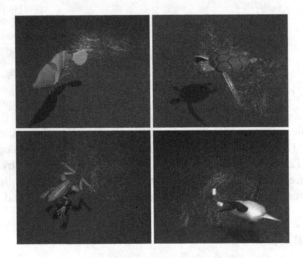

Fig. 1.   Flow streamlines of animal swimmers by a grid-based fluid method [9]

Cetacean flippers stabilize the body and create different motions. Their shape varies from the long, tapering tip of the humpback whale to the short, rounded flipper of the killer whale [38]. A thick layer of skin streamlines a dolphin's body [39]. Dolphins are high speed swimmers, with low drag and high propulsion partly due to their shape [11]. Some shark species have less buoyancy than their weight, so must keep moving to maintain depth [13]. Boxfish can turn 180 degrees instantly using their caudal fin as a rudder [24]. The sunfish steers itself using its pectoral fins [41]. The jet system of the squid provides propulsion for high speed forward motion [43].

Jellyfish motion is not fully understood (Fig. 2 [14, 50]). Its bell motion produces pulsing jets that provide propulsion [45]. Jellyfish have passive tentacles that create a drag force [50]. Fluid simulation of soft-bodied jellyfish with tentacles is complex due to the interaction of elastic bodies and water [48].

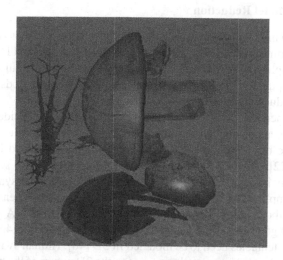

Fig. 2. Jellyfish swimming hydrodynamics by a particle-based fluid method [14]

Octopus open and close their arms to produce jet propulsion [46]. Anguilliform type swimmers propel themselves forwards by producing propagating waves. This behavior is widespread among species ranging from nematodes to eels [51]. An elongated ribbon-like fin creates a sinusoidal waveform for propulsion in electric and knife fish [52]. Electric fish are able to swim just as easily backwards as forwards, and rapidly switch direction.

4.2 Humans

Optimal swimming for animals and humans are a trade-off between minimal drag, maximum propulsion and minimal physical exertion. In human races, the underwater phases of dives and turns generate higher swimming speeds. Submerged gliding has a lower drag force, as the contribution from wave drag is negligible at sufficient depth. This is why the submerged dolphin-kick stroke is typically used after starts and turns in races. The human body assumes a streamlined pose, with the arms outstretched beyond the top of the head [27] and the legs kicking in unison [12]. Surface waves, splashes and bubbles do not have an impact on this submerged stroke [10]. The human dolphin-kick is bio-inspired by cetacean motion [12, 53]. Human swimmers therefore try to adopt similar behavior to fish in order to maximize speed [29].

Underwater swimming forms a significant time proportion in races [31]. The prone glide position is the most basic stroke [18], and when near the surface causes waves resulting in the wave drag effect [19]. During breaststroke, the swimmer gets a sharp push forwards when the arms are moved back, and then slows down a little due to drag when the arms are moved forward [15]. Drafting in triathlon races (when a swimmer is immediately behind another) is done to enable force transference [32].

5   Computational Fluid Dynamics Modeling

5.1   Geometry Model Reduction

Surface swimming modeling must consider the water surface, splashes and bubbles. The swimmer is a deforming surface that is two-way coupled to the fluid [11]. For grid-based fluid methods, simplifying the swimmer's geometry can reduce the number of cells and speed up the computation. Similarly for particle-based fluid methods the number of particles can be reduced to speed up the computation.

When a swimmer's shape is symmetric its gait may also be considered symmetric. A symmetry plane can be applied to some animal shapes (frog, turtle, manta ray, [9]). A symmetry plane bisecting a turtle improves computational speed by reducing the number of cells [22]. The wake behind a 3D swimming eel has two separate vortices, while a 2D eel only has one vortex [9]. If a 3D geometry has radial symmetry like in a squid, it can be simplified to a 2D axi-symmetric geometry [43]. When only the fish fin is in motion then body deformation can be ignored [23, 41, 42]. A jellyfish can be simplified to a 2D geometry if the geometry has radial symmetry [14, 44, 45, 50, 54]. However, jellyfish tentacles need to be modeled in 3D [48]. Human swimmers can only be modeled in 2D when limbs are stationary due to the 3D nature of the human body [31, 32, 37]. With human 2D simulation there are major differences to 3D results [31]. 3D computer aided design (CAD) geometry models can be produced by the laser scanning of real animal specimens ([39]: dolphin; [24]: boxfish; [43]: squid) and real human swimmers [10, 12, 13, 19, 20, 26, 27, 29, 30, 34].

5.2   Fluid Discretization Methods

Fluid methods used to discretize the flow domain can be divided into traditional engineering grid-based methods for better accuracy, or emerging particle and hybrid-based methods for better 3D visualization and computational efficiency. The grid-based fluid methods use a stationary grid, except for the geometry of moving objects (the swimmer). The Lagrangian particle-based fluid methods are mainly derivatives of the Smooth Particle Hydrodynamics method (SPH) by Monaghan [55, 56]. The Lagrangian method tracks flow as it moves through the domain, and discretizes the fluid (only where it is located) using particles. For swimming the approach is still predominantly to use grid-based methods for better accuracy. No CFD study has made a comparison between grid-based and particle-based methods for swimming.

For animal swimming grid-based fluid methods predominate [1, 9, 21–25, 38, 39, 41–52, 54, 58]. For human swimming, grid-based fluid methods also predominate [8, 10, 15, 17–20, 26, 28–37]. Particle-based fluid methods are therefore used less often for animal [11, 14, 40, 48] and human swimming [12, 13, 16, 27].

There are different grid-based fluid methods used for swimming. The studies of articulated rigid bodies of swimming animals [9] and a biomechanical human swimmer [8] use the classic staggered Marker And Cell (MAC) method [57]. In the latter study which includes human bones and muscles [8], the particle level set method [59, 60] is used to capture the water surface. Level-set methods are widely used in animation, because of their ability to model and render a smooth surface interface. High resolution grids are required in the boundary layer around the body of a human swimmer in the prone-glide position [18, 34, 36].

The grid-based Immersed Boundary Method [61] is used for complex immersed moving geometry boundaries, and therefore used for submerged animal [23, 41, 42, 52] and human swimming [10, 26, 53]. A momentum exchange-based Immersed boundary-Lattice Boltzmann Method (MEIB-LBM) is used for jellyfish swimming [44].

The SPH particle-based fluid method is ideal for water surface modeling, including droplet splashes and two-way solid-fluid coupling. However, SPH has infrequently been used for swimming: dolphins and sharks [11], trout [40] and humans [12, 13, 27]. To simulate elastic bodies like jellyfish, a particle-based fluid method may be used [50]. However, the SPH method approximates incompressibility with large pressure gradient forces and can be computationally expensive. Grid-based fluid methods are often more accurate, but are also computationally slow. As a compromise, the hybrid-based semi-Lagrangian Stable Fluids method [62] is unconditionally stable, though it adds numerical dampening. It uses grid-based and semi-Lagrangian methods.

A hybrid fluid method is used to model a swimming jellyfish [14, 48]. For the Lagrangian part, the moving semi-implicit (MPS) method is used, that has similarities to the SPH method. The Stable Fluids method is used to simulate surface and submerged human swimmers [15, 16]. It is suggested by researchers that the Stable Fluids method is promising for swimming fluid simulation for animation (Fig. 3, [16]).

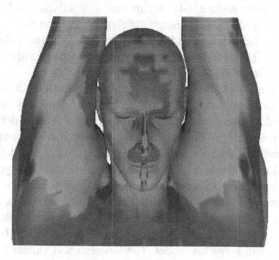

Fig. 3. Near body flow around submerged dolphin-kick by a grid-based fluid method [16]

5.3 Turbulence Modeling and Vortex Shedding

Grid-based discretization methods categorize fluids as laminar, turbulent or in the laminar-turbulent flow regime, by using the dimensionless Reynolds number. There are fluid vortices predicted around a dolphin's flipper, when using the standard k-omega turbulence model [38]. A dolphin and a shark both exhibit strong vortices (Fig. 4, [11]) generated by the oscillatory motions of their tails [11]. A simulation of the laminar-turbulent transition around another dolphin [39, 58] uses the Gamma-Re transition turbulence model. A CFD model of a swimming turtle uses the k-omega shear stress transport (SST) viscosity turbulence model [22]. The motion of a fin of a sunfish also exhibits vortex structures [23, 42]. The wake behind a boxfish is turbulent, but the boundary layer is laminar. To account for turbulence at such relatively low Reynolds numbers, the Menter Shear Stress Transport (Transition SST) model is used [24]. For a ribbon-fin fish the flow is laminar or may transition to turbulent [52].

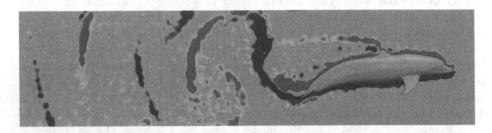

Fig. 4. Vorticity around a dolphin by a grid-based fluid method [11]

A swimming jellyfish produces radial symmetric rotating currents called vortex rings [44, 45, 49, 54, 63]. Measurements around a jellyfish reveal that the flow does not develop into the turbulent regime [64]. A simulation of jellyfish with laminar flow is undertaken in another study [54]. There are differences between the wake structures of 2D and 3D swimming eel simulations [9, 51]. A lamprey [25] has a Reynolds number comparable to eels [65]. A frog has a Reynolds number that is within the transitional laminar and turbulent region [21].

For a human dolphin-kick, there is a wake generated from the lower legs and feet [12]. Small vortex structures are shed from the head and hips [10]. A study uses the Boussinesq-based eddy viscosity turbulence model for a human dolphin-kick [53]. Vortices around a prone-glide swimmer are formed by concave and convex body geometry features, and predicted using the Spalart-Allmaras turbulence model [18]. Turbulent fluid zones are predicted [34] where there are sudden geometrical changes in body shape (head, shoulders, elbows, hips, knees and feet). The standard k-epsilon turbulence model is used for flow around a prone-glide swimmer [30], and compares accurately with measurements [31]. Simulations using the standard k-omega turbulent model for a prone-glide swimmer [19] demonstrate better performance in the boundary layers, compared to the standard k-epsilon model. The k-omega SST (Shear Stress Transport) turbulence model is used for another prone-glide swimmer [20]. Turbulence models (Spalart-Almaras, k-epsilon, k-omega, Realizable k-epsilon, RNG k-epsilon) are compared for a prone-glide swimmer. Comparison with experimental data [37] reveal that the standard k-ω turbulence model is the most accurate turbulence model for prone-glide human swimming [35, 36].

5.4 Solid-Fluid Coupling

The traditional method of two-way solid-fluid coupling is by prescribing fluid velocities to be equal to the solid velocities at the solid-fluid interface, and then integrating the pressure to get force boundary conditions on the solid boundary [1, 8]. Secondary phenomena like body deformation and swaying are caused by fluid vortices, and predicted using two-way solid-fluid coupling [1].

A two-way coupled rigid solid body model is a simplification of a deformable body model. Articulated rigid body modeling can be used for the swimming gaits of a variety of animals [9]. Two-way coupling works by the fluid exerting pressure forces on the rigid solid body of the swimmer, while at the same time the kinematics of the rigid body by locomotion affects the pressure distribution of the fluid [9]. An example of self-propulsive swimming is a frog, that disturbs the water fluid by the classic frog kick, and produces hydrodynamic forces back onto its own body [21]. Self-propulsion is therefore the two-way coupling between body dynamics and fluid hydrodynamics.

The Immersed Boundary Method (IBM) [66] can model unstructured deforming boundaries, with animal locomotion kinematics as input to the moving mesh boundary. The immersed boundary method is used for solid-fluid coupling of a fish fin [23, 41, 42], jellyfish [44, 50], ribbonfish [52], and the human dolphin-kick [10, 26, 53].

Solid-fluid coupling of jellyfish in a flow current is undertaken [49] using the Moving-Grid Finite-Volume Method (MGVFM). Another method for a jellyfish combines the lattice Boltzmann method (LBM), and the immersed boundary method (IBM). It employs a Cartesian grid for the LBM solving the fluid flow, and a Lagrangian grid for the IBM solving the moving boundary [44].

An advanced CFD study suggests that a human swimmer can include biomechanical modeling, with the hard bones and soft tissues coupled (Fig. 5, [8]). The coupling uses an interleaved approach in this study. Animation studies generally exclude muscles and bones, because it is complex and to improve computational efficiency.

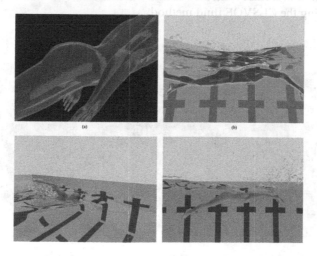

Fig. 5. Biomechanical surface swimming by a grid-based fluid method [8]

A major strength of the SPH particle-based fluid method is that it can handle complex deforming boundaries. This method is used in some studies of dolphins and shark [11] and humans [12, 13, 27] A hybrid method known as moving semi-implicit (MPS) is used to model solid-fluid coupling in a jellyfish [14, 48] The jellyfish umbrella is calculated as fluid particles and deformed in the same manner as a fluid.

5.5 Multi-phase Flow

Swimming simulation requires multi-phase flow modeling for predicting the shape of the water surface, splashes, air re-entrainment, bubbles and froth. Multi-phase flow modeling can be neglected for submerged swimming, such as the human dolphin-kick [10, 13]. For grid-based fluid methods, the grid resolution determines whether droplets and bubbles are captured [17]. For submerged swimming it is common to neglect the motion of the water surface, and model it instead as a flat plane, and therefore ignore multi-phase flow models. A boundary type used for the water surface in submerged swimming is a zero pressure boundary, where the flow enters and leaves the top of the flow domain [1, 9, 24, 49]. Another boundary used is the no gradient (no slip) condition [10, 23, 26, 29]. Another boundary condition used is a symmetry plane [33, 34, 36, 37].

Surface swimming such as a trout in a river [40] can provide other interesting scenarios, such as a whale jumping out of water (breaching) [9]. Human surface swimming can include other sports such as diving, water polo and artistic swimming [8].

For human surface swimming a dynamic water surface is often modeled [8, 13, 17–20]. A biomechanical surface human swimmer [8] employs a MAC grid, and uses a particle-level-set fluid method [59, 60] to model the water surface interface. An animation of a human swimmer interacts with the water surface to produce splashes and bubbles (Fig. 6, [17]). The water surface is modeled using the coupled level-set and volume-of-fluid method (CLSVOF) [67]. A problem with the VOF method is the recovery of a smooth surface from the volume fraction distribution. This problem can be resolved using the CLSVOF fluid method.

Fig. 6. Bubbles, splashes and water surface effects by a grid-based fluid method [17]

Human swimming strokes near the water surface are modeled using a grid-based [15] and a semi-Lagrangian fluid method [62]. Swimming animations using motion capture data of breaststroke, crawl, butterfly and backstroke strokes are able to demonstrate surface and splashing effects [15].

In sports science, a backstroke swimmer [13] demonstrates surface and splashing motion, using a particle-based fluid method. A prone-glide swimmer [18–20] demonstrates water surface effects, using a grid-based fluid method. The Volume of Fluid (VOF) two-phase flow model is used to predict the water surface shape around a swimmer in a prone-glide position [19, 20].

Surface human swimming simulation is able to predict the disturbance of the water surface without splashing [19, 20]. Some studies progress further, and include droplet splashes but without bubbles [8, 13, 15]. Only one study progresses even further to predict splashes and bubbles surrounding a surface human swimmer [17].

A major strength of the particle-based SPH fluid method is its ability to handle complex splashes [68, 69]. The SPH method is used for submerged swimming [11, 12, 27]. Splashes and surface waves using the SPH method are captured for a human backstroke swimmer [13]. The more traditional grid-based fluid methods are used for water surface modeling of surface human swimmers [8, 15, 17, 19, 20]. Only one study uses a particle-based fluid method (SPH) for predicting surface splashes [13].

6   Conclusions

The Navier Stokes fluid flow equations used in swimming simulation are able to predict vortex shedding, water surface motion, splashes and bubbles. For human swimming the modeling of the free water surface is more prevalent then animal swimming. Level-set fluid methods are used by animators to predict the free water surface, sometimes coupled with a volume of fluid method. Modeling swimming animals as articulated rigid bodies avoids the complexity of deformable body modeling. Articulated rigid bodies are not used for deformable marine invertebrates.

For animal and human swimming, the approach is predominantly to use grid-based fluid methods for better accuracy. The SPH fluid method is ideally suited for surface swimming and two-way solid-fluid coupling. Hybrid-based fluid methods are also used: MPS for animals and Stable Fluids for humans.

Different flow regimes are used to classify different types of animals. The standard k-omega turbulence model is preferred for prone-glide human swimmers. For the human dolphin-kick fluid vortices are predicted around the legs and feet. Vortices around a prone-glide human swimmer are predicted around changes in body shape.

Solid-fluid coupling is modeled using an articulated rigid body of a swimmer, and having the fluid exerting pressure forces on the rigid body, while the kinematic locomotion of the rigid body affects the hydrodynamics. Self-propulsion of swimming is modeled by two-way coupling between solid body dynamics and hydrodynamics. Secondary phenomena such as body deformation and swaying are caused by vortex shedding, and modeled correctly by two-way solid-fluid coupling. The immersed boundary grid-based method is often used in swimming for solid-fluid coupling.

Surface swimming fluid simulation requires multi-phase flow models, for water surface motion, splashes, bubbles and froth. For submerged swimming it is usual to model the water surface as a flat plane. Multi-phase flow modeling can be entirely neglected for swimming that is sufficiently submerged. Fluid simulation research on surface swimming predicts the shape of the water surface but without splashes. While other research progresses to include splashes but not bubbles. The fluid simulation of a human surface swimmer that includes splashes and bubbles has been modeled once.

Acknowledgment. Research supported through funding and training by The Centre for Digital Entertainment (CDE) and Engineering and Physical Sciences Research Council (EPSRC). The research leading to these results has been partially supported by the People Programme (Marie Curie Actions) of the European Union's Seventh Framework Programme FP7/2007-2013/under REA grant agreement n° [612627].

References

1. Lentine, M., Tómas Grétarsson, J.T., Schroeder, C., Robinson-Mosher, A., Fedkiw, R.: Creature control in a fluid environment. IEEE Trans. Vis. Comput. Graph. **17**(5), 682–693 (2011)
2. Furukawa, M., Watanabe, M., Fukumoto, A., Suzuki, I., Yamamoto, M.: Swimming Animats with Musculoskeletal structure (2012)
3. Yang, P.F., Laszlo, J., Singh, K.: Layered dynamic control for interactive character swimming. In: ACM SIGGRAPH/Eurographics Symposium on Computer Animation, pp. 39–47. Eurographics Association (2004)
4. Nakashima, M., Nakano, T.: Simulation analysis of an octopus-inspired propulsion mechanism. J. Aero Aqua Bio-mechanisms. **4**(1), 49–55 (2015)
5. Nakashima, M.: Modeling and simulation of human swimming. J. Aero Aqua Bio-mechanisms **1**(1), 11–17 (2010)
6. Rudolf, D., Mould, D.: Animating Jellyfish through Observational Models of Motion. Department of Computer Science (2004)
7. Malik, S., Morris, N., Yang, P.: Physically-based Animation of Humanoid Swimming (2002)
8. Si, W., Lee, S.-H., Sifakis, E., Terzopoulos, D.: Realistic biomechanical simulation and control of human swimming. ACM Trans. Graph. **34**(1), 1–15 (2014)
9. Tan, J., Yuting, G., Turk, G., Liu, K.: Articulated swimming creatures. ACM Trans. Graph. **30**(4), 1 (2011)
10. Von Loebbecke, A., Mittal, R., Russell, M., Hahn, J.: A computational method for analysis of underwater dolphin kick hydrodynamics in human swimming. Sports Biomech. **8**(1), 60–77 (2009)
11. Cohen, R., Cleary, P.: Computational studies of the locomotion of dolphins and sharks using Smoothed Particle Hydrodynamics. In: Lim, C.T., Goh, J.C.H. (eds.) 6th World Congress of Biomechanics (WCB 2010). IFMBE Proceedings, vol. 31, pp. 22–25. Springer, Heidelberg (2010)
12. Cohen, R.C.Z., Cleary, P.W., Mason, B.: Simulations of human swimming using Smoothed Particle Hydrodynamics. In: 7th International Conference on CFD in the Minerals and Process Industries, Melbourne, Australia (2009)

13. Cohen, R.C.Z., Cleary, P.W., Mason, B.: Improving understanding of human swimming using Smoothed Particle Hydrodynamics. In: Lim, C.T., Goh, J.C.H. (eds.) 6th World Congress of Biomechanics (WCB 2010). IFMBE Proceedings, vol. 31, pp. 174–177. Springer, Heidelberg (2010)

14. Lazunin, V., Savchenko, V.: Artificial jellyfish: evolutionary optimization of swimming. In: The 20th International Conference in Central Europe on Computer Graphics, Visualization and Computer Vision. EuroGraphics Proceedings of WSCG (2012)

15. Kwatra, N., Wojtan, C., Carlson, M., Essa, I., Mucha, P.J., Turk, G.: Fluid simulation with articulated bodies. IEEE Trans. Vis. Comput. Graph. **16**(1), 70–80 (2010)

16. Truong, D.-T., Chow, Y.-Y., Fang, A.C.: Visualization and simulation of near-body hydrodynamics using the Semi-lagrangian fluid simulation method. In: 15th Pacific Conference on Computer Graphics and Applications, PG 2007, pp. 219–228. IEEE (2007)

17. Mihalef, V., Kadioglu, S., Sussman, M., Metaxas, D., Hurmusiadis, V.: Interaction of two-phase flow with animated models. Graph. Models **70**(3), 33–42 (2008)

18. Sato, Y., Hino, T.: CFD simulation of flows around a swimmer in a prone glide position. Suiei Suichu Undo Kagaku. **13**(1), 1–9 (2010)

19. Mantha, V.R., Marinho, D.A., Silva, A.J., Rouboa, A.I.: The 3D CFD study of gliding swimmer on passive hydrodynamics drag. Braz. Arch. Biol. Technol. **57**(2), 302–308 (2014)

20. Banks, J., James, M.C., Turnock, S.R., Hudson, D.A.: An analysis of a swimmer's passive wave resistance using experimental data and CFD simulations (2014)

21. Fan, J., Zhang, W., Zhu, Y., Zhao, J.: CFD-based self-propulsion simulation for frog swimming. J. Mech. Med. Biol. **14**(6), 1440012-1–1440012-10 (2014)

22. Dudley, P.N., Bonazza, R., Jones, T.T., Wyneken, J., Porter, W.P.: Leatherbacks swimming in silico: modeling and verifying their momentum and heat balance using computational fluid dynamics. PLoS ONE **9**(10), e110701 (2014)

23. Dong, H., Bozkurttas, M., Mittal, R., Madden, P., Lauder, G.V.: Computational modeling and analysis of the hydrodynamics of a highly deformable fish pectoral fin. J. Fluid Mech. **645**, 345 (2010)

24. Van Wassenbergh, S., Van Manen, K., Marcroft, T.A., Alfaro, M.E., Stamhuis, E.J.: Boxfish swimming paradox resolved: forces by the flow of water around the body promote manoeuvrability. J. R. Soc. Interface **12**, 1–11 (2014)

25. Tytell, E.D., Hsu, C.Y., Williams, T.L., Cohen, A.H., Fauci, L.J.: Interactions between internal forces, body stiffness, and fluid environment in a neuromechanical model of lamprey swimming. Proc. Nat. Acad. Sci. **107**(46), 19832–19837 (2010)

26. Von Loebbecke, A., Mittal, R., Fish, F., Russell, M.: Propulsive efficiency of the underwater dolphin kick in humans. J. Biomech. Eng. **131**(5), 054504-1–054504-4 (2009)

27. Cohen, R.C.Z., Cleary, P.W., Mason, B.R.: Simulations of dolphin kick swimming using smoothed particle hydrodynamics. Hum. Mov. Sci. **31**(3), 604–619 (2012)

28. Sato, Y., Hino, T.: a computational fluid dynamics analysis of hydrodynamic force acting on a swimmer's hand in a swimming competition. J. Sports Sci. Med. **12**(4), 679 (2013)

29. Hochstein, S., Pacholak, S., Brücker, C., Blickhan, R.: Experimental and Numerical Investigation of the Unsteady Flow around a Human Underwater Undulating Swimmer. In: Tropea, C., Bleckmann, H. (eds.) Nature-Inspired Fluid Mechanics. Notes on Numerical Fluid Mechanics and Multidisciplinary Design, vol. 119, pp. 293–308. Springer, Heidelberg (2012). doi:10.1007/978-3-642-28302-4_18

30. Novais, M., Silva, A., Mantha, V., Ramos, R., Rouboa, A., Vilas-Boas, J., Luís, S., Marinho, D.: The effect of depth on drag during the streamlined glide: a three-dimensional CFD analysis. J. Hum. Kinet. **33**, 55–62 (2012)

31. Marinho, D., Barbosa, T., Rouboa, A., Silva, A.: The hydrodynamic study of the swimming gliding: a two-dimensional computational fluid dynamics (CFD) analysis. J. Hum. Kinet. **29**, 49–57 (2011)
32. Silva, A.J., Rouboa, A., Moreira, A., Reis, V.M., Alves, F., Vilas-Boas, J.P., Marinho, D.A.: Analysis of drafting effects in swimming using computational fluid dynamics. J. Sports Sci. Med. **7**(1), 60 (2008)
33. Popa, C.V., Zaidi, H., Arfaoui, A., Polidori, G., Taiar, R., Fohanno, S.: Analysis of wall shear stress around a competitive swimmer using 3D Navier-Stokes equations in CFD. Acta Bioeng. Biomech. **13**(1), 3–11 (2011)
34. Popa, C.V., Arfaoui, A., Fohanno, S., Taïar, R., Polidori, G.: Influence of a postural change of the swimmer's head in hydrodynamic performances using 3D CFD. Comput. Methods Biomech. Biomed. Eng. **17**(4), 344–351 (2014)
35. Arfaoui, A., Popa, C.V., Taïar, R., Polidori, G., Fohanno, S.: Numerical streamline patterns at swimmer's surface using RANS equations. J. Appl. Biomech. **28**(3), 279–283 (2012)
36. Zaïdi, H., Fohanno, S., Taïar, R., Polidori, G.: Turbulence model choice for the calculation of drag forces when using the CFD method. J. Biomech. **43**(3), 405–411 (2010)
37. Zaïdi, H., Taïar, R., Fohanno, S., Polidori, G.: An evaluation of turbulence models in CFD simulations of underwater swimming. Ser. Biomech. **24**, 1–5 (2009)
38. Weber, P.W., Howle, L.E., Murray, M.M., Fish, F.E.: Lift and drag performance of odontocete cetacean flippers. J. Exp. Biol. **212**(14), 2149–2158 (2009)
39. Pavlov, V., Riedeberger, D., Rist, U., Siebert, U.: Analysis of the relation between skin morphology and local flow conditions for a fast-swimming dolphin. In: Tropea, C., Bleckmann, H. (eds.) Nature-Inspired Fluid Mechanics. Notes on Numerical Fluid Mechanics and Multidisciplinary Design, vol. 119, pp. 239–253. Springer, Heidelberg (2012)
40. Taverna, L., Chellali, R., Rossi, L.: 3D simulation of robotic fish interactions with physics-based underwater environment. In: OCEANS 2010 IEEE, pp. 1–4. IEEE Sydney (2010)
41. Ramakrishnan, S., Mittal, R., Lauder, G.V., Bozkurttas, M.: Analysis of maneuvering fish fin hydrodynamics using an immersed boundary method. In: AIAA 2008 38th Fluid Dynamics Conference and Exhibit. AIAA, Seattle, Washington (2008)
42. Mittal, R., Dong, H., Bozkurttas, M., Lauder, G., Madden, P.: Locomotion with flexible propulsors: II. Computational modeling of pectoral fin swimming in sunfish. Bioinspiration Biomimetics **1**(4), S35–S41 (2006)
43. Tabatabaei, M., Olcay, A.B., Gokçen, G., Heperkan, H.A.: Drag force and jet propulsion investigation of a swimming squid. In: EPJ Web of Conferences, vol. 92 (2015)
44. Yuan, H.Z., Shu, S., Niu, X.D., Li, M., Hu, Y.: A numerical study of jet propulsion of an oblate jellyfish using a momentum exchange-based immersed boundary-lattice boltzmann method. Adv. Appl. Math. Mech. **6**(3), 307–326 (2014)
45. Sahin, M., Mohseni, K., Colin, S.P.: The numerical comparison of flow patterns and propulsive performances for the hydromedusae Sarsia tubulosa and Aequorea victoria. J. Exp. Biol. **212**(16), 2656–2667 (2009)
46. Sfakiotakis, M., Kazakidi, A., Pateromichelakis, N., Ekaterinaris, J.A., Tsakiris, D.P.: Robotic underwater propulsion inspired by the octopus multi-arm swimming. Robotics and Automation (ICRA). In: 2012 IEEE International Conference, pp. 3833–3839. IEEE (2012)
47. Van Rees, W.M., Gazzola, M., Koumoutsakos, P.: Optimal shapes for anguilliform swimmers at intermediate Reynolds numbers. J. Fluid Mech. **722**, R3-1–R3-12 (2013)
48. Hirato, J., Kawaguchi, Y.: Calculation model of jellyfish for simulating the propulsive motion and the pulsation of the tentacles. In: 18th International Conference on Artificial Reality and Telexistence (2008)

49. Inomoto, T., Matsuno, K., Yamakawa, M., Asao, S., Ishihara, S.: Numerical Simulation of flows around jellyfish in a current. In: ICCM 2015, Auckland, NZ (2015)
50. Rudolf, D., Mould, D.: An Interactive fluid model of jellyfish for animation. In: Ranchordas, A., Pereira, J.M., Araújo, Hélder J., Tavares, João Manuel R.S. (eds.) VISIGRAPP 2009. CCIS, vol. 68, pp. 59–72. Springer, Heidelberg (2010). doi:10.1007/978-3-642-11840-1_5
51. Kern, S., Koumoutsakos, P.: Simulations of optimized anguilliform swimming. J. Exp. Biol. 209(24), 4841–4857 (2006)
52. Shirgaonkar, A.A., Curet, O.M., Patankar, N.A., MacIver, M.A.: The hydrodynamics of ribbon-fin propulsion during impulsive motion. J. Exp. Biol. 211(21), 3490–3503 (2008)
53. Mittal, R.H., Dong, M., Bozkurttas, A., Von Loebbecke, A., Najjar, F.: Analysis of flying and swimming in nature using an immersed boundary method. Urbana51 (2006)
54. Matevž, D., Bajcar,T., Širok., B.: Numerical investigation of flow in the vicinity of a swimming jellyfish. Eng. Appl. Comput. Fluid Mech. 3(2), 258–270 (2009)
55. Monaghan, J.: Smoothed particle hydrodynamics. Ann. Rev. Astron. Astrophys. 30(1), 543–574 (1992)
56. Monaghan, J.: Smoothed particle hydrodynamics. Rep. Prog. Phys. 68(8), 1703–1759 (2005)
57. Harlow, F., Welch, J.: Numerical calculation of time-dependent viscous incompressible flow of fluid with free surface. Phys. Fluids 8(12), 2182 (1965)
58. Riedeberger, D., Rist, U.: Numerical simulation of laminar-turbulent transition on a dolphin using the γ-Re θ model. In: Nagel, W., Kröner, D., Resch, M. (eds.) High Performance Computing in Science and Engineering '11, pp. 379–391. Springer, Heidelberg (2012)
59. Enright, D., Marschner, S., Fedkiw, R., Animation and rendering of complex water surfaces. ACM Trans. Graph. 21(3), 736–744 (2002)
60. Foster, N., Fedkiw, R.: Practical animation of liquids. In: 28th Annual Conference on Computer Graphics and Interactive Techniques, pp. 23–30. ACM (2001)
61. Peskin, C.: The immersed boundary method. Acta Numer. 11, 479–517 (2002)
62. Stam, J.: Stable fluids. In: 26th Annual Conference on Computer Graphics and Interactive Techniques, pp. 121–128. ACM Press/Addison-Wesley Publishing Co. (1999)
63. Lazunin, V., Savchenko, V.: Vortices formation for medusa-like objects. In: ECCOMAS CFD 2010 (2010)
64. Ichikawa, S., Yazaki, Y., Mochizuki, O.: Flow induced by jellyfish. Phys. Fluids 18(9), 091108 (2006)
65. Tytell, E.: The hydrodynamics of eel swimming II. Effect of swimming speed. J. Exp. Biol. 207(19), 3265–3279 (2004)
66. Mittal, R., Iaccarino, G.: Immersed boundary methods. Annu. Rev. Fluid Mech. 37, 239–261 (2005)
67. Sussman, M., Puckett, E.: A coupled level set and volume-of-fluid method for computing 3D and axisymmetric incompressible two-phase flows. J. Comput. Phys. 162(2), 301–337 (2000)
68. Li, S., Liu, W.: Meshfree and particle methods and their applications. Appl. Mech. Rev. 55(1), 1 (2002)
69. Cleary, P.W., Prakash, M., Ha, J., Stokes, N., Scott, C.: Smooth particle hydrodynamics: status and future potential. Prog. Comput. Fluid Dyn. Int. J. 7(2–4), 70 (2007)

Motion Capture and Estimation of Dynamic Properties for Realistic Tree Animation

Shaojun Hu[1], Peng He[1], and Dongjian He[2]($\boxtimes$)

[1] College of Information Engineering, Northwest A&F University, Xianyang, China
[2] College of Mechanical and Electronic Engineering,
Northwest A&F University, Xianyang, China
hdj168@nwsuaf.edu.cn

Abstract. The realistic animation of real-world trees is a challenging task because natural trees have various morphology and internal dynamic properties. In this paper, we present an approach to model and animate a specific tree by capturing the motion of its branches. We chose Kinect V2 to record both the RGB and depth of motion of branches with markers. To obtain the three-dimensional (3D) trajectory of branches, we used the mean-shift algorithm to track the markers from color images generated by projecting a textured point cloud onto the image plane, and then inversely mapped the tracking results in the image to 3D coordinates. Next, we performed a fast Fourier transform on the tracked 3D positions to estimate the dynamic properties (i.e., the natural frequency) of the branches. We constructed static tree models using a space colonization algorithm. Given the dynamic properties and static tree models, we demonstrated that our approach can produce realistic animation of trees in wind fields.

Keywords: Motion capture · Kinect · Dynamic property · Tree

1 Introduction

The realistic modeling and animation of vegetation is a significant problem because of the inherent complexity of plants. The reconstruction of static tree models from images and point clouds has been widely studied; however, there are few studies that explore the scheme for simulating the swaying of trees in a wind field. Recently, motion capture has been extended from tracking human movement to simulating plant motion. A passive optical system has been used in tree and maize motion capture [10,17], and realistic animation can be achieved using the motion capture data. However, an optical system is expensive and motion capture is limited for indoor trees. In contrast to an optical system, video-based motion capture uses a camera, which has the advantage of low-cost and portability [3,4,15]. Although all the aforementioned motion capture and animation methods generated reasonable results, the studies did not explore the vibration relationship of branches.

© Springer International Publishing AG 2017
J. Chang et al. (Eds.): AniNex 2017, LNCS 10582, pp. 18–34, 2017.
https://doi.org/10.1007/978-3-319-69487-0_2

In our work, we use Kinect to capture static tree point clouds and tree motion in a pulling and releasing experiment, and then study the motion trajectory and dynamic properties (i.e., natural frequency) of branches. Based on a single-view point cloud of a tree captured by Kinect, we use a space colonization (SC) algorithm to reconstruct a static tree model. Then, we calculate the relative rotation angle between a parent branch and a child branch, and extract the dynamic properties of branches using a fast Fourier transform (FFT). Finally, we generate tree animations using the static tree model and the extracted parameters. In this paper, we address the problem of outdoor motion capture by taking advantage of a low-cost depth sensor, Kinect V2. The contributions of this paper are as follows:

- a low-cost method to capture and estimate the dynamic properties of a real-world tree with hierarchical structures; and
- a physics-guided model to animate trees in wind fields using the extracted properties and static tree models.

2   Related Work

Dynamic Property Estimation. Tree dynamic properties play an important role in branch pruning and vibration harvesting. In the early years, the dynamic properties of trees were measured using the relationship between the height and diameter at the breast (DBII) of tree branches [11,12] or a strain-stress data logger [8]. In the past decade, researchers have used computer vision based methods to measure the dynamic properties of trees. Sun et al. [15] used video clips of tree motion to extract parameters, and used those parameters to synthesize the motion of an artificial tree model. Long et al. [10] used a passive optical motion capture system to capture the motion of an indoor tree in a wind field, and extracted the wind field to drive the motion of the reconstructed model. Both Sun et al. and Long et al. extracted parameters based on force-displacement measurement, whereas in our work, we propose extracting parameters based on the rotation angle. Wang et al. [16] used three synchronized Kinect V1s to capture the motion of indoor potted plants, and used FEM to estimate Young's modulus and the damping coefficient. Unlike the work of Wang et al., we use Kinect V2 to capture the motion of outdoor trees.

Tree Animation. The study of the dynamic tree model began in the late 1990s. The first work that simulated the stochastic motion of trees and grass was by Shiya and Fournier [14]. Because our work is related to data-driven animation, we only discuss the closest works regarding that approach. Diener et al. [3] used video-captured motion data to drive the artificial tree model. Long et al. [10] used the extracted wind field from a three-dimensional (3D) sequence of reflective markers to drive the motion of a captured tree. Although Long et al. and Diener et al. made use of captured data to simulate motion, they did not establish a relation between the extracted parameters and physics-based animation model. Wang et al. [16] obtained Young's modulus and damping coefficients, and used an FEM model to simulate the deformation of a small potted plant; however, this is time-consuming for a complex tree structure. The latest work of data-driven tree animation was proposed by Hu et al. [6]. The researchers used a camera or mobile phone to capture the motion of a tree outdoors. In our work, we take advantage of Kinect V2, which can be used outdoors in weak light and simultaneously capture the depth and RGB of tree motions.

3   Overview

Our motion capture and data-driven animation system consists of three parts:

First, we use Kinect V2 to collect the motion of a tree, which is driven by a pulling and releasing experiment. To obtain the rotation angle in 3D coordinates, we project the textured point cloud of tree motion onto the image plane first, and then perform tracking in the image plane. When we obtain the trajectory in a two-dimensional (2D) image, we map it to 3D coordinates inversely, and calculate the rotation angle based on the 3D trajectory. Based on the 3D rotation angle, we use an FFT on it and obtain the spectrum of motion in the frequency domain. Motion capture and parameter analysis are introduced in Sects. 4 and 5, respectively.

When we obtain the dynamic parameters, we use an SC algorithm to generate the skeleton of a point cloud captured by Kinect outdoors. Once the static tree model is reconstructed and the dynamic parameters are acquired, we establish the relation between the dynamic parameters and physics-based animation model, and then synthesize tree motion. We discuss this in Sect. 6.

In Sect. 7, we present the results and analysis of our study and limitations are also included.

4   Motion Capture

Many approaches have been proposed to capture tree motions in wind or using a pulling and releasing experiment [1,3,8,10]. The main equipment includes a strain-stress data logger [8], an electromagnetic tracking system [1], and a camera [3]. Instead of the aforementioned devices, we use a low-cost depth sensor to perform motion capture. Specifically, we record the motion of a tree using Microsoft Kinect V2, which can capture motion outdoors and provide depth of scene. Figure 1a shows our motion capture system, which consists of a Kinect V2 sensor and a desktop PC, which can be used to collect the motion data of a tree outdoors.

We selected two outdoor Magnolia trees with heights and DBH of approximately 2.6 m and 2.4 cm, respectively, and 3.3 m and 4.94 cm, respectively. To reduce occlusion, we conducted the capture in winter on a leafless tree. Because of self-similarity in branching, it is difficult to search for features in motion data. To perform accurate and efficient tracking for a tree with uncertain features is beyond the scope of our work; thus, for simplicity, we pasted red makers with a width of approximately 3 cm on a selected branch. Because of the limitation

Fig. 1. Scene setting of tree motion capture and captured data using Kinect: (a) capture system; (b) back-projection image of textured point cloud; (c) point cloud.

of the precision of Kinect, it cannot detect tiny branches; thus, we pasted red markers on the first three level of branches, and for levels higher than three, we marked selected parts of them. Tree motion was driven by pulling and releasing branches. To reduce measurement errors, the Kinect direction was set approximately perpendicular to the motion plane.

Unlike video-based motion analysis approaches, our aim is to study tree motion and dynamic parameters in 3D space. However, tracking the motion of branches in a point cloud is difficult; thus, we propose performing 2D tracking first and then mapping the 2D position to 3D coordinates. Hence, not only do we obtain a creditable result, but also reduce the implementation complexity. Figure 1b shows the back-projection of a textured point cloud and Fig. 1c shows the point cloud. From the recorded data shown in Fig. 1c, we observed that the captured data preserved the main branch of the tree in both the back-projection image and original point cloud.

5 Parameter Estimation

5.1 Semi-automatic Tracking

To obtain the motion trajectory and natural frequency of branches, we need to track the motion of branches. Before capturing, we bound red markers on branches to provide a good feature to track. As described in the previous section, we projected the textured point cloud onto a 2D image; thus, we performed 2D tracking first. The mean-shift algorithm is efficient for color-based feature tracking [2] and we tracked a window with a fixed size during the tracking session; hence, we used the algorithm to track the markers on branches. The workflow is as follows:

Step 1: Select the tracked object. Because of the multi-markers in tree branches, we interactively selected a tracking target.

Step 2: Build a tracking model. Based on the CamShift algorithm, we set the tracking trait as a red hue channel, and built a tracking model with a histogram of the selected target.

Step 3: Calculate the probability of the image. According to the histogram of the tracking target, the back-projection of the current frame is calculated.

Sept 4: Calculate the mean-shift vector. The mean-shift vector is calculated using the center and centroid of the tracking window.

Step 5: Calculate the stable tracking window. After *Step 4*, we obtain the centroid and mean-shift vector, and move the tracking window to the new centroid along with the mean-shift vector. We repeat *Steps 4* and *5*, and the mean-shift algorithm converges to a stable target area.

Step 6: Track the object continuously. To achieve continuous tracking of the object, we set the next frame, starting with the tracking window as the current frame's stable tracking window, and repeat *Steps 4–6* until all frames are processed.

Constrained by the precision of Kinect and motion blur caused by high-speed movement, the tracking feature becomes weak and tracking may be interrupted. In our work, we adopt two approaches to manage the miss-tracking problem.

The first approach is to consider frames with a weak tracking feature. We set the centroid of the tracking window at the current frame interactively when there were no features to track in the tracking window of the current frame.

To solve the problem of tiny branches with movement beyond the pre-designed search area, we increased the search area and then searched the target iteratively from four directions. Because of the locality of movement and continuous characteristic of the motion sequence, when increasing the search window, the target would definitely be tracked continuously.

Figure 2 shows the tracking results of one branch in selected frames, where the blue box represents the initial window position and the red box represents the stable tracking results.

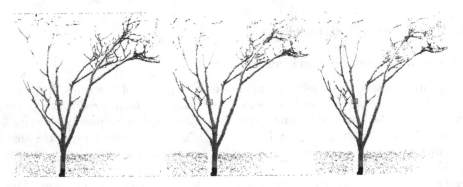

Fig. 2. Continuous frames of the tracking results of a marker using the mean-shift algorithm.

5.2   Motion Trajectory of a Branch

The motion trajectory of branches is complicated and unpredictable. James et al. [8] captured the motion of a branch using a strain and stress data logger in the north and west directions only, and synthesized the motion trajectory in the plane through this two-direction displacement. In our work, we obtained motion in the plane of branches using mean-shift tracking; however, motion in the plane cannot display the realistic trajectory of a branch. In a motion capture session, we obtained the textured point cloud by combining the image frame and corresponding depth, and projected the textured point cloud onto the image plane. To obtain the 3D position of an image pixel in the projection image as seen in Fig. 3, we retrieved a corresponding image from the point cloud according to the centroid, avoiding re-executing the coordinate transformation of Kinect based on the original depth.

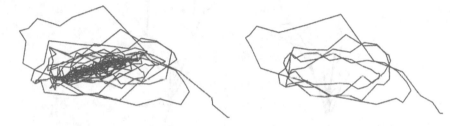

Fig. 3. Trajectory of a branch: (left) front view of the trajectory of the selected branch; (right) the first 80 frames of the selected branch.

5.3   Dynamic Property Estimation

Natural Frequency. Thus far, we have obtained the tracked feature position (3D) along frames. In each frame, we built an approximate hierarchical structure by connecting the feature positions represented by the tracked feature. Mapping the motion of branches to the approximate tree structure and calculating the rotation angle between a parent branch and a child branch rather than using displacement, we obtained the motion of a branch. Considering that the movement of branches is continuous and interrelated, the displacement of the sub-branches contains the displacement of the parent branches. To obtain the pure motion of a branch that eliminates the interference of the parent branches, we propose calculating the relative rotation angle to avoid the displacement of the parent branches in the global coordinate system. Therefore, if the parent branches are set as the reference coordinate system, the motion of the sub-branches relative to the parent branches can be obtained easily.

Figure 4 illustrates our relative rotation angle calculation approach. When pulling and releasing the tree, we obtained the ith frame, as shown in Fig. 4b, where the red arrow indicates the direction of the parent branch and θ_i represents rotation angle at the ith frame between the parent branch and the child branch. The calculation of θ_i uses a plain vector operation and triangular calculation principle described as follows:

$$\theta_i = \arccos\left(\frac{\boldsymbol{v}_{(AC)_i} \cdot \boldsymbol{v}_{(CD)_i}}{\left\|\boldsymbol{v}_{(AC)_i}\right\| \left\|\boldsymbol{v}_{(CD)_i}\right\|}\right). \tag{1}$$

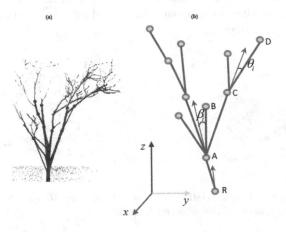

Fig. 4. Illustration of the rotation angle between the child branch and the parent branch: (a) approximate tree structure; (b) the ith frame.

We calculated the rotation angle in 3D coordinates using the method shown in Fig. 4 and obtained the rotation angle sequence in the time domain (as seen in Fig. 6). Motion in the time domain cannot reveal the inherent pattern of branch motion. Therefore, we converted the rotation angle sequence to a frequency domain using an FFT (as shown in Fig. 7). From the signal in the frequency domain, we can clearly analyze the inherent properties of motion. Figure 5 shows the hierarchical structure of our simplified tree, where the numbers 1–6 represent force-bearing points and the letters A–I and a–g represent branches.

Figure 6 shows the change in the rotation angles of four selected branches (C, D, I, F in Fig. 5 tree 1) in the time domain after tracking 409 frames and Fig. 7 shows the corresponding natural frequency of selected branches in Fig. 6. From the frequency domain spectrum results, we observed that each selected branch had one or more dominant frequency.

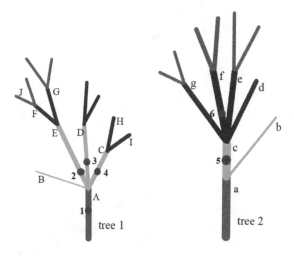

Fig. 5. Illustration of the simplified tree model.

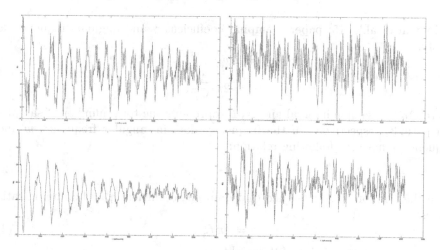

Fig. 6. Changes in the rotation angles: (top) branch C and branch D; (bottom) branch I and branch F.

Damping Ratio. In a pulling and releasing experiment, the movement of the tree stops because of damping. Damping is complicated and consists of several components. To date, the energy dissipation mechanism has not yet been fully elucidated and is usually determined using experimental methods. In practice, researchers relate damping to velocity, and use viscous damping to represent damping in most conditions.

In [7], James proposed several methods to calculate damping: a displacement curve fitting method, logarithmic decay method, and half-band method. Inspired by [15], we derived our damping ratio calculation approach.

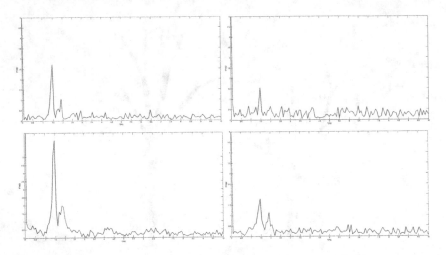

Fig. 7. Natural frequency of branches that correspond to Fig. 6.

In Sun et al.'s [15] paper, damping coefficient γ and angular frequency w satisfy:

$$\gamma = \Delta w$$
$$\Delta w = 2\pi \frac{\Delta v}{NT}, \tag{2}$$

where Δv is a sample interval and N, T represents the total number of samples and periods, respectively. In the frequency domain, angular frequency w and frequency f have the following relation:

$$w = 2\pi f. \tag{3}$$

From the work of [15], we learned that damping coefficient γ and damping ratio ξ satisfy

$$\gamma = 4\pi f \xi. \tag{4}$$

Substituting (3) and (4) into (2), we obtain

$$4\pi f \xi = 2\pi \Delta f. \tag{5}$$

We simplify (5), and derive our damping ratio calculation formula in the frequency domain:

$$\xi = \frac{\Delta f}{2f}, \tag{6}$$

where Δf represents the frequency variation after the frequency attenuates to half.

5.4   Pattern of the Natural Frequency

To explore the relationship between the natural frequency of different branches, we conducted three comparison experiments on two Magnolia trees. The three

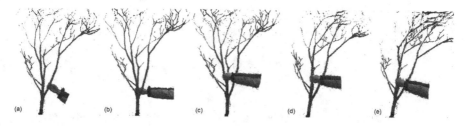

Fig. 8. Different force-bearing point and force applied to branches: (a–c) the different force-bearing points; (d–e) a different force at the same force-bearing point.

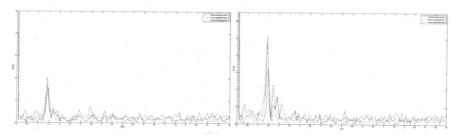

Fig. 9. Natural frequency comparison of the same branch with a force exerted at a different position: (left) branch C; (right) branch I.

experiments were designed as follows: (1) apply approximate force at different positions of different branches; (2) use similar tree species with different tree structures; and (3) apply different forces at the same position of the same branch. Figure 8 shows one frame of motion capture in the comparison experiments.

Figure 9 shows the results for different force-bearing points with an approximate force exerted on them. From the spectrum of the natural frequency, we observed that the first dominant natural frequencies were almost the same (approximately 1.5 Hz). Figure 10 shows the results of different tree structures for one pulling and releasing test. We selected four branches from two trees, and the response spectrum of the vibration shows that the dominant natural frequency of each tree was the same (with tree 1 at 1.5 Hz and tree 2 at 1.2 Hz). Figure 11 shows the results of different forces at the same forced point. Similarly, the natural frequency of different branches was almost the same, but a larger force had a peak value greater than the smaller force.

As shown in Figs. 9, 10 and 11, we can clearly conclude that the first dominant natural frequency of the first three levels of branches were the same.

Figure 12 shows the spectrum of branch J at different forced points. Clearly, high level branches show more complicated vibrations (multiple modal), but they also have in common that they have one dominant frequency near 2.4 Hz.

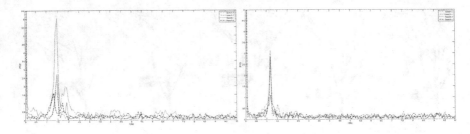

Fig. 10. Natural frequencies of two different tree structures.

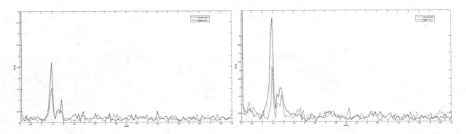

Fig. 11. Influence of different pulling forces on the natural frequency on the same branch: (left) branch A; (right) branch I.

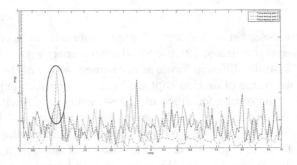

Fig. 12. Spectrum of branch J at different force-bearing points.

6   Tree Modeling and Animation

6.1   Tree Modeling

The generation of tree models is a challenging task which has been studied widely in recent years. In our paper, we chose point cloud based tree modeling because tree point clouds are easy to capture using Kinect. Runions et al. [13] proposed an SC algorithm to generate the tree model of an artificial point cloud and canopy. The SC algorithm resolves branch intersection effectively, and its principle is based on plant growth theory, which is illustrated as competing space for growth between skeleton nodes. In our work, after capturing the tree point cloud using Kinect, we used an SC algorithm to generate the tree skeleton. Instead of rendering the tree using an L-system, we designed a skeleton node data structure and branch data structure, and constructed a tree hierarchy structured using a self-implemented engine. Finally, we generated a tree geometric model with generalized cylinders, for which the radius of a branch was estimated using the pipe model.

6.2   Tree Animation

Because we obtained the static tree model and dynamic properties of branches, we then used the model and parameters to animate the tree. Many approaches have been proposed to animate tree movement in a wind field. To generate tree motion using a static model and dynamic parameters, we need to determine a feasible physics-based model to implement data-driven tree animation. Hu et al. [4] proposed a tree animation model based on modal analysis, which takes the branch frequency and damping ratio into account. Inspired by Hu et al.'s work, we assumed that a branch was a curved beam and used a simplified physics-based tree animation model.

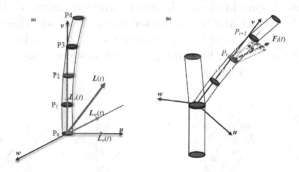

Fig. 13. Our curved branch deformation model.

As seen in Fig. 13a, four segments that consisted of a curved beam (P_0P_1, P_1P_2, P_2P_3, P_3P_4) and located in local coordinate ($\boldsymbol{u}, \boldsymbol{v}, \boldsymbol{w}$) were subjected to a local net force F(t).

Similar to Hu et al.'s [4] method, we took advantage of modal analysis to establish and solve the dynamic equation of branch motion. From the frequency signal (as seen in Figs. 9, 10 and 11), we assumed that the first dominant frequency had a significant impact on motion. Based on this assumption, we only considered the first dominant mode because the remaining modes were small. The dynamic equation that combines the measured parameters is

$$\ddot{x}(t) + 4\pi \xi f \dot{x}(t) + 4\pi^2 f^2 x(t) = \frac{|\boldsymbol{F}(t)|}{m}, \tag{7}$$

where f and ξ are the natural frequency and damping ratio of the first mode, respectively, m is the mass branch, and $x(t)$ is the displacement of the branch. We decomposed F(t) into the $(\boldsymbol{u}, \boldsymbol{v}, \boldsymbol{w})$ coordinate, and represented it as $(F_u(t), 0, F_w(t))$ because we considered that the branch did not stretch in the $\boldsymbol{v}$ direction. Equation (7) can be solved using the explicit Euler method, and we converted the displacement $x(t)$ to an elasticity force according to $\boldsymbol{F}'(t) = 4\pi^2 f^2 \boldsymbol{x}(t)$ to control the deformation of the curved branch.

Our final aim was to calculate the rotation angle along with the force direction (as seen in Fig. 13b). Similar to Ref. [5], we converted the curved beam to a spring system and resolved the rotation angle using Hooke's law, which explains that a bending angle is proportional to a bending moment. For further information on the calculation of the rotation angle, see Ref. [5].

7 Results and Limitations

All the modeling and animation tests were performed on a desktop PC with an Intel Core i3 Duo CPU at 3.8 GHz and an NVIDIA GeForce GTX 750 video card.

Modeling Results. Figure 14 shows the reconstruction results of the tree point cloud captured by Kinect and reconstructed using an SC algorithm. Comparing the point cloud and generated tree geometric model, we conclude that the tree model preserved the detail of branching and tiny branches, and agreed with the original captured point cloud.

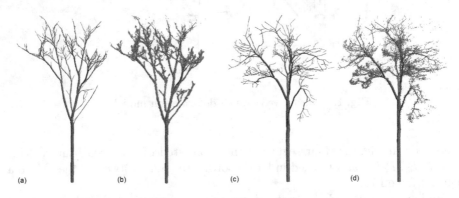

(a)   (b)   (c)   (d)

Fig. 14. Reconstructed static tree model using an SC algorithm. (a, c) Two reconstructed tree models; (b, d) the tree models agreed with the point clouds.

Parameter Estimation. Table 1 shows the parameters of the marked branches captured by Kinect. The results show that some branches vibrated at a frequency of 1.39 Hz, but more than 85 % of the branches vibrated at a frequency of 1.46 Hz. From the response spectrum of the vibration, we clearly know that higher level branches demonstrated a more complex vibration modal (as shown in Fig. 12), but it also contained the main stem vibration modal at 1.46 Hz. Based on this assumption, we only extracted the first mode, which had a natural frequency of 1.46 Hz, and exploited this frequency to build a dynamic equation of branch motion.

Figure 15 shows the damping ratio relation of selected branches corresponding to Table 1. The damping ratios were disorganized; however, we approximately thought that branches with a larger force pulling on them would have a higher damping ratio, with the presupposition that we ignored the measurement error. Because there were fewer captured branches in the reconstructed model, we used the statistical characteristics of the acquired data of some branches to interpolate the damping ratio of the remaining branches. For a more detailed illustration of damping ratio estimation, see Ref. [4].

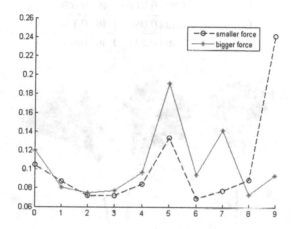

Fig. 15. Damping ratio of branches with different forces.

Animation Results. Figure 16 shows the animation of two Magnolia trees in a wind field generated by our method. The wind field was generated using $1/f^{\beta}$ noise [9]. One advantage of our physics-based tree model with extracted parameters is the capability to respond to any external force and any model by tuning the parameters.

Limitations. Although we could efficiently reconstruct a static tree model from a Kinect-V2-captured point cloud, constrained by the precision of the device, the detailed branches in the canopy may have been lost. Additionally, during the motion capture session, tiny branches could not be captured because of the precision of Kinect. Second, we only discussed the first three levels of branches' frequency patterns and only used one dominant frequency to generate tree motion. Thus, researching more levels of a branch's natural frequency will be a challenging and interesting issue.

Table 1. Parameters of selected branches.

Branch ID	Small force		Large force	
	f	ξ	f	ξ
A	1.46	0.104	1.46	0.120
C	1.46	0.086	1.46	0.081
D	1.46	0.072	1.46	0.075
E	1.46	0.072	1.46	0.074
B	1.46	0.084	1.39	0.077
I	1.46	0.133	1.46	0.096
H	1.46	0.069	1.46	0.191
F	1.39	0.077	1.46	0.094
G	1.39	0.089	1.46	0.141
J	1.46	0.241	1.46	0.093

Fig. 16. Several frames from the animation of two different trees corresponding to Fig. 14 in a wind field.

8   Conclusion

We proposed a semi-automatic approach to track the markers on a branch and mapped the 2D tracking results to 3D to obtain the 3D trajectory. Based on the 3D trajectory, we derived physical parameters (i.e., the natural frequency and damping ratio) of an outdoor tree. To measure the motion of a branch, we proposed a relative rotation angle principle to calculate the rotation angle, of the branch in local coordinates. To analyze the natural frequency and damping ratio of branches, we converted the vibration of a branch in the time domain to the frequency domain using FFT analysis. Then, we applied the extracted parameters and the static tree model that was reconstructed using an SC algorithm to a physics-based tree animating model. The animation results showed that our approach was feasible for generating realistic tree animations from motion captured data.

Supplementary

An accompanying video can be accessed at Demo link: http://pan.baidu.com/s/1c1HWZPu.

Acknowledgment. We thank Dr. Maxine Garcia and Shujie Deng for editing the English text of a draft of this manuscript. The work is supported by the NSFC (61303124) and the Fundamental Research Funds for the Central Universities (Z109021708).

References

1. Adelin, B., Julien, D., Pascal, H., Boris, A., Nicolas, D., Lionel, R., Bruno, M.: A robust videogrametric method for the velocimetry of wind-induced motion in trees. Agric. For. Meteorol. **184**, 220–229 (2014)
2. Comaniciu, D., Ramesh, V., Meer, P.: Kernel-based object tracking. IEEE Trans. Pattern Anal. Mach. Intell. **25**(5), 564–577 (2003)
3. Diener, J., Reveret, L., Fiume, E.: Hierarchical retargetting of 2d motion fields to the animation of 3d plant models. In: Proceedings of the 2006 ACM SCA, Switzerland, pp. 187–195 (2006)
4. Hu, S., Chiba, N., He, D.: Realistic animation of interactive trees. Vis. Comput. **28**(6–8), 859–868 (2012)
5. Hu, S., Fujimoto, T., Chiba, N.: Pseudo-dynamics model of a cantilever beam for animating flexible leaves and branches in wind field. Comput. Animation Virtual Worlds **20**(2–3), 279–287 (2009)
6. Hu, S., Zhang, Z., Xie, H., Igarashi, T.: Data-driven modeling and animation of outdoor trees through interactive approach. Vis. Comput. **33**(6), 1017–1027 (2017)
7. James, K.R.: A dynamic structural analysis of trees subject to wind loading. In: Phd's dissertation. The University of Melbourne, Victoria, Australia (2010)
8. James, K.R., Haritos, N., Ades, P.K.: Mechanical stability of trees under dynamic loads. Am. J. Bot. **93**(10), 1522–1530 (2006)
9. Khorloo, O., Gunjee, Z., Sosorbaram, B., Chiba, N.: Wind field synthesis for animating wind-induced vibration. Int. J. Virtual Reality **10**(1), 53–60 (2011)
10. Long, J., Porter, B., Jones, M.: Animation of trees in wind using sparse motion capture data. Vis. Comput. **31**(3), 325–339 (2015)
11. Moore, J.R., Maguire, D.A.: Natural sway frequencies and damping ratios of trees: concepts, review and synthesis of previous studies. Trees **18**(2), 195–203 (2004)
12. Moore, J.R., Maguire, D.A.: Natural sway frequencies and damping ratios of trees: influence of crown structure. Trees **19**(4), 363–373 (2005)

13. Runions, A., Lane, B., Prusinkiewicz, P.: Modeling trees with a space colonization algorithm. In: Proceedings of the Third Eurographics Conference on Natural Phenomena, NPH 2007, pp. 63–70. Eurographics Association, Aire-la-Ville, Switzerland (2007)
14. Shinya, M., Fournier, A.: Stochastic motion-motion under the influence of wind. Comput. Graph. Forum **11**(3), 119–128 (1992)
15. Sun, M., Jepson, D.A., Fiume, E.: Video input driven animation (vida). In: 9th IEEE International Conference on Computer Vision, Nice, France, pp. 96–103. IEEE (2003)
16. Wang, B., Wu, L., Yin, K., Ascher, U., Liu, L., Huang, H.: Deformation capture and modeling of soft objects. ACM Trans. Graph. **34**(4), 1–12 (2015)
17. Xiao, B., Guo, X., Zhao, C.: An approach of mocap data-driven animation for virtual plant. IETE J. Res. **59**(3), 258–263 (2013)

MPM Based Simulation for Various Solid Deformation

Yuntao Jiang[1]($\boxtimes$), Tao Yang[1], Jian Chang[2], and Shi-Min Hu[1]

[1] Tsinghua University, Beijing, China
jhodinger@gmail.com, yangtao9009@gmail.com, shimin@tsinghua.edu.cn
[2] Bournemouth University, Poole, UK
jchang@bournemouth.ac.uk

Abstract. Solid materials are responsible for many interesting phenomena. There are various types of them such as deformable objects and granular materials. In this paper, we present an MPM based framework to simulate the wide range of solid materials. In this framework, solid mechanics is based on the elastoplastic model, where we use von Mises criterion for deformable objects, and the Drucker-Prager model with non-associated plastic flow rules for granular materials. As a result, we can simulate different kinds of deformation of deformable objects and sloping failure for granular materials.

Keywords: Solid simulation · MPM · Elastoplastic model

1 Introduction

Solid materials exist everywhere in our daily life, and are responsible for many interesting phenomena. Deformable objects, such as chewing gum, toothpaste, and bread dough, undergo elastic and plastic deformation when pressed or stretched. While granular materials, like sand and grain, generate plastic flow and slope failure under large deformation. The numerical simulation of these different materials has been a problem of long standing interest and challenge.

Material Point Method (MPM) is gaining popularity in computer graphics for simulating solid materials, due to its ability to combine the advantage of both Lagrangian and Eulerian approaches. Recently MPM has been successfully applied to simulate granular materials such as sand, and has effectively generated the flow pattern and sloping phenomena [8].

In this work, we show the constitutive models which have been applied in SPH framework also work well in MPM, sometimes even more stable. We use the linear model for elastic deformation, and different yield criterion for the plastic deformation for different materials [1].

In this paper we present an MPM based framework for the wide range of solid materials including deformable objects and granular materials. We introduce a modified version of the Drucker-Prager model with non-associated plastic flow rules for plastic flow of granular materials. The overall framework has a stable running performance without the need of extensive tuning, and thus provides a handy tool for complex solid simulation.

© Springer International Publishing AG 2017
J. Chang et al. (Eds.): AniNex 2017, LNCS 10582, pp. 35–44, 2017.
https://doi.org/10.1007/978-3-319-69487-0_3

2   Related Work

2.1   SPH Simulation

SPH shares much with MPM, so here we briefly introduce some SPH based works. SPH was first applied to simulate elastic solid materials by Libersky and Petschek [9]. Gray et al. [6] extended this early work with a method for overcoming the tensile instability that would otherwise lead to numerical fracture. In these works, the strain in deformed solid materials is updated with velocity gradient.

To simulate different materials, different yield criterions are used. Cleary and Das [4] used Von Mises plasticity and linear isotropic hardening to simulate elastoplastic deformation of deformable objects. Bui et al. [3] implemented the Drucker-Prager model with associated and non-associated plastic flow rules to simulate large deformation and post-failure of granular materials, and An et al. [1] extended this work to 3D cases.

In computer graphics, the strain of solid materials is typically computed by comparing the current shape of the solid materials with a reference shape. Müller et al. [10] proposed a particle-based method for elastic, plastic and melting solid materials, using Green-Saint-Venant strain to determine the stress tensor. To approximate the Jacobian of the deformation vector field, a Moving Least Squares approach is employed. Solenthaler et al. [11] use SPH to approximate the Jacobian of the deformation field, which can handle coarsely sampled and coplanar particle configurations. Becker et al. [2] extended their work with a corotational approach to correctly handle rotations. The method using the reference shape can maintain the original shape well, but is unsuitable for applications with extremely large deformations and topological changes.

Yan et al. [15] presented an SPH framework to uniformly handle the interaction between elastoplastic solid and multiple fluids. This framework uses the velocity gradient to update the strain, as in [1,6]. Here we follow this method, and extend the solid part with our MPM method.

2.2   MPM Simulation

Material Point Method (MPM) [14] has been applied to simulate a wide range of solid materials in the past two decades. Stomakin et al. [12] used MPM for simulating snow, and introduced a novel MPM method for heat transport, melting and solidifying materials [13]. Jiang et al. [7] tuned the model in [12] to simulate granular materials. Later Klár et al. [8] introduced the Drucker-Prager plastic flow model into MPM to simulate sand dynamics, and Daviet and Bertails-Descoubes [5] presented a semi-implicit scheme for granular materials.

Our MPM method is similar to the works mentioned above, but we adopt the constitutive model which has been used in the SPH based work, showing that MPM based method is equally flexible and more stable than SPH for these applications.

3 Solid Mechanics

The motion of solid materials obeys conservation of mass and conservation of momentum. Since the conservation of mass is naturally preserved by the particle representation, we here only focus on the conservation of momentum

$$\frac{D\boldsymbol{v}}{Dt} = \frac{1}{\rho}\nabla \cdot \boldsymbol{\sigma} + \boldsymbol{g} \tag{1}$$

where $\boldsymbol{v}$ is the velocity, ρ is the density, $\boldsymbol{g}$ is the gravity, and $\boldsymbol{\sigma}$ is the Cauchy stress tensor determined by the constitutive model of solid materials.

3.1 Elastic Constitutive Model

In this section we briefly introduce the elastic constitutive model used by all the solid materials in our framework, and leave the plasticity to Sect. 3.2.

The stress tensor $\boldsymbol{\sigma}$ can be written as

$$\boldsymbol{\sigma} = -P\boldsymbol{I} + \boldsymbol{s} \tag{2}$$

where P is the pressure, and $\boldsymbol{s}$ is the deviatoric stress tensor. According to the Hookie's law, the rate of change of $\boldsymbol{s}$ is given by

$$\frac{D\boldsymbol{s}}{Dt} = 2G(\dot{\epsilon} - \frac{1}{3}Tr(\dot{\epsilon})\boldsymbol{I}) \tag{3}$$

where G is the shear modulus, $Tr(\cdot)$ is the trace operator, and $\dot{\epsilon}$ is the strain rate tensor, which is given by

$$\dot{\epsilon} = \frac{1}{2}(\nabla\boldsymbol{v} + \nabla\boldsymbol{v}^T)$$

$$\boldsymbol{\omega} = \frac{1}{2}(\nabla\boldsymbol{v} - \nabla\boldsymbol{v}^T) \tag{4}$$

where $\boldsymbol{\omega}$ is Jaumannn rotation tensor, which is later used to handle rotations. The velocity gradient tensor ∇v is computed with MPM, which is stated in detail in Sect. 4.

The pressure P can be computed either in SPH scheme or with the constitutive model, and is updated with the constitutive model as

$$\frac{DP}{Dt} = -KTr(\dot{\epsilon}) \tag{5}$$

where K is the bulk modulus.

Considering the effect of the rotation, the final equation for updating the stress tensor $\boldsymbol{\sigma}$ is given as

$$\frac{D\boldsymbol{\sigma}}{Dt} = 2G(\dot{\epsilon} - \frac{1}{3}Tr(\dot{\epsilon})\boldsymbol{I}) + KTr(\dot{\epsilon})\boldsymbol{I} + \boldsymbol{\omega}\boldsymbol{\sigma} - \boldsymbol{\sigma}\boldsymbol{\omega} \tag{6}$$

It is worth mentioning that this approach can handle only small rotations, and approaches like those in [2] or [7] are required to handle larger rotations.

3.2   Von Mises Plasticity

When the deformation of deformable objects goes beyond a threshold, the objects are unable to recover their initial shape, and the irreversible part of the deformation is called plastic deformation. The criterion to decide when and how the plastic deformation will take place is called yield criterion.

For deformable objects, the Von Mises criterion is commonly applied:

$$f(J_2) = J_2 - Y^2 = 0 \tag{7}$$

where Y is a parameter determining the yield stress, and J_2 is the second principal invariant of deviatoric stress tensor $\mathbf{s}$, given by: $J_2 = \frac{1}{2}\mathbf{s} : \mathbf{s}$.

Similar to [15], we assume the solid material has an elastic response at first, calculating a trial stress tensor $\boldsymbol{\sigma}_{tr}$ according to Eq. (6), and we can get the trial deviatoric stress tensor by

$$\mathbf{s}_{tr} = \boldsymbol{\sigma}_{tr} - \frac{1}{3}Tr(\boldsymbol{\sigma}_{tr})\mathbf{I} \tag{8}$$

If $f(J_2) > 0$, then yield happens, and we update $\mathbf{s}$ as:

$$\mathbf{s} = \mathbf{s}_{tr}\sqrt{\frac{Y}{J_2}} \tag{9}$$

Then the stress tensor $\boldsymbol{\sigma}$ is calculated by

$$\boldsymbol{\sigma} = \mathbf{s} + \frac{1}{3}Tr(\sigma_{tr})\mathbf{I} \tag{10}$$

3.3   Drucker-Prager Model

For granular materials, we use the Drucker-Prager model with non-associated plastic flow rules here. As in [1], the yield condition $f(I_1, J_2)$ and plastic potential function $g(I_1, J_2)$ have the following forms, respectively

$$f(I_1, J_2) = \sqrt{J_2} + \alpha_\phi I_1 - k_c = 0 \tag{11}$$

$$g(I_1, J_2) = \sqrt{J_2} + \alpha_\psi I_1 - C \tag{12}$$

where I_1 and J_2 are, respectively, the first and second invariants of the stress tensor $\boldsymbol{\sigma}$; C is an arbitrary constant; α_ϕ and k_c are Drucker-Prager's constants, which are related to the Coulomb's material constants c (cohesion) and ϕ (internal friction); α_ψ has the same expression as α_ϕ and is related to the dilatancy angle ψ. These are given as

$$\alpha_\phi = \frac{tan\phi}{\sqrt{9 + 12tan^2\phi}} \quad k_c = \frac{3c}{\sqrt{9 + 12tan^2\phi}}$$

$$\alpha_\psi = \frac{tan\psi}{\sqrt{9 + 12tan^2\psi}} \tag{13}$$

The stress-strain relationship is given by

$$\frac{D\sigma}{Dt} = 2G(\dot{\epsilon} - \frac{1}{3}Tr(\dot{\epsilon})\mathbf{I}) + K\dot{\epsilon} + \omega\sigma - \sigma\omega$$
$$- \dot{\lambda}(3\alpha_\psi K\mathbf{I} + \frac{G}{\sqrt{J_2}}s) \tag{14}$$

where $\dot{\lambda}$ is the rate of change of the plastic multiplier

$$\dot{\lambda} = \begin{cases} \dfrac{3\alpha_\phi KTr(\dot{\epsilon}) + (G/\sqrt{J_2})s : \dot{\epsilon}}{9\alpha_\phi\alpha_\psi K + G} & f(I_1, J_2) > 0 \\ 0 & f(I_1, J_2) \le 0 \end{cases} \tag{15}$$

4 Material Point Method

In MPM particles (material points) are used to track mass, momentum and stress. Specifically, particle p holds position x_p, velocity v_p, mass m_p, and stress σ. The Lagrangian treatment of these quantities makes the advance step fairly simple. To compute the spatial derivatives of velocity and stress, a regular background Eulerian grid is used.

In each timestep, we first transfer the mass and momentum from particles to the grid, and we compute the velocity gradient at the particles with the grid information. Then we can update the stress on the particles. The forces on grid nodes are computed, and the velocites of the grid nodes are updated. Finally the updated velocity is transferred back to the particles.

4.1 Interpolation Scheme

To transfer the quantities of particles to the grid, we use a shape function defined as

$$N_i^h(x_p) = \begin{cases} \frac{1}{8}(1 + N_x N_{Ix})(1 + N_y N_{Iy})(1 + N_z N_{Iz}) & , I \in \{N_p\} \\ 0 & , \text{otherwise} \end{cases} \tag{16}$$

where $\mathbf{N}_x = (N_x, N_y, N_z)$ are the natural coordinates of the evaluation position x_p, $\mathbf{N}_I = (N_{Ix}, N_{Iy}, N_{Iz})$ are the natural coordinates of the grid node, and $\{N_p\}$ are the eight nodes of the grid cell containing x_p.

The definition of the natural coordinates is given as

$$\mathbf{N}_x = \frac{2(x_p - x_c)}{h} \tag{17}$$

where x_p is the evaluation position, h is the grid spacing, and x_c is the position of the center of the cell where x_p lies. Thus the natural coordinate of a position inside the cell ranges from $(-1, -1, -1)$ to $(1, 1, 1)$.

For more compact notation, we will use $\omega_{ip} = N_i^h(\boldsymbol{x}_p)$ and $\nabla\omega_{ip} = \nabla N_i^h(\boldsymbol{x}_p)$. To transfer a scalar A from grid to a particle p, we use the shape function as the interpolation function

$$A_p = \sum_i A_i \omega_{ip}$$

$$\nabla A_p = \sum_i A_i \nabla\omega_{ip} \tag{18}$$

And likewise, to transfer particle data to a grid node i, we have

$$A_i = \sum_p A_p \omega_{ip}$$

$$\nabla A_i = -\sum_i A_p \nabla\omega_{ip} \tag{19}$$

As the node i is shared by eight grid cells, all the particles in these cells contribute to the scalar. The minus sign comes from the fact that $\nabla' N_i^h(\boldsymbol{x}_i) = -\nabla N_i^h(\boldsymbol{x}_p)$, where ∇' means the derivative operator acts on $\boldsymbol{x}_i$.

4.2 Full Method

Here we outline the full update procedure.

1. **Rasterize particle data to the grid.** The first step is to transfer the mass and momentum from particles to the grid. The mass is transferred using the weighting function $m_i^n = \sum_p m_p \omega_{ip}^n$. And to conserve momentum, the velocity is transferred as $\boldsymbol{v}_i^n = \sum_p \boldsymbol{v}_p^n m_p \omega_{ip}^n / m_i^n$. The density is transferred as $\rho_i^n = \frac{m_i^n}{\sum_p (m_p/\rho_p)\omega_{ip}^n}$.

2. **Compute particle velocity gradient.** Giving the grid cell that a particle p lies in, the velocity gradient at the particle is computed with the velocities of the cell's eight nodes: $\nabla\boldsymbol{v}_p^n = \sum_i \boldsymbol{v}_i^n (\nabla\omega_{ip}^n)^T$.

3. **Update particle stress** $\boldsymbol{\sigma}_p^n$ with the constitutive model in Sect. 3.

4. **Update velocities on grid** $\boldsymbol{v}_i^*$ with $\dfrac{D\boldsymbol{v}}{Dt} = -\dfrac{1}{\rho_i^n}(\boldsymbol{\sigma}_p^n \nabla\omega_{ip}^n) + g$.

5. **Grid-based body collisions** on $\boldsymbol{v}_i^*$.

6. **Update particle velocities.** The new particle velocities are $\boldsymbol{v}_p^{n+1} = (1 - \alpha)\boldsymbol{v}_{PICp}^{n+1} + \alpha\boldsymbol{v}_{FLIPp}^{n+1}$, where the PIC part is $\boldsymbol{v}_{PICp}^{n+1} = \sum_i \boldsymbol{v}_i^{n+1} \omega_{ip}^n$ and the FLIP part is $\boldsymbol{v}_{FLIPp}^{n+1} = \boldsymbol{v}_p^n + \sum_i (\boldsymbol{v}_i^{n+1} - \boldsymbol{v}_i^n)\omega_{ip}^n$. We use $\alpha = 0$ for deformable objects and $\alpha = 0.05$ for granular materials.

7. **Particle-based body collisions** on $\boldsymbol{v}_p^{n+1}$ with boundaries.

8. **Update particle positions** using $\boldsymbol{x}_p^{n+1} = \boldsymbol{x}_p^n + \Delta t \boldsymbol{v}_p^{n+1}$.

4.3 Grid-Based Collision Between Different Objects

The most common way of solving the interaction between different objects in MPM is to use multiple grids, one for each object.

We can easily detect the collision of different objects by the overlap of the nodes of different grids, and add collision constraints upon these nodes.

Let's suppose two objects A and B are colliding with each other, and node i_A and i_B are overlapping with each other. The collision would happen if the following condition is satisfied:

$$(v_{iB} - v_{iA})\nabla m_{iA} < 0 \tag{20}$$

where v_{iA} and v_{iB} are the velocity of node i_A and i_B respectively, and ∇m_{iA} is the mass gradient of object A defined as $\nabla m_{iA} = \sum_p m_{pA}\nabla\omega_{ipA}$, which can be seen as the surface normal of object A pointing outwards.

Hence the collision is handled at the surface of the objects, and only happens when the two object are moving toward each other, and is ignored when they are separating.

Then the velocities at node i is modified as

$$\Delta v_{iA} = (v_{iB} - v_{iA})\frac{m_{iA}m_{iD}}{m_{iA} + m_{iB}}$$
$$\Delta v_{iB} = -\Delta v_{iA} \tag{21}$$

This form of constraint ensures conservation of momentum, and enforces the two nodes to move at the same speed. The penetration is automatically avoided in this way. Although it gives very stable results, it leads to a perfectly inelastic collision, and causes considerable energy lost, so it is not suitable for highly dynamic applications.

5 Results

We have simulated several examples to demonstrate the effectiveness of our method, including deformable objects of different plasticity, granular materials, and the interaction between them.

In Fig. 1, a dropping bunny (left), if undergoing pure elastic deformation, bounces up and recover its shape (middle). When plastic deformation happens (right), it can no longer maintain its initial shape and fails to bounce up.

For granular materials, we set up a notched sand block as one of the cases in [8]. In Fig. 2, the block falls down and forms a pile of sand at last. The friction between the ground and the sand is necessary for generating the sloping failure, and we use a friction force proportional to the pressure.

In Fig. 3 we show a bunny dropping onto a sand ball. The sand ball itself is undergoing deformation, and the bunny hits on it and sinks into the pile of sand in the end.

Fig. 1. A bouncing elastic bunny (middle) and a plastic bunny (right).

Fig. 2. Sliding and sloping failure of granular materials.

6   Discussion and Conclusion

Comparison with SPH method. MPM is more stable. There is no need to add artificial viscosity to eliminate the tensile and numerical instability. The constitutive models formerly implemented in SPH method can be easily transferred to MPM, and generate good results. However, because the interpolation of velocities from the grid to the particles brings in a loss of information, the phenomena like fragmentations and cracks require different methods to handle, which will be our future work. The APIC method [7] can also be implemented to better preserve the information between the interpolation process, which remains to be tested.

Limitations. The constitutive model we used for solid materials split the strain into two additive part, the elastic strain and the plastic strain. While this is

Fig. 3. Interaction between an elastic object and granular materials.

simple and also a good approximation to the exact problem, to truly handle finite deformation, it is better to use a multiplicative approach. Also we would like to investigate more models, hardening, and transitions between different kinds of materials. Besides, the visualization of different materials and their combination requires further study.

Conclusion. We have presented a MPM framework for simulating various solid materials including deformable objects and granular materials. The constitutive models applied in previous SPH based works can be easily adopted to our framework. The collision of different objects are handled in a stable way with the use of the grid.

Acknowledgements. This work is supported by the People Programme (Marie Curie Actions) of the European Union's Seventh Framework Programme FP7/2007-2013/ under REA grant agreement n° [612627].

References

1. An, Y., Wu, Q., Shi, C., Liu, Q.: Three-dimensional smoothed-particle hydrodynamics simulation of deformation characteristics in slope failure. Geotechnique **66**, 670–680 (2016)
2. Becker, M., Ihmsen, M., Teschner, M.: Corotated sph for deformable solids. In: Proceedings of the Fifth Eurographics Conference on Natural Phenomena (NPH 2009), pp. 27–34. Eurographics Association, Aire-la-Ville (2009). http://dx.doi. org/10.2312EG/DL/conf/EG2009/nph/027-034
3. Bui, H.H., Fukagawa, R., Sako, K., Ohno, S.: Lagrangian meshfree particles method (SPH) for large deformation and failure flows of geomaterial using elasticplastic soil constitutive model. Int. J. Numer. Anal. Methods Geomech. **32**(12), 1537–1570 (2008). http://dx.doi.org/10.1002/nag.688 http://dx.doi.org/10.1002/nag.688
4. Cleary, P.W., Das, R.: The potential for SPH modelling of solid deformation and fracture. In: Reddy, B.D. (ed.) IUTAM Symposium on Theoretical, Computational and Modelling Aspects of Inelastic Media. IUTAM BookSeries, vol. 11, pp. 287–296. Springer, Dordrecht (2008). doi:10.1007/978-1-4020-9090-5_26
5. Daviet, G., Bertails-Descoubes, F.: A semi-implicit material point method for the continuum simulation of granular materials. ACM Trans. Graph. **35**(4), 102:1–102:13 (2016). http://doi.acm.org/10.1145/2897824.2925877
6. Gray, J., Monaghan, J., Swift, R.: SPH elastic dynamics. Comput. Methods Appl. Mech. Eng. **190**(49), 6641–6662 (2001). http://www.sciencedirect.com/science/article/pii/S0045782501002547
7. Jiang, C., Schroeder, C., Selle, A., Teran, J., Stomakhin, A.: The affine particle-in-cell method. ACM Trans. Graph. **34**(4), 51:1–51:10 (2015). http://doi.acm.org/10.1145/2766996
8. Klár, G., Gast, T., Pradhana, A., Fu, C., Schroeder, C., Jiang, C., Teran, J.: Drucker-prager elastoplasticity for sand animation. ACM Trans. Graph. **35**(4), 103:1–103:12 (2016). http://doi.acm.org/10.1145/2897824.2925906
9. Libersky, L.D., Petschek, A.G.: Smooth particle hydrodynamics with strength of materials. In: Trease, H.E., Fritts, M.F., Crowley, W.P. (eds.) Advances in the Free-Lagrange Method Including Contributions on Adaptive Gridding and the Smooth Particle Hydrodynamics Method. Lecture Notes in Physics, vol. 395, pp. 248–257. Springer, Heidelberg (1991). doi:10.1007/3-540-54960-9_58

10. Müller, M., Keiser, R., Nealen, A., Pauly, M., Gross, M., Alexa, M.: Point based animation of elastic, plastic and melting objects. In: Proceedings of the 2004 ACM SIGGRAPH/Eurographics Symposium on Computer Animation (SCA 2004), pp. 141–151. Eurographics Association, Aire-la-Ville (2004). http://dx.doi.org/10.1145/1028523.1028542
11. Solenthaler, B., Schlfli, J., Pajarola, R.: A unified particle model for fluidsolid interactions. Comput. Animat. Virtual Worlds 18(1), 69–82 (2007). http://dx.doi.org/10.1002/cav.162
12. Stomakhin, A., Schroeder, C., Chai, L., Teran, J., Selle, A.: A material point method for snow simulation. ACM Trans. Graph. 32(4), 102:1–102:10 (2013). http://doi.acm.org/10.1145/2461912.2461948
13. Stomakhin, A., Schroeder, C., Jiang, C., Chai, L., Teran, J., Selle, A.: Augmented MPM for phase-change and varied materials. ACM Trans. Graph. 33(4), 138:1–138:11 (2014). http://doi.acm.org/10.1145/2601097.2601176
14. Sulsky, D., Chen, Z., Schreyer, H.: A particle method for history-dependent materials. Comput. Methods Appl. Mech. Eng. 118(1), 179–196 (1994). http://www.sciencedirect.com/science/article/pii/0045782594901120
15. Yan, X., Jiang, Y.T., Li, C.F., Martin, R.R., Hu, S.M.: Multiphase SPH simulation for interactive fluids and solids. ACM Trans. Graph. 35(4), 79:1–79:11 (2016). http://doi.acm.org/10.1145/2897824.2925897

Sampling Hierarchical Position-Based Dynamics Simulation

Meili Wang[1], Hua Zheng[1], Kun Qian[2], Shuqin Li[1(✉)],
and Xiaosong Yang[2]

[1] Northwest A&F University, Xianyang 712100, Shaanxi, China
lsq_cie@nwsuaf.edu.cn
[2] Bournemouth University, Poole, UK

Abstract. The representation of detail is an essential part of animation. However, realistically and efficiently simulating details of folds and wrinkles in cloth has always been a huge challenge. Although the position-based dynamics method can simplify and generally depict details, grids are so fine that the simulation frame is far from satisfactory. The hierarchical position-based dynamics method provides an improved scheme. However, it is not capable of optimizing all grids effectively. In addition, during the coarsening process of the hierarchical selection procedure, some polygonal parts do not have effective convergence speed. We propose a voxelization-based sampling method. The proposed sampling method not only applies to any hierarchical grid but also avoids the uneven convergence speed of local simulation through particle selection. Experimental results show that the hierarchical sampling model proposed in this paper can accelerate the convergence of all layers of details.

Keywords: Position-based dynamics · Hierarchical position-based dynamics · Deformation · Sampling

1 Introduction

The Position-based dynamics (PBD) [1] allows robust simulation of dynamic systems in real time, and PBD can be widely applied in simulating physical phenomena, such as the dynamics of deformable objects and fluids. The advantages of PBD simulation are that it gives control over explicit integration and removes typical instability problems; meanwhile, the positions of vertices and parts of objects can be manipulated directly during simulation. The explicit position-based solver is easy to understand and implement. However, the PBD simulation method comes at the price of much slower convergence.

The hierarchical position-based dynamics (HPBD) simulation method [2] has faster convergence than the PBD method while maintaining the ability to process general nonlinear constraints, and makes real-time simulation possible at a higher level of detail that satisfies interactive applications, such as computer games. However, the main problem with the HPBD method is that a poor quality grid is produced if a coarse grid is generated in arbitrary order. To overcome the disadvantages of the HPBD method,

© Springer International Publishing AG 2017
J. Chang et al. (Eds.): AniNex 2017, LNCS 10582, pp. 45–55, 2017.
https://doi.org/10.1007/978-3-319-69487-0_4

we propose an adaptive-sampling HPBD method that generates even and regular sampling for mesh representation.

2 Related Works

PBD method has been widely used for deformable and rigid bodies simulation owing to its simplicity. A complete survey of the PBD method can be found in [1]. The main feature of the PBD method is its direct control over vertex positions, which eliminates the overshooting problem of force-based methods. The physical properties of simulated objects are determined by the constraints applied. Various constraints have been designed to solve different scenarios in deformation applications; e.g., shape-matching constraints [3, 4], strain-limiting constraints [5], collision detection [6], melting constraints [7], and continuous-material constraints [8]. The main disadvantage of PBD is the low convergence rate resulting from the Gauss–Seidel and Jacobian constraint solvers. These solvers solve the constraints one at a time, resulting in the slow propagation of information on the mesh.

Various techniques have been proposed to improve the convergence of PBD method. Adding additional geometrical constraints to confine the movement of particles is the most widely used technique. For example, the long-range attachment [9] constraint is a simple and robust constraint that confines the distance between unconstrained particles and attachments (e.g., in the case of an inextensible rod) and prevents stretching in cloth simulation. However, these techniques only improve the convergence rate of attached vertices. Wang et al. [10] proposed a Chebyshev semi-iterative approach for accelerating projective and position-based dynamics. The approach affects the projective dynamics of the PBD method. Modeling a multi-grid structure is a more general approach to accelerating the convergence rate. The HPBD method proposed in [2] refines the original mesh to a multi-layer coarse mesh. The coarse mesh provides motion prediction for the fine layer, which can effectively reduce the effect of information propagation on the mesh. However, the mesh generation method is not particularly robust and may generate poor-quality meshes, as will be discussed in Sect. 3.

Voxelization represents the surface of a 3D model with small cubes called voxels. In this way, the model data can be converted into a regular signal that is important for extracting efficient feature descriptors. The concept of voxelization was proposed by Kaufman in 1986 [11]. The simplest and most commonly used voxelization is binary voxelization, where the value of voxelization is either 0 or 1. Rueda et al. [12] proposed a simple and robust algorithm without gridding, but this algorithm only generates regular grids. Huang et al. [13] proposed a fast voxelization that can realize a 6-neighborhood closure or a 26-neighborhood closure, and ensure the authenticity, minimization, and correspondence of voxelization.

In this paper, we propose employing a voxelization sampling-based [14] hierarchical mesh generation method to voxelize the vertices, sides, and surfaces of a 3D model, thus generating a correct voxel model of the object from which features can be extracted, which can improve the mesh quality in HPBD simulation and allow faster convergence.

3 Main Problems and Error Generation in HPBD Simulation

3.1 Summary of the Main Problems of HPBD

The result of PBD simulation depends on time step, iteration, and constraint traversal order. The stiffness of the PBD system increases as the iteration increases. The relationship between the iteration and stiffness is nonlinear, which makes it difficult to choose parameters for rescaling stiffness according to the iteration because the PBD solver is an approximation of implicit Euler integration that is solved in Gaussian or Jacobian style. Such a solution will converge slowly because the constraint sets are mostly unfeasible, resulting in incompatibility between different constraint sets and oscillation.

The use of multiple grids is one of the most common methods of solving the convergence problem of PBD method. The HPBD method is based on multiple grids and applies a certain rule for the generation of each layer's mesh. A multi-grid coarse mesh (coarse level) is generated according to the original mesh (fine level), using the movement of the coarse mesh for motion prediction of the fine-level mesh. That is, the coarse mesh provides movement guidance for the fine mesh, reducing the time for information propagation on the mesh (i.e., accelerating the convergence). The main problem with the HPBD method is that generating the coarse grid in an arbitrary order produces a poor-quality grid.

We describe the process of HPBD error generation and highlight problems in Sect. 3.2.

3.2 Reproducing a Problematic HPBD Generation Process

The process of HPBD error generation can be described as selecting the particle subsets at each level; generating the *cardinality-n* constraints for coarser levels; and choosing p_j among the coarse neighbors of p_i.

The particle p_j is the coarse particle that the fine particle collapses to, while C represents the *cardinality-n* constraints.

To select particle subsets, we first define the original coordinates as shown in Fig. 1 (1). The resulting subsets are indicated as black points. In contrast, the white points are fine particles. The generation process is the same as that in HPBD simulation.

To generate coarser levels, we need to choose the particle p_j where the particle p_i will collapse to. We first compute the average position of the coarse neighbors of p_i using the original positions of the particles. The neighbor closest to the average position is then selected as p_j.

The particles are traversed row by row in order. The black particles selected for the next level are called coarse particles. We then introduce the generation process on a polygonal mesh rather than a triangular mesh.

We denote the first point of the first line by $P(1, 1)$, the second point of the first line by $P(1, 2)$, the first point of the second line by $P(2, 1)$, and so on.

To simplify the original mesh, we start at the first fine particle $P(1, 1)$ and calculate the average distance between $P(1, 1)$ and its neighbors. We then compare the differences with the average distance, and obtain the minimum difference p_j that it is certain

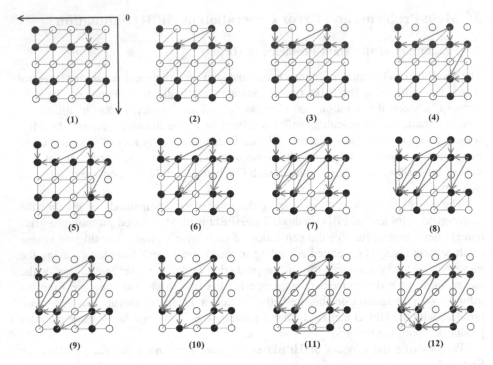

Fig. 1. Process of HPBD problem generation.

the fine particles collapse into. In Fig. 1(1), we see that p_j for $\mathbf{P}(1, 1)$ is $\mathbf{P}(2, 2)$. We next simplify the constraint to generate the coarse mesh. As in HPBD simulation, the fine particle $\mathbf{P}(1, 1)$ and p_j ($\mathbf{P}(2, 2)$) have a common point of adjacency.

The constraints for $\mathbf{P}(1, 1)$, that are removed, connected with adjacent coarse particles, without updating the constraints that coarse points corresponding to the fine particle are connected to its inclusion point p_j. In the example shown in Fig. 1(4), the particle p_j corresponding to the fine particle $\mathbf{P}(3,1)$ is $\mathbf{P}(4,2)$, and the particle $\mathbf{P}(2,1)$ adjacent to the fine particle $\mathbf{P}(3,1)$ is not constrained to $\mathbf{P}(4,2)$. We thus need to delete the original constraints and add a new constraint from $\mathbf{P}(2, 1)$ to $\mathbf{P}(4, 2)$ along a new edge. In Fig. 1(9) and (10), the resulting rough polygons show that it does not work well as HPBD described. It is also seen in Figs. 1(3) and (4) that there are unilateral constraints.

3.3   Defective Results of HPBD Simulation

When the quality of the coarse mesh is unsatisfactory, the irregular distribution of the point cloud results in undetected collisions at the coarse level. The coarse-level mesh provides motion guidance for the fine layer, which can also be considered as a constraint provided by the coarse layer. When the coarse mesh does not detect a collision, it provides a false motion prediction for the fine layer. If the fine layer captures the collision, the vertices in the collision invoke the solution of the collision constraint, contradicting the position delta provided by the coarse mesh. If there are low number of iterations and hierarchical layers, the contradiction becomes obvious especially when using a Jacobian-style solution.

The result of such contradictions between coarse mesh constraints and collision constraints is instability. Even using the relaxation strategy proposed in [15] may lead to poor stability because the vertices in a collision change between a collided state and an un-collided state, and the vertices will finally oscillate on the boundary of the collider or completely run into the collider. Figure 2 shows the results of the HPBD method caused by the poor quality of the generated mesh.

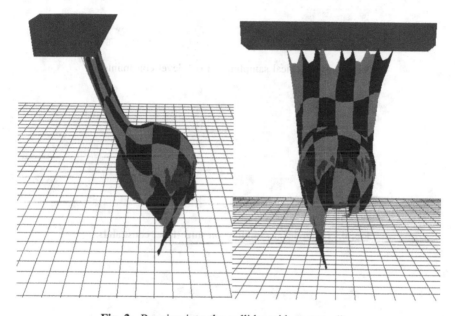

Fig. 2. Running into the collider with poor quality.

4   Multi-grid Generation Based on Importance Sampling

4.1   Voxelization-Based Sampling

The HPBD method proposed in [2] uses both irregular and regular sampling for mesh representation. However, the irregular mesh cannot perform well in collision detection when dealing with large holes as discussed above, while the regular mesh can result in misidentification and lose important geometric information. Therefore, better voxelization sampling is needed for constructing the mesh. A voxelization-based adaptive sampling method is ideal for capturing different levels of detail. In this paper, we apply voxelization down-sampling to efficiently distribute the samples on the mesh. The idea is to generate the hierarchical mesh structure by applying voxelization sampling to the original mesh and then to remesh the sampled points to generate the coarse simulation mesh. The link between each hierarchical layer during simulation is the same as that of the method proposed in [14].

The results of hierarchical sampling are shown in Figs. 3, 4 and 5. The results of our method are shown on the left while the results of the original HPBD method are shown on the right. It can be seen that our method improves uniformity and solves the unilateral and polygonal problems, thus accelerating local convergence.

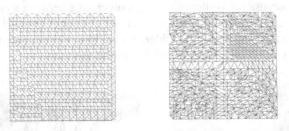

Fig. 3. Hierarchical sampling on one-level constraints.

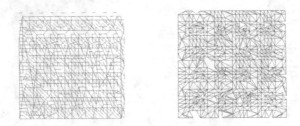

Fig. 4. Hierarchical sampling on three-level constraints.

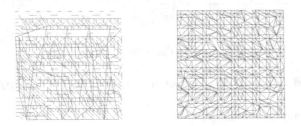

Fig. 5. Hierarchical sampling on five-level constraints.

4.2   Building Links Between Layers

We obtain an even coarse mesh by sampling rather than using the HPBD particle subset selection algorithm. We compute the fine points according to the sampled values. For example, if the sampling points are X_1, X_2 and X_3, as shown in Fig. 6, then the weights w_1, w_2, w_3 represent how the coarse particles update the positions of the original fine particles respectively. The positions of the fine particles are computed by Eq. 1.

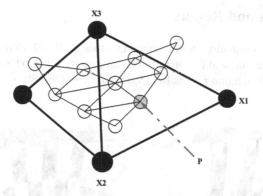

Fig. 6. Sampling example.

We have $X_1, X_2, X_3 \in R^3, P \in R^3, w_1, w_2, w_3 \in R$, and

$$P = w_1X_1 + w_2X_2 + w_3X_3. \tag{1}$$

This equation is equivalent to

$$\begin{pmatrix} P_x \\ P_y \\ P_z \end{pmatrix} = \begin{pmatrix} X_{1x} & X_{2x} & X_{3x} \\ X_{1y} & X_{2y} & X_{3y} \\ X_{1z} & X_{2z} & X_{3z} \end{pmatrix} \cdot \begin{pmatrix} w_1 \\ w_2 \\ w_3 \end{pmatrix}, \tag{2}$$

where P is the position matrix for the fine particle p. A is the position matrix for the parents of particle p, and W is the weight matrix. We have

$$P = A \cdot W, \tag{3}$$

$$W = A^{-1} \cdot P. \tag{4}$$

In this way, it can be determined that a fine particle has at least three parents.

We compute the weights of the coarse particle in the update of the positions of the fine particles and avoid the generation of non-triangular polygons.

We use Eq. 5 to update the position of particle p_i:

$$p_i \leftarrow p_i + \sum_{j \in P_i} w_{ij}(p_j - q_j), \tag{5}$$

where p_i is the set of indices of the parents of particle i, and w_{ij} is the affected weight of the parent p_j of p_i.

5 Experiments and Results

Figure 7 compares simulation results obtained using HPBD (left) and our method (right). These simulations had five iterations with gravity set to 0.98 and three layers in the hierarchy. The simulation results for 15 iterations and gravity set to 0.28 are shown in Fig. 8.

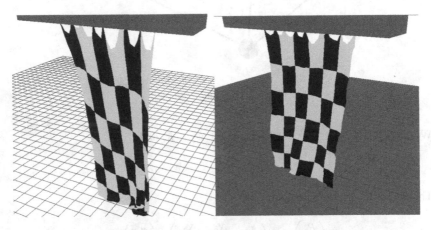

Fig. 7. Simulation comparison for gravity of 0.98.

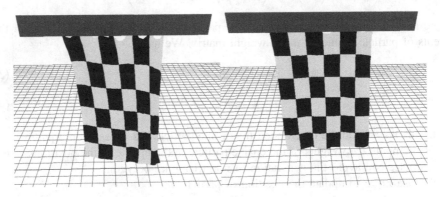

Fig. 8. Simulation comparison for gravity of 0.28.

We compare the spring relative change rate (SRCR) [2] among the PBD method, the HPBD method, and our proposed method in Table 1. For the results in Table 1, the original mesh contains 961 particles, the number of iterations is set to five, and gravity is set to 0.98. The SRCR for the PBD method is 67% while that for the HPBD method at level 1 is 63%. For our proposed method, the SRCR is 38% with 400 sampling

Table 1. Comparison of the SRCR among PBD, HPBD and our proposed method.

Methods	PBD	HPBD	Sample-1	Sample-2
Level 1	67%	63%	38	46
Level 2		48%	29	34
Level 3		41%	26	26

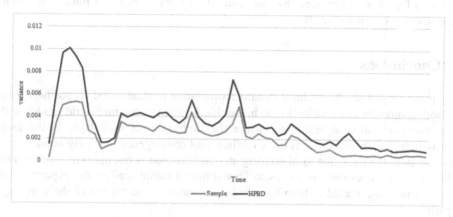

Fig. 9. Stability of collision tests.

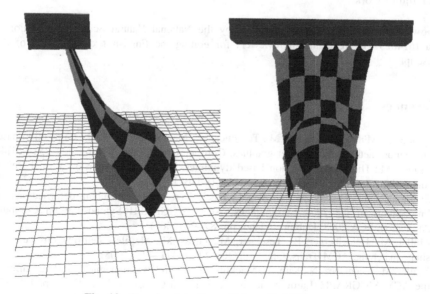

Fig. 10. Running into the collider with improvement.

particles (Sample 1) and 46% with 200 sampling particles (Sample 2). The same tendency can be seen at levels 2 and 3. These results indicate that the proposed method has a higher SRCR. If we change gravity to 0.28 and increase the number of iterations to 15, then the SRCR is 43% for the PBD method and 13% for the HPBD method, but only 7% for our method.

The computation time was 97 ms for PBD, 34 ms for HPBD, and 45 ms for our method.

Finally, the stability of the collision tests for five iterations and gravity set to 0.98 is shown in Fig. 9. It can be seen that our method fixes the problem of running through the collider, as seen in Fig. 10.

6 Conclusions

This paper proposed a hierarchical dynamic simulation method based on position. The method samples from a distribution to hierarchically construct a multi-grid model, and uses the voxelization algorithm to ensure the uniformity of each layer in the grid distribution. The overall effect is more realistic and convergence is greatly accelerated, thus avoiding the issue that local convergence acceleration is not uniform for different grid states. The question remains as to how different samples affect the experimental results, which is reflected in both the number of samples and the use of the sampling algorithm.

Although our sampling method improves the quality of cloth simulation, different sample sizes and reconstruction affect the convergence rate. This will be another topic of our future work.

Acknowledgments. This work was funded by the National Natural Science Foundation of China (61402374). We thank all reviewers for editing the English text of a draft of this manuscript.

References

1. Bender, J., Müller, M., Otaduy, M., Teschner, M., Macklin, M.: A survey on position-based simulation methods in computer graphics. Comput. Graph. Forum **33**(6), 228–251 (2014)
2. Müller, M.: Hierarchical position based dynamics. In: The Workshop on Virtual Reality Interactions & Physical Simulations, pp. 1–10. DBLP (2008)
3. Steinemann, D., Otaduy, M., Gross, M.: Fast adaptive shape matching deformations. In: Proceedings of the 2008 Eurographics, ACM SIGGRAPH Symposium on Computer Animation, SCA 2008, Dublin, Ireland, pp. 87–94 (2008)
4. Müller, M., Heidelberger, B., Teschner, M., Gross, M.: Meshless deformations based on shape matching. ACM Trans. Graph. (TOG) **24**(3), 471–478 (2005)
5. Müller, M., Chentanez, N., Kim, T., Macklin, M.: Strain based dynamics. In: Proceedings of the ACM SIGGRAPH, Eurographics Symposium on Computer Animation, pp. 149–157. Eurographics Association (2014)
6. Müller, M., Chentanez, N., Kim, T., Macklin, M.: Air meshes for robust collision handling. ACM Trans. Graph. (TOG) **34**(4), 1–9 (2015)

7. Müller, M., Keiser, R., Nealen, A., Pauly, M., Gross, M., Alexa, M.: Point based animation of elastic, plastic and melting objects. In: Proceedings of the 2004 ACM SIGGRAPH, Eurographics Symposium on Computer Animation, pp. 141–151. Eurographics Association (2004)
8. Bender, J., Koschier, D., Charrier, P.: Weber D: Position-based simulation of continuous materials. Comput. Graph. **44**, 1–10 (2014)
9. Li, Y., Christie, M., Siret, O., Kuopa, R.: Cloning crowd motions. In: Lee, J., Kry, P. (eds.) Proceedings of the 11th ACM SIGGRAPH, ACM SIGGRAPH Symposium on Computer Animation, SCA 2012, Lausanne, Switzerland, pp. 201–210 (2012)
10. Wang, H.: A chebyshev semi-iterative approach for accelerating projective and position-based dynamics. ACM Trans. Graph. **34**(6), 1–9 (2015)
11. Kaufman, A., Shimony, E.: 3D scan-conversion algorithms for voxel-based graphics. In: Proceedings of the 1986 Workshop on Interactive 3D Graphics, pp. 45–76. ACM, New York (1987)
12. Rueda, A., Segura, R., Feito, F., Miras, J., Ogyar, C.: Voxelization of solids using simplicial coverings. In: Proceedings of the 12th Internet Conference in Central Europe on Computer Graphics Visualization and Computer Vision (2004)
13. Yagel, R., Filippov, V., Kurzion, Y., Huang, J.: An accurate method for voxelizing polygon meshes. In: Proceedings of the 1998 IEEE Symposium on Volume Visualization, pp. 119–126. IEEE, New York (1998)
14. Chang, H., Lai, Y., Yao, C., Hua, K., Niu, Y., Liu, F.: Geometry-shader-based real-time voxelization and applications. Vis. Comput. **30**(3), 327–340 (2014)
15. Macklin, M., Müller, M., Chentanez, N., Kim, T.: Unified particle physics for real-time applications. ACM Trans. Graph. **33**(4), 153 (2014)

Fast and Robust Point-in-Spherical-Polygon Tests Using Multilevel Spherical Grids

Jing Li[1,2(✉)], Han Zhang[1], and Wencheng Wang[2,3]

[1] State Key Laboratory of Integrated Information System Technology,
Institute of Software, Chinese Academy of Sciences, Beijing, China
lijing2015@iscas.ac.cn
[2] State Key Laboratory of Computer Science, Institute of Software,
Chinese Academy of Sciences, Beijing, China
[3] The University of Chinese Academy of Sciences, Beijing, China

Abstract. Point-in-spherical-polygon determination is widely required in applications over the earth. However, existing methods for point-in-polygon tests cannot be applied directly, due to non-Euclidean computation over the spherical surface. Thus, it is general to transform a spherical polygon into a planar polygon via projection, and then perform point-in-polygon tests. Unfortunately, this is expensive and may cause determination errors. In this paper, we propose to subdivide the spherical grid cells iteratively, and apply the ray-crossing method locally in grid cells, which is by one of our previous works. As a result, this not only avoids expensive transformation computation, but also guarantees robust determination for point-in-spherical-polygon tests. Experimental results attest our effectiveness, and show an acceleration of five orders of magnitude over a popularly used method.

Keywords: Point-in-spherical-polygon test · Multilevel grid · Ray-crossing

1 Introduction

Applications over the earth have been increasing rapidly, e.g. space exploration, mobile communication, and internet monitoring. Here, a fundamental operation is determining whether a point is inside a spherical polygon, called as a *point-in-spherical-polygon test*. As the concerned polygon over the earth generally has many edges, and the query points are normally in a very large number, it is a challenge to run fast point-in-spherical-polygon tests.

Though there have been a lot of methods for point-in-polygon tests on a plane, they cannot be directly employed for point-in-spherical-polygon tests, due to the non-Euclidean computation over the spherical surface. With regard to this, it is commonly adopted to transform a spherical polygon to a planar polygon by projecting it onto a plane through a certain projection, e.g. cylindrical projection, and then perform point-in-polygon tests on the plane. Besides a high cost, such a treatment unfortunately suffers from the distortion of transforming a curved

© Springer International Publishing AG 2017
J. Chang et al. (Eds.): AniNex 2017, LNCS 10582, pp. 56–66, 2017.
https://doi.org/10.1007/978-3-319-69487-0_5

spherical edge to a straight planar edge, which would cause determination errors due to the precision problem.

Realizing that performing the analysis directly in the non-Euclidean spherical surface [1] can avoid the precision problem caused by projection, Bevis and Chatelain [2] extended the traditional ray-crossing method to treat spherical polygons. It is a popular robust method for point-in-spherical-polygon tests till now [3,4]. It works by first specifying a point X inside the polygon, then connecting the query point Q with X and counting the polygon edges that XQ intersects with. If the counted number is even, this means Q is inside the polygon, otherwise it is not. Similar to the planar ray-crossing method, this method needs to check every edge of the spherical polygon. Moreover, it requires a considerable amount of trigonometric calculations to determine whether two spherical line segments intersect with each other, which is more costly than additions or multiplications. Therefore, though the method can avoid errors due to projection, its testing speed is not fast. This also prevents it from applications, especially those that need to process many points in real time.

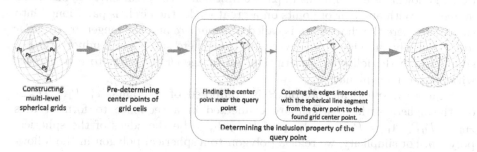

Fig. 1. The workflow of our method for fast and robust point-in-spherical-polygon tests.

In this paper, we address this challenge by presenting a fast point-in-spherical-polygon test method with the distortion problem well solved. In our method, we first build grid cells along longitudes and altitudes, and iteratively subdivide the grid cells that contain polygonal edges until the edges in a grid cell are in a smaller number than a set threshold value. Afterwards, with such a constructed multilevel spherical grid, we adopt one of our previous works to perform point-in-polygon tests [5] for query points. It is by predetermining the inclusion property of the center points of the cells as a prior, and then applying the ray crossing method locally in the cell that contains the query point by producing the line segment from the query point to the center point of the cell. Since each cell contains not many edges, the method is very fast. For the details, please refer to reference [5].

During the grid construction and point determination, one basic operation is to judge whether two spherical line segments intersect with each other, which is more difficult than the intersection test between two line segments on the plane. Instead of solving the problem by projection or by calculating angles in the non-Euclidean space as done in existing works, we perform the test directly in the three dimensional space. As we know, the smallest distance between two points on the sphere surface is the smaller arc of the *great circle* passing through these two points, the located plane of the circle contains the sphere center. The edges of a polygon and the spherical line segments we generate to connect center points and query points on the sphere surface are all on their corresponding great circles. Thus, to determine whether a spherical line segment intersects with an edge of the spherical polygon, we can calculate the relative positions of the two vertices of the spherical line segment against the plane that contains the edge. In this way, not only much computation can be saved, but also errors caused by projection are avoided. Figure 1 shows the workflow of our method.

2   Our Algorithm

2.1   Conventions and Definitions

Before introducing our algorithm, we first clarify some definitions and conventions. Following the definitions in [2], we first define the great circle as discussed in Sect. 1. With any pair of points on a great circle, the circle is partitioned into two arcs, where the shorter arc is called a *minor arc* and the longer arc a *major arc*. Generally, an edge of a polygon on the sphere surface is a minor arc. For simplicity, in the following description, an arc generally refers to a minor arc without special explanation.

Suppose a spherical polygon S is composed of n points, $P_0, P_1, ..., P_{n-1}$ on the sphere surface, which are connected in a sequence to form n arcs $A_0 = P_0P_1, A_1 = P_1P_2, ..., A_{n-1} = P_{n-1}P_0$, to be the edges of the spherical polygon. For simplicity, we refer a polygon to a spherical polygon in the following discussion.

Suppose S is viewed from outside the sphere and it does not contain holes. We define the region on the left-hand side is inside the spherical polygon while the region on the right-hand side is outside, when traveling along the polygon edges in the anti-clockwise sequence. When S contains nested holes, we define the holes at the odd levels of the hierarchy for the nested holes are oriented in a clockwise direction, whereas the holes at the even levels are oriented in the opposite direction (e.g. anti-clockwise direction). Under such conventions, the definition of the inside/outside region of a polygon remains unchanged. For the polygon in Fig. 1, $P_0P_1P_2$ is the outer boundary of the polygon and $P_3P_4P_5$ is the boundary of a hole at the first level.

The location of a point P on the sphere surface is specified by its latitude (λ) and longitude (ϕ), denoted by $P(\lambda, \phi)$, $\lambda \in [-90°, 90°]$, $\phi \in [-180°, 180°]$. The point-in-spherical-polygon test is defined as given a query point Q and a polygon S on the sphere surface, determine if Q is inside S.

2.2   Constructing Multilevel Spherical Grids

In the spherical space, the longitude-latitude grid (called as *grid* in short) is the most commonly used coordinate system. It uniformly partitions the lines of longitude and latitude into segments and then generates regions by these segments. Owing to the uniform property, indexing in a grid is straightforward and easy to implement. However, for global applications, the distribution of polygons is usually very uneven. Polygons with tiny edges (comparing to the sphere's radius) may distribute sparsely on the whole surface of the sphere. In such a case, a uniform grid may contain a large number of small cells, most of which are empty, wasting too much storage. Therefore, we construct multilevel spherical grids. That is, we first construct a global uniform longitude-latitude grid without a high resolution to cover the whole sphere surface, and dispatch polygon edges into its cells. Then, we subdivide the cells having too many polygon edges into uniform sub-grids, which form the second-level grids. Such a subdivision process is repeated iteratively until the edges in each grid cell are fewer than a set threshold or the constructed levels reach a set value. As the cells to be subdivided are only in the regions with many edges, there are many large cells to reduce the number of cells and the storage requirement.

The resolutions for grids on each level are set as follows. According to our observation, in global applications, spherical polygons usually have many short edges and occupy small regions. So, it is better to construct a coarse grid for the first-level grid and finer grids for other levels. Therefore, we give a fixed low resolution for the first-level grid and calculate the resolutions for the sub-grids at other levels by the number of edges they contain. Equation 1 lists the formula for calculating the grid resolutions.

$$
\begin{cases}
M_\lambda(i,j) = R_\lambda, M_\phi(i,j) = R_\phi & i = 1, j = 1 \\
M_\lambda(i,j) = l_\lambda(i,j)\sqrt{kN(i,j)/(l_\lambda(i,j)l_\phi(i,j))} & 1 < i \le MAXD, 1 \le j < M_i \\
M_\phi(i,j) = l_\phi(i,j)\sqrt{kN(i,j)/(l_\lambda(i,j)l_\phi(i,j))}
\end{cases}
$$

$$(1)$$

In Eq. (1), (i,j) denotes the jth grid on the ith level, M_λ and M_ϕ are the number of cells for the grid in the latitude direction and the longitude direction respectively. l_λ and l_ϕ are the size of the grid in the latitude direction and the longitude direction respectively, which is measured by the degree of latitude and longitude. N is the number of edges in the grid. $MAXD$ is the set maximum level of the multilevel grids. M_i is the total number of grids at the ith level. k is a coefficient. R_λ and R_ϕ are two empiric values. In our implementation, $MAXD, k, R_\lambda$ and R_ϕ are set to 4, 1.0, 10 and 20 respectively.

In dispatching an edge into grid cells, we first trace the edge and find the cells crossed by the edge, which is by calculating the intersections of the edge with the boundaries of grid cells sequentially along the edge, then record the edge in all these crossed cells. Note that cares should be taken for the polygon edge crossing the line at Longitude 180°, because the value of longitude jumps at the crossing point. In this case, we split the edge into two edges at the crossing point and dispatch the two edges respectively.

2.3 Predetermining Center Points of Grid Cells

After the multilevel grids are constructed, we determine the inclusion property of all the center points in the grid cells. These predetermined center points will be used as priors to promote the determination of query points. We start the determination of center points from the first-level grid, and then process the grids level by level until the grids at the deepest level are processed.

For each grid at each level, we take the similar measure as [5] to determine the center points by using the ray-crossing method locally. That is, for two neighboring center points, O_1 and O_2, we connect them with an arc segment. If the inclusion property of O_1 is known, the inclusion property of O_2 can be derived by counting the intersections between the arc segment and the polygon edges in the cells crossed by the arc segment using the rules listed in Table 1.

Table 1. Rules of determining the inclusion property of a point by another center point with known property.

Property of O_1	Priority of the intersection count	Property of O_2
Inside	Odd	Outside
Inside	Even	Inside
Outside	Odd	Inside
Outside	Even	Outside

To determine all the center points, we connect center points one by one with arc segments to form a traversal path, as illustrated in Fig. 2. When the first center point on the path is determined, the following center points on the path can be determined one by one with the counted intersections locally as described above. Similar to [5], a singular case may appear that a center point overlaps an edge or a vertex of the polygon. To this, we take the same measure as [5] that just mark the center point as singular and continue to treat the next center point on the path. Figure 2 shows this process.

Though the basic processing steps are similar to [5], there are two main differences when performing it on the sphere surface. The first one is for determining the intersection between two line segments. Here, we need to calculate the intersection of two arc segments (one is an edge of the polygon, and the other is an arc segment connecting two center points). The second is how to determine the first center point on a traversal path. In the planar case, it can be determined by finding a point outside the grid's bounding box, which is sure to be outside the polygon. However, this is infeasible for the first-level grid on the sphere surface as the grid covers the whole sphere surface. For a grid on the other levels, it is still sophisticated to find a point with known inclusion property outside the grid because the region outside the grid may belong to the grids on other levels. For these problems, we propose two solutions, as discussed below.

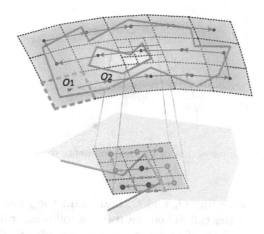

Fig. 2. The process of determining center points of multilevel grids. Inside, outside and singular center points are denoted by green, red and orange points respectively. Cells marked by orange boundaries are the starting cells of the paths for determination. (Color figure online)

To determine whether two arc segments intersect with each other, we make use of the relative positions of the vertices of an arc segment against the plane passing through the other arc segment and the sphere's center. Specifically, suppose AB and CD are two arc segments to be tested, O is the sphere's center, γ_{AB} is the plane passing through AB and O, and γ_{CD} is the plane passing through CD and O, then AB intersects with CD if and only if A and B are on different sides of γ_{CD} and C and D are on different sides of γ_{AB}, as showed in Fig. 3.

Note that in the determination, one arc segment is an edge of the polygon, and the other is an arc segment connecting two center points. According to the definition in Sect. 2.1, an arc segment refers to a part of a great circle. This means the arc is on the plane of the great circle through the sphere's center. In the implementation, longitude and latitude are transformed to rectangular coordinates and all the calculations are carried out in a rectangular coordinate system. The relative position of a vertex against a plane can be obtained by the normal of the plane. Taking the vertex C and the plane γ_{AB} as an example, suppose $\overline{OA}$, $\overline{AB}$ and $\overline{AC}$ are directed straight line segments and $w = (\overline{OA} \times \overline{AB}) \cdot \overline{AC}$, then if $w > 0$, C is on the left side of γ_{AB} (or the arc segment AB), similarly, if $w < 0$, C is on the right side of γ_{AB} (or the arc segment AB).

In [2], determining the intersection of arcs is handled directly on the sphere's surface by comparing the angles between arcs, which involves many trigonometric functions. Comparing to this, the measure proposed here can save a large amount of computation as only simple additions and multiplications are needed.

In determining the first center point on the traversal path for a grid, instead of finding a point outside the grid, we determine it by the edges in the same cell. As showed in Fig. 4, O_i is the center point of a non-empty cell $Cell_i$ (i.e. it contains edges). AB is an edge in $Cell_i$ and C is the midpoint of AB. We generate

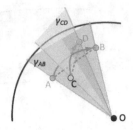

Fig. 3. Determining the intersection of two arc segments directly in the three dimensional space.

an arc segment by connecting O_i and C, and count the intersections between O_iC and the edges in the cell. Then we use the following rules to determine the inclusion property of O_i: if O_i is on the left side of AB, then O_i is inside the polygon when the counted number for intersections is even, otherwise it is outside. Similarly, if O_i is on the right side of AB, then O_i is inside the polygon when the counted number for intersections is odd, otherwise it is outside. In Fig. 4, O_iC does not intersect any edge and O_i is on the left side of AB, so O_i is inside the polygon. The relative position of O_i to AB is calculated as described above.

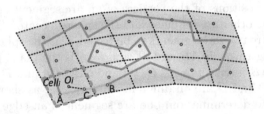

Fig. 4. Determining the inclusion property of the first center point on a traverse path

2.4 Point-in-Spherical-Polygon Test

With the constructed multilevel grids and the predetermined grid center points, we determine a query point as follows. Firstly, we search for a non-singular grid center point close to the query point in the multilevel grids. Specifically, we start the search from the first-level grid. We first find the grid cell that the query point falls in. If the cell's center point is singular, we search other cells around the cell gradually from near to far until a cell with non-singular center point is found. If the cell is a leaf node (i.e. it is not subdivided), the search is finished. If the cell is at a middle node, indicating that it is subdivided and has a sub-grid, we enter the sub-grid and search for a cell which has a non-singular center point and near the query point. Repeat such a searching process until a leaf node with a non-singular center point is found. Then, an arc segment is generated by connecting the cell's center point and the query point. By counting the intersections of the arc segment with the edges in the cells crossed by the arc segment, the query point can be determined by the same rule for predetermining center points, as showed in Table 1.

Figure 5 shows an example. In the figure, Q falls in the cell bounded by orange lines. As the cell has a sub-grid, we enter the sub-grid and search for the cell that Q falls in. Thus, the cell bounded by purple lines is found. As the cell does not have a sub-grid and it has a non-singular center point O, then O is selected as the nearest non-singular center point to Q. So we connect Q with C by an arc segment. As O is inside the polygon and QC dose not intersect any edge, it is determined that Q is inside the polygon.

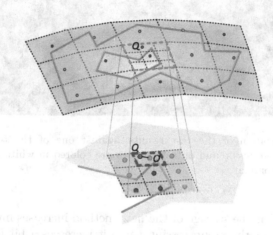

Fig. 5. Determining a query point locally with multilevel grids and predetermined center points

3   Results and Discussion

To test the performance of our method, we performed tests on a laptop installed with an Intel(R) Atom(TM) x7 1.6 GHz CPU, 4 GB RAM and Win10 operation system. We made two sets of experiments, one for testing the time and storage performance, and the other for testing the accuracy.

For the first set of experiments, we selected 7 spherical polygons with similar shape, whose number of edges are in a range from 2,927 to 92,781. Figure 6 shows one of them. For each polygon, we generated 1,000,000 query points randomly distributed within the bounding box of the polygon. We tested the time and storage cost for our new method. We also implemented the method of [2] for comparison, which is still one of the popular solutions for point-in-spherical-polygon tests. As described in Sects. 2 and 3, this method needs a large amount of trigonometric calculation to determine the intersection of arcs, which is too slow for testing 1,000,000 points. Because of this, we improved the method of [2] by using our method proposed in Sect. 2 to determine the intersection between arc segments. As the method does not need auxiliary structure and preprocessing, we only recorded its total time for determining all query points. Table 2 lists the statistical results.

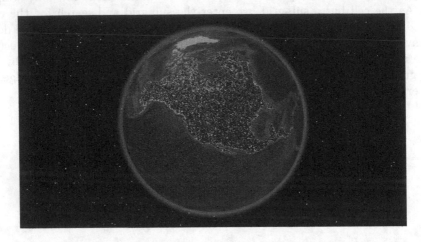

Fig. 6. The visualization of the test results against one of the tested polygons, NorthAmerica7, where inside and outside points are colored in white and red respectively. (Color figure online)

Results show that the storage of the new method increases linearly with the number of edges. For the preprocessing time, it increases a bit faster than the linear growth. As for the total time of determining the query points, it decreases with the increase of the number of edges. This is because test polygons are obtained by sampling one original data. When a polygon has more edges, the edges tend to be shorter, which is in favor of decreasing the number of intersections because shorter edges are likely to overlap fewer cells. Comparing to the improved method of [2], our method achieves an acceleration of about five orders of magnitude, as given in Table 2. Though our method needs additional space for storing grids and extra time for constructing grids, both the storage cost and preprocessing time are within a reasonable range. Note that even including the preprocessing time, our new method is still much faster, achieving an acceleration of several magnitudes. Clearly, with these advantages, our method is very suitable for fast determining many query points against large scale polygons with many edges, which is an increasingly popular requirement in modern global applications.

For the second set of experiments, we select a polygon, Antarctica, which overlaps the South Pole, to test the determination accuracy of the new method. As errors are more likely to appear near the boundary of a polygon, we generated 9,409 query points around the polygon's boundary, which has 54 edges. For each point, the distance from the point to the nearest edge is within 5% of the average length of polygon edges. To compare with our method, we implemented

Table 2. Performance comparison of our method against the improved method of [2]

Polygon	Edge#	St(KB)[a]	T_p(s)[b]	T_q(s)[c]	T_{q-SRC}(s)[d]	$Acce.ratio_1$[e]	$Acce.ratio_2$[f]
NorthAmerica0	2,927	244	0.068	0.96	2,652	2,762	2,579
NorthAmerica1	4,909	425	0.12	0.88	4,381	4,977	4,380
NorthAmerica2	9,253	831	0.23	0.71	8,318	11,714	8,848
NorthAmerica3	19,637	1721	0.54	0.6	17,668	29,446	15,497
NorthAmerica4	32,138	2750	0.94	0.54	28,953	53,616	19,562
NorthAmerica5	47,982	4092	1.51	0.49	43,369	88,507	21,684
NorthAmerica6	70,926	5947	2.49	0.45	63,883	141,961	21,728
NorthAmerica7	92,781	7729	3.56	0.43	83,635	194,499	20,960

[a] St: the storage required for the auxiliary structure by our method.
[b] T_p: the preprocessing time of our method, which includes both the time for constructing the grids and the time for predetermining the center points.
[c] T_q: the total time for determining all the query points by our method.
[d] T_{q-SRC}: the total time for determining all the query points by the improved ray-crossing method.
[e] $Acce.ratio_1$: the acceleration ratios, computed as $Acce.ratio_1 = (T_{q-SRC} - T_q)/T_q$.
[f] $Acce.ratio_2$: the acceleration ratios, computed as $Acce.ratio_2 = (T_{q-SRC} - T_p - T_q)/(T_p + T_q)$.

a projection-based method which is usually used in practice. It first projects a polygon to a plane by azimuthal projection and then uses a planar ray-crossing method.

When a spherical polygon is projected on the plane, the polygon edges will become planar curves. So the planar polygon obtained by the projection is a polygon with curved edges. To carry out ray-crossing method on the plane, straight edges are generated by connecting the vertices of the planar polygon. Therefore, if a query point's projection falls in the region between a curved edge and its corresponding straight edge, errors may appear, e.g., the point's projection is determined outside the polygon by the straight edge while in fact it is inside the polygon.

Such errors caused by projection were verified by our results. Figure 7 shows the polygon Antarctica and the query points after the azimuthal projection. Figure 7(a) and (b) show the test results by the projection-based method and our method respectively, where inside and outside points are marked by purple and orange points respectively. The regions causing errors are illustrated in green. By the enlarged views, it is clear that points falling in the problem regions are mistakenly classified as outside the polygon. In contrast, all such points are correctly determined by our method as showed by the enlarged view in Fig. 7(b). This is because our method does not use projection which intrinsically avoids such errors. Figure 7(c) shows the projection of mistakenly determined points with the projection based method, which are illustrated by red points. With a statistical investigation, about 15.6% of query points are judged incorrectly by the projection-based method while all the query points are correctly determined by our method.

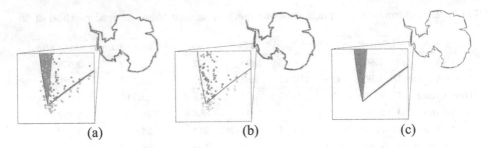

(a)   (b)   (c)

Fig. 7. Results of the accuracy test of the polygon "Antarctica".

4   Conclusion

In summary, we present a fast and robust method for point-in-spherical-polygon tests. By constructing multi-level grids and predetermining grid center points, point-in-spherical-polygon test can be carried out rapidly with local operations. Here, we develop a novel measure to fast determine whether two arc segments are intersected with each other, through computing relative positions of points against a plane. As a result, we can significantly promote point-in-spherical-polygon tests. As shown by experimental results, our robustness and efficiency are attested, and we can even obtain an acceleration of five orders of magnitude over a popularly used method.

Acknowledgment. This work is partially supported by the sub-project of the National Key Research and Development Program of China (No. 2016QY01W0101), the National Natural Science Foundation of China (Nos. 60873182, 61379087, U1435220, and 61661146002), and the EU FP7 funded project AniNex (FP7-IRSES-612627).

References

1. Raskin, R.G.: Spatial analysis on the sphere. Technical report 94-7. University of California, Santa Barbara (1994)
2. Bevis, M., Chatelain, J.-L.: Locating a point on a spherical surface relative to a spherical polygon of arbitrary shape. Math. Geol. **21**(8), 811–828 (1989)
3. Nedrich, M., Davis, W.J.: Detecting behavioral zones in local and global camera views. Mach. Vis. Appl. **24**, 579–605 (2013)
4. Bello, L., Coltice, N., Tackley, P.J., Muller, R.D., Cannon, J.: Assessing the role of slab rheology in coupled plate-mantle convention models. Earth Planet. Sci. Lett. **430**, 191–201 (2015)
5. Li, J., Wang, W.-C.: Fast and robust GPU-based point-in-polyhedron determination. Comput. Aided Des. **87**, 20–28 (2017)

Character Modeling and Dynamics

Repurpose 2D Character Animations for a VR Environment Using BDH Shape Interpolation

Simone Barbieri[1,2,3(✉)], Ben Cawthorne[3], Zhidong Xiao[2],
and Xiaosong Yang[2]

[1] Centre for Digital Entertainment, Bournemouth University, Poole, UK
sbarbieri@bournemouth.ac.uk
[2] Bournemouth University, Poole, UK
[3] Thud Media, Cardiff, UK

Abstract. Virtual Reality technology has spread rapidly in recent years. However, its growth risks ending soon due to the absence of quality content, except for few exceptions. We present an original framework that allows artists to use 2D characters and animations in a 3D Virtual Reality environment, in order to give an easier access to the production of content for the platform. In traditional platforms, 2D animation represents a more economic and immediate alternative to 3D. The challenge in adapting 2D characters to a 3D environment is to interpret the missing depth information. A 2D character is actually flat, so there is not any depth information, and every body part is at the same level of the others. We exploit mesh interpolation, billboarding and parallax scrolling to simulate the depth between each body segment of the character. We have developed a prototype of the system, and extensive tests with a 2D animation production show the effectiveness of our framework.

Keywords: Virtual Reality · Animation · 2D characters in 3D environment · Shape interpolation · Billboarding · Parallax scrolling

1 Introduction

In the last few years, the interest in Virtual Reality technology has greatly grown. The increase in the graphical processing power has, in fact, allowed consumers to get high-end experiences with a reasonable price. Despite the strong interest towards this technology, the quality content is still very limited at the moment, so the entire platform, at least for the entertainment industry, risks becoming merely a gimmick or a tech demo [28].

In the recent years, *indie games* have spread widely and have become an important reality in the video game industry [23]. Many of these games are realized by very few people, or, in some cases, even by single individuals, such as *Braid* [10] or *Undertale* [17]. Moreover, a large number of these games are realized in 2D. In traditional platforms, in fact, 2D represents a more economic and immediate alternative to the 3D animation, which is particularly diffuse in

J. Chang et al. (Eds.): AniNex 2017, LNCS 10582, pp. 69–85, 2017.
https://doi.org/10.1007/978-3-319-69487-0_6

(a)   (b)   (c)   (d)

Fig. 1. Two examples of 2D characters placed in a 3D environment using our framework. (a), (b) Copyright ©, Esoteric Software. (c), (d) Copyright ©, Toot Enterprises Limited.

video games, but it is becoming increasingly popular in animation as well. As a matter of fact, while 2D animation requires as much skill as 3D animation, it is still faster to produce, since it has a dimension less to take in account while animating. The 2D asset production is also less expensive and faster to realize.

As Virtual Reality places the user in the center of a 3D environment, many content creators that could bring quality products for the platform are stopped by the cost of the production of a full 3D environment and characters. Using 2D characters in VR would definitely reduce the production cost. However, there is an important challenge to solve in order to use 2D character in a 3D environment. 2D characters and animations, in fact, do not have any depth information. When they are inserted in a 3D context, without any revision, they would appear just flat, and they would ruin the user's immersion in the VR experience.

In this paper, we address this problem by presenting an original framework to retarget 2D animation contents for Virtual Reality application. We combine two classical computer graphics techniques – billboarding and parallax scrolling – with a new shape interpolation method to simulate the depth in 2D characters and animations, in order to exploit them in a 3D VR environment.

The problem we aim to solve with this paper could be considered as an extension of the problem to make appear and interact 2D objects with a 3D environment. Depending on the medium, this problem is solved in different ways. For video games, for example, it is often used the previously cited billboarding, which rotates the 2D elements in the environment towards the camera, in order to not let the user see that they are actually 2D. This technique is used especially with user interface, but also for effects, background elements – trees, clouds – or characters. This happens, for example in the video game *Mario Kart 64* [22], where the characters are prerendered from 3D models, but in the actual game they appear as 2D sprites. For what concerns films, it is easier to handle the problem. The camera in a film is, in fact, controlled by the director and the user will never have the chance to watch somewhere that has not been settled by the director himself. Thus, inserting 2D elements is a straightforward task, usually performed by visual effects compositors. An example could be seen in the film *Who Framed Roger Rabbit* [35], in which cartoon characters interact with the real world. For traditional animation, letting the character interact with 3D objects requires a similar procedure. With VR, it must be considered that a user can watch in any direction at any time, and even slightly move inside a predefined area, hence a traditional composite cannot be realized.

The rest of the paper is organized as follows: in Sect. 2 we present a brief review of the related work; in Sect. 3 we give an exhaustive explanation of the system, including a detailed description of the three technologies we combined for our framework; in Sect. 4 we show and analyze the results we obtained with the proposed system; in Sect. 5 we draw our conclusions and explain the future works that could be done to improve the framework.

2   Related Work

Merging 2D and 3D. In this paper, we present a method that combines together 2D characters in a 3D environment. In computer graphics there are several subfields that attempt a similar task, or, more generally, merging 2D and 3D elements. Due to the great amount of different subfields in this category, we introduce in this section only the groups we believe are the most close and relevant to our work.

One of these subfields is the hybrid animation [25], which combines 2D and 3D animation media. There are several examples of 2D films that include 3D objects. One of the most remarkable example is *The Iron Giant* [9], which features an entire 3D character, the Iron Giant itself, in a 2D animated film. In 2002, in the film *Spirit: Stallion of the Cimarron* [4], DreamWork Pictures revealed a technology to use 3D characters while the camera is significantly far away from them, to "take over" a 2D animation when the camera gets closer [15]. In the same year, Walt Disney Pictures, in the film *Treasure Planet* [14], presents a hybrid character, namely a 2D character with 3D components.

Sýkora and colleagues [29] introduce a method to allow users to specify depth inequalities in some sections of a 2D character, in order to generate a 2.5D pop-up. This technique has different objectives, such as enhancing the perception of depth in a 2D character, producing 3D-like shading or even stereoscopic images. This method, however, produces several artefacts due to the incorrect estimation of the contour thickness. Jain et al. [21] propose a technique for adding a 3D secondary motion – the motion of objects in response to the one from a primary character – to a 2D character exploiting physical effects. Usually this kind of effects are hand-animated and they are particularly time-consuming. Their method, however, integrates simulation methods to replicate cloth motion.

To generate 3D animation from 2D sketches is another technique which combine 2D and 3D together. Similarly to the work presented in this paper, these techniques have to solve a depth problem, although they have to infer the depth, which is absent in the drawing, while we have to simulate it in order to display the characters correctly in a 3D environment. Davis and colleagues [16] are the first to introduce a specific method to pose articulated figures with sketches. Their tool requires as input a keyframe sequence sketched from the artist and the system will reconstruct all the possible 3D poses that match the input sketch and those have a valid ranking score, which is computed according to a set of heuristics. The 3D poses are ordered by their ranking score, and users can select the pose that is the closest to their idea. However, this method has a few problems, such as the necessity of users to specify the template of the skeleton through a configuration file and the manual annotation of the sketch. These problems are addressed by Mao et al. [24], who present a tool in which users do not need to manually specify the template of the skeleton any more; in fact, now they can select one from a list categorised by gender, ethnicity and age. Then the user draws the stick figure, by using the thickness of a connection between two joints to express the depth of that body part. Jain et al. [20] propose a method to recreate a hand-drawn animation in a 3D environment. The generated animation consists of a reconstruction of motion captured poses, which matches the user's animation, but does not exactly follow the animator's drawing. The main difference with the previous methods is that this method exploits a database to reconstruct the animation.

More recent works in this subfield allow posing characters with very few lines. Guay and colleagues [18], for instance, take the concept of the "line of action", a technique used in drawing to grant a dynamic look to a character, and, while giving it a formal definition, they use it to pose a 3D character with a single stroke. Hahn et al. [19] introduce an original concept: the sketch abstraction. Fundamentally, it is a way to connect the character's rigging to the 2D input sketch. The abstraction is bounded to some points in the mesh. Then, it establishes a correspondence between the abstraction and the input sketch, which can be computed with a straightforward in-order correspondence by considering the drawing direction, or by using the closest-point matching between the two sets of points. The final posing is therefore retrieved by solving an optimization problem. Barbieri et al. [7] propose a method to automatically compute the sketch abstraction, thus removing a redundant task for users in the previous method.

The final subfield of computer graphics related to our work we introduce is the crowd simulation, which is the reproduction of the movement of a vast number of character at the same time, typically in a 3D environment. One of the techniques used to display this amount of entities is the image-based rendering. Tecchia et al. [30] follow this approach, by using pre-generated impostors [27] – textured polygons that face the camera and replace more complex objects – rendered from different viewpoints. Depending on the position of the user, the most appropriate impostor is displayed. This method has a downside of requiring a huge amount of memory, as it requires a rendering of each character, from different perspectives and multiple frames for each of them. Aubel et al. [5] solve this problem by using dynamically generated impostors. In this way, no storage is used for impostors that are not active in the scene. In addition to the movement of the camera, for the generation of the images for the impostors they have to take in account the self-deformation too, as the characters are not static objects. They solve the problem by updating the impostor only if the distance between some pre-determined points in the character's skeleton changes significantly. Yang and colleagues [34] combine this two approaches by using both pre-generated snapshots and synthesized new ones dynamically. To produce the new images, they use segments of the pre-generated one, thus avoiding the rendering of the geometric model multiple times.

2D Shape Interpolation. The interpolation of planar shapes is a well-known problem in computer graphics and there exist many approaches in literature which address this problem. Besides offering an exhaustive review of the most relevant classical methods of mesh morphing, Alexa [2] provides a comprehensive explanation of the terminology and mathematical background required for the proper understanding of the problem.

The As-Rigid-As-Possible (ARAP) technique [3] aims to generate rigidity-preserving interpolations. By blending the interior of the shape rather than the boundaries, it creates locally least-distorting in-between shapes. It linearly blends the rotation and scaling components of the transformation for each pair of triangles from the source and target shapes, to consequently reconstruct the shape sequence. Despite this method offers a better control on local distortions compared to classic methods, it also produces artefacts if the source and target shapes present a large-scale deformation. To solve this problem, Choi et al. [13] and Baster et al. [8] used a different procedure to choose the rotation angles and thus guarantee coherence between adjacent triangles.

Xu et al. [33] related the rigid interpolation to the Poisson problem, thus offering a formal mathematical definition to the problem. However, this method is almost identical to [3]. The main difference is the weighting, which allows the result not to depend significantly on the tessellation of the mesh. Nonetheless, this method undergoes the same problem of [3], presenting distorted results whether large rotations are applied.

Weber and Gotsman [32] presented a method to produce smooth conformal mappings by blending the *angular factor* – the local orientation change induced by the mapping – on the shape's boundary. Chen et al. [11] extended their method by supporting the wider class of quasi-conformal mappings, in order to provide interpolations with a bounded amount of conformal distortion. Chien et al. [12] improved [11] by presenting an algorithm two orders of magnitude faster. Moreover, the method from Chien et al. is meshless, thus provides results with increased smoothness.

3   2D Characters in a 3D Environment

The proposed framework allows users to repurpose 2D characters and animations in a 3D, VR environment. Our system simulates the depth between the different body parts of the characters by moving them in the scene according to the

Fig. 2. The input of the system. Every character is split up into different body parts, as on the left(Copyright ©, Esoteric Software), and it is provided drawn from eight different perspectives, as on the right (Copyright ©, Magic Mall, Cloth Cat Animation).

position of the viewer. It exploits 3 different techniques: billboarding [1], parallax scrolling [6] and 2D shape interpolation [12]. As shown in Fig. 2, the system requires as input a character split in different body parts. Moreover, each body part has to be provided drawn from eight different perspectives.

The body parts are placed all on the same plane $\mathcal{P}$, the billboard, which will be rotated constantly facing the user. To determine the rotation matrix of the billboard which rotates around the y-axis, and with the viewer looking towards the negative z-axis, we first compute the eye vector from the model view matrix M:

$$\vec{V}_{eye} = M^{-1} \begin{pmatrix} 0 \\ 0 \\ -1 \\ 0 \end{pmatrix}.$$

The rotation θ about the y-axis is then computed as:

$$cos\theta = \vec{V}_{eye} \cdot \vec{V}_{front},$$
$$sin\theta = \vec{V}_{eye} \cdot \vec{V}_{right},$$

where

$$\vec{V}_{front} = (0, 0, 1),$$
$$\vec{V}_{right} = (1, 0, 0).$$

The rotation matrix R around the y-axis:

$$R = \begin{bmatrix} cos\theta & 0 & sin\theta \\ 0 & 1 & 0 \\ -sin\theta & 0 & cos\theta \end{bmatrix} \qquad (1)$$

is then concatenated to the M matrix. The matrix MR is therefore used to transform the billboard geometry. Figure 3 shows an example of billboarding. A similar operation is used to rotate the billboard around the x-axis too, however the rotation is attenuated by an arbitrary value ξ.

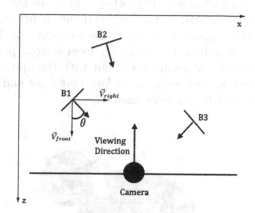

Fig. 3. This example shows how the billboarding works. B1, B2 and B3 are the billboards, which always face the camera.

On the billboard, the body parts move according to the movement of the user and to the parallax scrolling. When the viewer turns around the character, the body components in the closest half of the character's body move in the viewer's opposite direction, while the ones in the farthest half move in the same direction. The central part, such as the torso, however, does not move at all, except for the rotation due to the billboarding. Furthermore, according to parallax scrolling, the closest parts move faster. The reversed movement of the farthest component is explained by the *negative speed* of their movement, as they move *slower* than the closest parts. A layer λ is assigned to each body part of the character that should move when the camera is rotated. λ represents the proximity of the body part with the user; a higher λ corresponds to a body part that is closer to the user. The torso's λ is 0, so it will not move. For the closest parts, it will be positive, while negative for the farthest ones. When the camera is moved by a translation T_{camera}, the body parts will simply be moved by:

$$T_{bodypart} = \frac{T_{camera} \cdot \lambda}{\zeta}, \qquad (2)$$

where ζ is a balancing parameter.

λ is computed automatically by the system. When the user provides the character, it is analyzed from 4 perspectives: front, left, right and rear. Based on the position of each component from each perspective, it will be assigned a different λ. We use the left and right perspective to compute the front and rear λ values, and vice versa. For each view point, the starting point $\lambda = 0$ is placed in the middle point, but it could be replaced by the user. The others λ are assigned on the opposite direction of the z-axis for the left and right perspectives, or the x-axis for the front and rear ones, at regular intervals. However, for the rear and left perspective, the signs of these values are changed. Figure 4 shows an example of this process just on the head of the character. In the figure, the $\lambda = 0$ position has been changed. The other values are then assigned in the opposite direction of the z-axis, so the eyes and the mouth will be assigned a λ value of 1, while the chignon is assigned the value of -2. These values are used when the user is watching the character from a front perspective. In the rear perspective, the same values are used, but with the opposite sign. For the intermediate perspectives, front right, front left, rear right and rear left, we use the same λ values of the left and right ones.

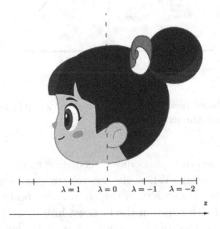

Fig. 4. An example of how the λ value is assigned to each component. In this example the left side of the character's head is taken into account. The reported values are not assigned to the body parts on the left side, but on the front one, and on the rear one with opposite sign.

As long as the user does not move significantly around the character, the shape interpolation is not applied. When the user surpasses a certain threshold, the perspective changes, and the interpolation is employed to change the appearance of each body part. Figure 5 shows the different perspective angles and the thresholds.

The 2D shape interpolation is employed to produce a smooth transition during the change of perspective when the user turns around the character. Without it, the body parts would just sharply change shape whenever the user surpasses

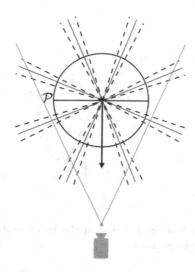

Fig. 5. The character from the top. The arrow is the viewing direction of the character. The red lines mark the points in which the perspective of the character changes. The dashed lines indicate the threshold for the interpolation. (Color figure online)

a certain angle. We divide the surface of the body part into two sections. The *joint part – jp –* is the section that appears in both the source and target surfaces. The rest is the *margin*. We define as *appearing margin – am –* the one in the target mesh, while as *disappearing margin – dm –* the one in the source. We highlight, however, that the difference between appearing and disappearing margin is based only on the walking direction of the user. Thus, they are not fixed as appearing or disappearing. The user is required to manually identify the joint part and the margin part of the mesh. Figure 6 shows an example of these sections.

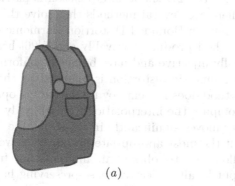
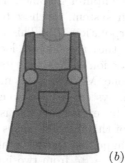

Fig. 6. The same body part from two different perspectives. The red section of these two body parts is the joint part. The blue parts are the margins (Copyright ©, Magic Mall, Cloth Cat Animation). (Color figure online)

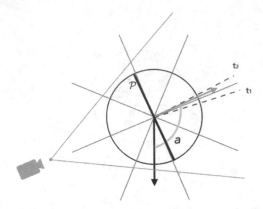

Fig. 7. In this example, the camera is between the two thresholds, and the angle a is computed for the correct interpolation.

The interpolation is applied only if the user is between the two thresholds. We define the interpolation as i^t, where $t \in [0, 1]$, $t = 0$ at the starting threshold and $t = 1$ at the ending threshold. Depending on the position of the user, a certain i^t is computed and shown.

Let us define a as the angle between the character viewing direction and the vector from the character's position to the user's position, as illustrated by Fig. 7, t is simply computed from a and the two thresholds:

$$t := \frac{a - t_1}{t_2 - t_1}, \tag{3}$$

where t_1 and t_2 are the angles of the first and second thresholds respectively.

Each interpolation i^t is a composition of two distinct operations. For what concerns the joint part of the shape, a classic shape interpolation method is applied. As we mentioned in Sect. 2, the 2D shape interpolation is particularly studied in computer graphics. There are several methods that solve this problem. For our system, we chose to rely on Bounded Distortion Harmonic (BDH) Shape Interpolation [12]. This method produce "provably good"[26] harmonic mappings – they are smooth, locally injective and have bounded conformal isometric distortion – such that its geometric distortion is bounded by the input mapping's one. Moreover, this method does not employ mathematical optimization. As our system requires to compute the interpolation for each body part of each character every time the user moves significantly in the scene, the parallel capability of this method makes it the most appropriate for our framework.

BDH shape interpolation allows us to obtain an interpolating function $f : [0, 1] \times \Omega \to \mathbb{R}^2$ from two input locally injective sense-preserving harmonic mappings $f^0, f^1 : \Omega \to \mathbb{R}^2$. The idea of the method is to interpolate the Jacobian J_f and then to integrate it to retrieve an interpolation. By identifying $\mathbb{R}^2$ with $\mathbb{C}$ and using the complex notation $z = x + iy$, they define a planar harmonic mapping as mapping $f : \Omega \to \mathbb{C}$ where $f(x + iy) = u(x, y) + iv(x, y)$ and the components u and v are harmonic. On a simply-connected domain Ω, any harmonic planar mapping f can be written as the sum of a holomorphic and an anti-holomorphic function:

$$f(z) = \Phi(z) + \overline{\Psi}(z). \tag{4}$$

For such mapping, $f_z = \Phi'$ is holomorphic and $f_{\bar{z}} = \overline{\Psi'}$ is anti-holomorphic.

This decomposition allows them to interpolate the similarity and anti-similarity parts of J_f independently by interpolating f_z and $f_{\bar{z}}$, as they are holomorphic and anti-holomorphic respectively. Thus, they obtain Φ and $\overline{\Psi}$, the holomorphic and anti-holomorphic components of the interpolated mapping. These two components are defined by the Cauchy complex barycentric coordinates [31]:

$$\Phi(z) = \sum_{j=1}^{n} C_j(z)\phi_j, \quad \Psi(z) = \sum_{j=1}^{n} C_j(z)\psi_j. \tag{5}$$

To compute f_z, Chien et al. [12] introduce a formula for f_z^t to linearly interpolate the angle of the closest rotation transformation by linearly interpolating the arguments of f_z^0 and f_z^1. This can be obtained by linearly interpolating the logarithms of f_z^0 and f_z^1, as expressed by this formula:

$$f_z^t = (f_z^0)^{1-t}(f_z^1)^t. \tag{6}$$

The following manipulation shows that these logarithms are linearly interpolated:

$$\begin{aligned}
f_z^t &= \exp\left((1-t)\log f_z^0\right) \cdot \exp\left(t \log f_z^1\right) \\
&= \exp\left((1-t)\log f_z^0 + t \log f_z^1\right) \\
&= |f_z^0|^{1-t} \cdot |f_z^1|^t \cdot \exp\left(i \cdot (1-t)\arg(f_z^0) + t \arg(f_z^1)\right).
\end{aligned}$$

f_z^t is essentially a holomorphic interpolation which linearly interpolates the argument. As such, it has to interpolate f_z^0 and f_z^1 so that the scaling constant is fixed.

For what concerns the anti-holomorphic part $f_{\bar{z}}$, Chien et al. introduce two different methods. Here we are going to discuss only the method we used for our framework. To compute $f_{\bar{z}}$ cannot be used the logarithmic interpolation, as $f_{\bar{z}}^1$ and $f_{\bar{z}}^1$ are typically 0 at points in Ω, and a logarithm for them cannot be defined.

A new quantity is introduced: $\eta = g_{\bar{z}}\overline{g_z} = \mu|g_z|^2$, which is anti-holomorphic and where g is a planar mapping. This quantity is linearly interpolated by the following formula:

$$\eta^t = (1-t)\eta^0 + t\eta^1, \tag{7}$$

Chien et al. also introduce a scaling function $\rho : [0,1] \to (0,1]$ such that $\rho(0) = \rho(1) = 1$, in order to check the geometric distortion bounds for each time t and scale η accordingly by preserving the bounds. We then obtain:

$$f_{\bar{z}}^t = \frac{\rho(t)\eta^t}{\overline{f_z^t}}. \tag{8}$$

Together, Eqs. 6 and 8 give us the formulae to compute f_z^t and $f_{\bar{z}}^t$, which, integrated, allow us to obtain the interpolated mappings.

For what concerns the margins, let us consider the plane $\mathcal{P}$ on which lay the mesh of each body part. We already mentioned that the mesh is split in two different parts: the joint part and the margin. Let us indicate the width of the margin as m_{width}. For an interpolation i^t, we cut the plane $\mathcal{P}$ along the y-axis at $x = m_{width} \cdot t$. If the margin is an appearing margin, the vertices on the closest part of the margin to the joint part will be added to the mesh. Instead, if it is a disappearing margin, the vertices on the farthest part of the margin to the joint part will be removed from the mesh. Whether these two parts are on the left or right part of the margin, it depends on the walking direction of the user. Algorithm 1 summarizes this procedure, which is shown in Fig. 8.

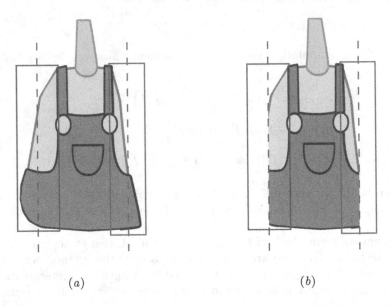

(a)   (b)

Fig. 8. An example of the interpolation of the margins at $t = 0.5$. The two different perspectives are those in Fig. 6. While the central part is the result of the deformation of the BDH interpolation, an intermediate state between the origin and target transformations, the other two sections, marked by the red and blue boxes, are the margins. As in this example we are considering $t = 0.5$, those sections are cut by half (Copyright ©, Magic Mall, Cloth Cat Animation). (Color figure online)

The parallax scrolling works on a higher level. In fact, while the interpolation operates distinctly for each body part, and only if the user is between two thresholds, the parallax scrolling constantly moves all the body parts of the character. To each body part, as the user moves in the scene, is applied the translation in Eq. 2.

As the character is a 2D figure, it lies on a 2D plane. The transformations applied by both the parallax scrolling and the shape interpolation do not add a third dimension to the mesh's vertices. Thus, the billboarding is just applied to the character's plane, and not individually to each component.

The whole procedure is performed every time the user moves, although the interpolation is executed only if the user is in particular positions, specifically between two thresholds. Algorithm 2 outlines the entire operation.

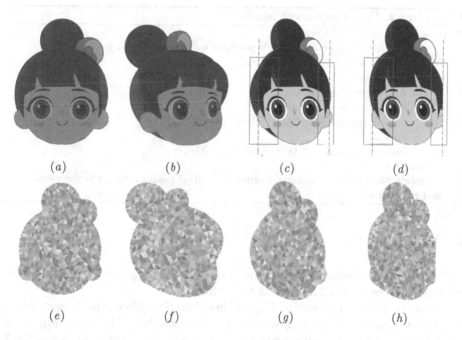

Fig. 9. An example of the interpolation process. In (a) and (b), the red sections are the joint parts, while the blue ones are the margins. (c) shows the interpolated joint part merged with the two margins, while in (d) the margins are cut and it shows the final interpolation at $t = 0.65$. It must be noticed that the deformation is on the mesh, not on the texture, which is just applied on it. In the second row, in (e), (f), (g) and (h), the deformation process on the meshes is shown (Copyright ©, Magic Mall, Cloth Cat Animation). (Color figure online)

Algorithm 1. Body part interpolation

1: **procedure** INTERPOLATEBODYPART(bodypart, angle)
2:      $t \leftarrow (angle - t_1)/(t_2 - t_1)$
3:      $bodypart_{jp} \leftarrow BDH(bodypart, t)$
4:      split margin at $x_{cut} \leftarrow m_{width \cdot t}$
5:      **if** margin is *am* **then**   ▷ in case of an *appearing margin*
6:           add to mesh vertices in the closest part of the margin to *jp*
7:      **else**   ▷ in case of a *disappearing margin*
8:           remove from mesh vertices in the farthest part of the margin to *jp*
9:      **end if**
10:     add vertices to mesh from the area $bodypart_{am} \cdot t$
11:     remove vertices from mesh from the area $bodypart_{dm} \cdot t$
12: **end procedure**

Algorithm 2. User's movement handler

1: **procedure** ONUSERMOVEMENT
2:      $\vec{u} :=$ vector between character's position and user's position
3:      $\vec{v} :=$ character's viewing direction
4:      $angle \leftarrow \arccos(\vec{u} \cdot \vec{v})$
5:      **for all** *bodypart* $\in$ *character* **do**
6:           **if** $t_1 \leq angle \leq t_2$ **then**
7:                InterpolateBodyPart(bodypart, angle)
8:           **end if**
9:           $bodypart_{position} + = (user_{translation} \cdot \lambda)/\zeta$
10:     **end for**
11:     rotate the character's plane around its central position towards the camera
12: **end procedure**

---

4   Results

In this section we discuss the experimental results we obtained while testing the proposed system with a 2D animation pipeline.

Figure 1(a) and (b), as well as Fig. 10, show how the different body parts move at the same time of a user, because of the parallax scrolling. The boy in Fig. 1 has the right arm and leg, as well as an eye and the mouth, in a front layer, hence the λ in the Eq. 2 is positive. The left arm and leg, instead, has a negative λ, as they are in the hindermost part of the character. In the end, the λ value for the torso and the head is 0. In the example in Fig. 1 the user is moving around the character in a counterclockwise sense – i.e. from the left to the right – therefore the body parts with positive λ are moving from the right to the left, in the opposite direction, while the ones in the rear side move in the same direction as the user. Moreover, as the forearm is closer to the user compared to the upper arm, it has a greater λ, therefore, it is moved more on the left.

Figure 9 shows instead an example of the interpolation of a body part between two different perspectives. Figure 9(a), the source, and Fig. 9(b), the target, show the body parts from which the interpolation is computed. These two images

(a)   (b)   (c)

Fig. 10. A complete example of our system. (a) shows the character from the front-right perspective, while in (b), it is in the middle of the transaction between that state and the front. Lastly, (c) shows the character from the front (Copyright ©, Magic Mall, Cloth Cat Animation).

represent the same body part, but from two different perspectives. In the two figures are also highlighted the joint part, in red, and the margins, in blue. In Fig. 9(c), the shared part is interpolated using BDH shape interpolation, and the two margins are added to the body part. In the figure, the appearing margin is surrounded by the red box, while the disappearing margin by blue box. The dashed lines mark the section of the margins that will be removed. In this particular example, $t = 0.65$. Figure 9(d) represents the final result of the computation. It can be noticed that there is some residue in the appearing margin, to the left of the dashed line. That is because that section of the hair is part of the joint section, thus it is not removed.

In the end, Fig. 10 show a complete transaction of the camera from the front-right perspective to the front one. It can be noticed in Fig. 10(b), in particular on the torso and the head, the interpolation of the two states. It can be also noticed the parallax scrolling on the arms and the legs.

Our tool is implemented as a Unity3D native plug-in. This allowed us to use Nvidia's CUDA to parallelize on the GPU as many operations as possible, in particular the interpolation.

5   Conclusion

In this paper we presented an original tool for repurposing 2D characters and animations for a 3D VR environment. This method relies on three different technologies, the billboarding, the parallax scrolling and the 2D shape interpolation, which are combined together as illustrated by algorithm 2. This novel approach to content creation for VR represents a valid alternative to classic 3D characters, by offering a more economic and faster way to produce products for the platform.

Although the system produces good results, we are aware of few limitations that affect it. For instance, at the moment the identification of the joint part and the margins of each body part must be manually set by users. Moreover, as the system is focused on repurposing of 2D characters, the other objects in the scene are 3D. There are two ways to handle the interaction of the 2D character with the scene. The first solution is to extend the system to make it work with every kind of objects; the second one is to use the 3D surroundings and to study a way to make them interact with the 2D character in a plausible way. Ultimately, it would be interesting to make a comparison with other 2D mesh interpolation methods.

References

1. Akenine-Moller, T., Haines, E.: Real-Time Rendering, 2nd edn. A.K. Peters Ltd. (2002)
2. Alexa, M.: Recent advances in mesh morphing. In: Computer Graphics Forum, vol. 21, pp. 173–198. Wiley Online Library (2002)
3. Alexa, M., Cohen-Or, D., Levin, D.: As-rigid-as-possible shape interpolation. In: Proceedings of the 27th Annual Conference on Computer Graphics and Interactive Techniques, pp. 157–164. ACM Press/Addison-Wesley Publishing Co. (2000)
4. Asbury, K., Cook, L., Howard, M., Katzenber, J., Soria, M.: Spirit: Stallion of the Cimarron. DreamWorks Pictures (2002)
5. Aubel, A., Boulic, R., Thalmann, D.: Real-time display of virtual humans: levels of details and impostors. IEEE Trans. Circuits Syst. Video Technol. **10**(2), 207–217 (2000)
6. Balkan, A., Dura, J., Eden, A., Monnone, B., Palmer, J.D., Tarbell, J., Yard, T.: Parallax scrolling. Flash 3D Cheats Most Wanted, pp. 121–164. Springer/Apress, Berkeley (2003). doi:10.1007/978-1-4302-0814-3_5
7. Barbieri, S., Garau, N., Hu, W., Xiao, Z., Yang, X.: Enhancing character posing by a sketch-based interaction. In: ACM SIGGRAPH 2016 Posters, p. 56. ACM (2016)
8. Baxter, W., Barla, P., Anjyo, K.I.: Rigid shape interpolation using normal equations. In: Proceedings of the 6th International Symposium on Non-photorealistic Animation and Rendering, pp. 59–64. ACM (2008)
9. Bird, B., Abbate, A., McAnuff, D.: The iron giant. Warner Bros. Feature Animation (1999)
10. Blow, J.: Braid (2008). http://braid-game.com/
11. Chen, R., Weber, O., Keren, D., Ben-Chen, M.: Planar shape interpolation with bounded distortion. ACM Trans. Graph. (TOG) **32**(4), 108 (2013)
12. Chien, E., Chen, R., Weber, O.: Bounded distortion harmonic shape interpolation. ACM Trans. Graph. (TOG) **35**(4), 105 (2016)
13. Choi, J., Szymczak, A.: On coherent rotation angles for as-rigid-as-possible shape interpolation. Technical report, Georgia Institute of Technology (2003)
14. Clements, R., Musker, J., Conli, R.: The treasure planet. Buena Vista Pictures (2002)
15. Cooper, D.: 2D/3D hybrid character animation on spirit. In: ACM SIGGRAPH 2002 Conference Abstracts and Applications, p. 133. ACM (2002)

16. Davis, J., Agrawala, M., Chuang, E., Popović, Z., Salesin, D.: A sketching inter-
    face for articulated figure animation. In: Proceedings of the 2003 ACM SIG-
    GRAPH/Eurographics Symposium on Computer Animation, pp. 320–328. Euro-
    graphics Association (2003)
17. Fox, T.: Undertale (2015). http://undertale.com/
18. Guay, M., Cani, M.P., Ronfard, R.: The line of action: an intuitive interface for
    expressive character posing. ACM Trans. Graph. (TOG) **32**(6), 205 (2013)
19. Hahn, F., Mutzel, F., Coros, S., Thomaszewski, B., Nitti, M., Gross, M., Sum-
    ner, R.W.: Sketch abstractions for character posing. In: Proceedings of the 14th
    ACM SIGGRAPH/Eurographics Symposium on Computer Animation,pp. 185–
    191. ACM (2015)
20. Jain, E., Sheikh, Y., Hodgins, J.: Leveraging the talent of hand animators
    to create three-dimensional animation. In: Proceedings of the 2009 ACM SIG-
    GRAPH/Eurographics Symposium on Computer Animation, pp. 93–102. ACM
    (2009)
21. Jain, E., Sheikh, Y., Mahler, M., Hodgins, J.: Augmenting hand animation with
    three-dimensional secondary motion. In: Proceedings of the 2010 ACM SIG-
    GRAPH/Eurographics Symposium on Computer Animation. pp. 93–102. Euro-
    graphics Association (2010)
22. Konno, H., Miyamoto, S.: Mario kart 64. Nintendo (1996)
23. Lipkin, N.: Examining indie's independence: the meaning of "indie" games, the
    politics of production, and mainstream cooptation. Loading. **7**(11) (2012)
24. Mao, C., Qin, S., Wright, D.: A sketch-based gesture interface for rough 3D stick
    figure animation. In: Eurographics (2005)
25. O'Hailey, T.: Hybrid Animation: Integrating 2D and 3D Assets. Taylor & Francis,
    Burlington (2010)
26. Poranne, R., Lipman, Y.: Provably good planar mappings. ACM Trans. Graph.
    (TOG) **33**(4), 76 (2014)
27. Schaufler, G.: Dynamically generated impostors. In: GI Workshop Modeling-
    Virtual Worlds-Distributed Graphics, pp. 129–136 (1995)
28. Scherba, T.: Virtual reality is about to go mainstream, but a lack of content
    threatens to hold it back (2016). https://techcrunch.com/2016/04/03/virtual-rea
    lity-is-about-to-go-mainstream-but-a-lack-of-content-threatens-to-hold-it-back/
29. Sýkora, D., Sedlacek, D., Jinchao, S., Dingliana, J., Collins, S.: Adding depth to
    cartoons using sparse depth (in) equalities. In: Computer Graphics Forum, vol. 29,
    pp. 615–623. Wiley Online Library (2010)
30. Tecchia, F., Chrysanthou, Y.: Real-time rendering of densely populated urban
    environments. In: Péroche, B., Rushmeier, H. (eds.) Rendering Techniques 2000,
    pp. 83–88. Springer, Vienna (2000)
31. Weber, O., Ben-Chen, M., Gotsman, C.: Complex barycentric coordinates with
    applications to planar shape deformation. In: Computer Graphics Forum, vol. 28,
    pp. 587–597. Wiley Online Library (2009)
32. Weber, O., Gotsman, C.: Controllable conformal maps for shape deformation and
    interpolation. In: ACM Transactions on Graphics (TOG), vol. 29, p. 78. ACM
    (2010)
33. Xu, D., Zhang, H., Wang, Q., Bao, H.: Poisson shape interpolation. Graph. Models
    68(3), 268–281 (2006)
34. Yang, Y., Wang, X., Chen, J.X.: Rendering avatars in virtual reality: integrating
    a 3D model with 2d images. Comput. Sci. Eng. 4(1), 86–91 (2002)
35. Zemeckis, R., Marshall, F., Watts, R.: Who framed roger rabbit. Buena Vista
    Pictures (1988)

Clothes Size Prediction from Dressed-Human Silhouettes

Dan Song[1], Ruofeng Tong[1(✉)], Jian Chang[2], Tongtong Wang[1],
Jiang Du[1], Min Tang[1], and Jian J. Zhang[2]

[1] State Key Lab of CAD&CG, Zhejiang University, Hangzhou, China
trf@zju.edu.cn
[2] NCCA, Bournemouth University, Poole, UK

Abstract. We propose an effective and efficient way to automatically
predict clothes size for users to buy clothes online. We take human height
and dressed-human silhouettes in front and side views as input, and estimate 3D body sizes with a data-driven method. We adopt 20 body sizes
which are closely related to clothes size, and use such 3D body sizes to
get clothes size by searching corresponding size chart. Previous image-
based methods need to calibrate camera to estimate 3D information from
2D images, because the same person has different appearances of silhouettes (e.g. size and shape) when the camera configuration (intrinsic and
extrinsic parameters) is different. Our method avoids camera calibration, which is much more convenient. We set up our virtual camera and
train the relationship between human height and silhouette size under
this camera configuration. After estimating silhouette size, we regress
the positions of 2D body landmarks. We define 2D body sizes as the
distances between corresponding 2D body landmarks. Finally, we learn
the relationship between 2D body sizes and 3D body sizes. The training
samples for each regression process come from a database of 3D naked
and dressed bodies created by previous work. We evaluate the whole
procedure and each process of our framework. We also compare the performance with several regression models. The total time-consumption for
clothes size prediction is less than 0.1 s and the average estimation error
of body sizes is 0.824 cm, which can satisfy the tolerance for customers
to shop clothes online.

Keywords: Clothes size prediction · Body size estimation · Regression
methods

1   Introduction

Suitable clothes size plays a vital role in successful transactions of shopping
clothes online. However, it is not easy for customers to achieve fitness when they
buy clothes online. On one hand, customers need to possess professional skills to
measure themselves with a special tool like a tape in a relatively private space.
On the other hand, customers have to check the size charts of items because of

J. Chang et al. (Eds.): AniNex 2017, LNCS 10582, pp. 86–98, 2017.
https://doi.org/10.1007/978-3-319-69487-0_7

various size standards for different countries and different clothes brands. In a word, the techniques for automatic clothes size suggestion are in demand. We adopt 20 body sizes (Fig. 2(b)) which are related to clothes size, including length information and girth information of 3D bodies. Given such 20 body sizes, clothes size can be obtained by searching corresponding size chart. Therefore, we put emphasis on the automatic estimation of 3D body sizes.

Images contain valuable information and are quite convenient to get, so we devote ourselves to automatic image-based methods. Generally speaking, there are two ways to predict body sizes using images. One way is to measure 3D body shapes which are reconstructed from images, while another way is to utilize body landmarks which are extracted from images.

Image-based human body reconstruction has attracted lots of researchers. Some researchers learn the relationship between 2D positions in image and corresponding depth information using a database of 3D bodies. Some investigators train a parametric human body model with a body database and use images as constraints to deform a template mesh. Some methods integrate both ideas illustrated above for body reconstruction. They firstly estimate rough bodies according to the appearances of silhouettes using machine learning methods. Then the bodies are refined geometrically to satisfy the body contours of silhouettes. Body sizes are acquired by measuring 3D bodies reconstructed with these methods.

A few works firstly detect landmarks from body contours and then predict body sizes using body landmarks. Various ways have been tried to detect landmarks positions, which are introduced in Sect. 2.1, but they have their limitations. Manual label requires a professional sense of landmarks locations and costs time and energy. Corner points detection restricts landmarks to be corner points and is very sensitive to the quality of silhouettes. Some researchers extract landmarks using Iterative Closest Point (ICP) for 2D curves which is time-consuming. Song et al. [1] adopt a 3D landmarks regression method which is very efficient and not sensitive to body contour appearances for using global information. However, they need camera calibration for regressing 3D landmarks from 2D silhouettes. Usually, machine learning methods are used to predict 3D body sizes from body landmarks.

Similar to the 3D landmarks regression method [1], we regress 2D landmarks from silhouettes. However, we do not calibrate camera but require height as input, which is much easier to get. Camera configuration (intrinsic and extrinsic parameters) has an influence on the size and shape of the human silhouette. The shape of the silhouette is affected little when the camera points to the center of human body at a relatively far distance in orthogonal view. The size of the silhouette is estimated using height under a fixed camera configuration. Then we regress the positions of 2D landmarks from resized silhouettes. Different from [1], we do not reconstruct 3D human body but learn body sizes using 2D landmarks. We introduce the framework and main processes of our method in Sect. 3 and evaluate them in Sect. 4.

For the specific task of body sizes estimation, the advantages of our method are summarized as: (a) automatic, (b) efficient (the total time-consumption is within 0.1 s), (c) effective (the average error is 0.824 cm) and (d) free of camera calibration. Previous methods can only satisfy part of the advantages stressed above. Additionally, our method is easy to be integrated into clothes shopping websites.

2   Related Work

2.1   Landmarks Detection Methods

Zhu et al. [2] manually label the positions of 2D landmarks. Lin and Wang [3] represent the front and side silhouettes with chain code [1] and detect corner points at 90-degree angles. They define body landmarks as some of these corner points with their criterions. Nguyen [4] define landmarks locations at a template body contour and detect landmarks for other body contours using Iterative Closest Point (ICP) for 2D curves. Cheng et al. [5] detect 2D body landmarks from a depth image of minimally-dressed people with a boosting tree regression method. Similar to [5], Song et al. [1] regress 3D landmarks from the front and side silhouettes of normally-dressed people. They design different feature descriptors for regression. They are inspired by the methods applied to human face such as face alignment [6–8] and face recognition [9].

2.2   Regression Methods

Regression is a statistical process for estimating the relationship among variables. For our tasks, we have tried linear and non-linear regression models and compare their results. Linear regression models are often fitted using the least squares approach, but they may also be fitted in other ways. Ridge regression [10] adds an $L2$-norm regularization to the linear least squares function. They are generally used when multicollinearity is present or when overfitting is a problem. Random forest [11] regression fits a number of classifying decision trees on various sub-samples of the dataset and use averaging to improve the predictive accuracy and control over-fitting. Gradient boosting regression [12] produces a prediction model in the form of an ensemble of weak prediction models, typically decision trees. Like other boosting methods, gradient boosting combines weak regressors into a strong one in an iterative manner. The successor regressor learns to correct its predecessor by reducing the residual. Support vector machine [13] (SVM) is used for classification and regression. In addition to linear classification, SVM can efficiently perform non-linear classification using kernel trick [14] by implicitly mapping their inputs into high-dimensional feature spaces.

---

[1] https://en.wikipedia.org/wiki/Chain_code.

2.3 Image-Based 3D Human Body Reconstruction

Chen and Cipolla [15] reconstruct 3D models from a single view by learning the relationship between 2D positions in an image and their corresponding depth information. They firstly use a template shape to encode the 2D positions in an image and corresponding depth information for 3D bodies in the database. Then they perform Principal Component Analysis (PCA) to reduce the dimension of 2D positions and depth information. Finally, they trained the Gaussian Process Latent Variable Model (GPLVM) from the combinational inputs of both 2D positions and depth information. Balan et al. [17] estimate 3D body shapes from dressed-human silhouettes in 4 views by optimizing a parametric human model (SCAPE [16]). They calibrate cameras for 4 views and set higher weight for exposed-skin parts. They optimize the body model through minimizing the pixels differences between silhouettes and projections of target mesh in 4 views. Boisvert et al. [18] reconstruct 3D human shape from front and side silhouettes by integrating both geometric and statistical priors. Firstly, they train a non-liner function connecting silhouettes appearances and body shapes to make a first approximation. Secondly, with body contours as constraints, body shapes are globally deformed along the principal directions of body database. Finally, they deform body shapes locally to ensure more fitness to input silhouettes.

3   Method

We take a pair of dressed-human silhouettes (front and side) and human height as input and get clothes sizes as output. We propose a data-driven method to efficiently estimate body sizes from dressed-human silhouettes. With body sizes in hand, we obtain clothes sizes by searching the size chart. Figure 1 shows the overview of our method which contains 4 processes. We use a database [1] of 3D naked and dressed bodies to learn: (a) the relationship between height and silhouette size under our virtual camera configuration; (b) the relationship between dressed-human silhouette and 2D body landmarks and (c) the relationship between 2D body sizes and 3D body sizes. The training data is introduced in Sect. 3.1 and the main processes are illustrated in the following sections.

3.1   Training Data Preparation

We use the training database constructed by previous work [1]. The training database has 1081×5 pairs of 3D naked and dressed bodies in total. The 3D naked bodies are synthesized from real bodies with a standard pose in MPI database [19]. The corresponding dressed bodies are acquired by dressing naked bodies with physically based cloth simulation. We get dressed-human silhouettes by projecting 3D dressed bodies in front and side views under our virtual camera configuration. The landmarks of 3D naked bodies are projected to 2D landmarks. 3D body sizes are computed by measuring 3D naked bodies in the database. In summary, our training data contains 3D body sizes, 2D landmarks and dressed-human silhouettes.

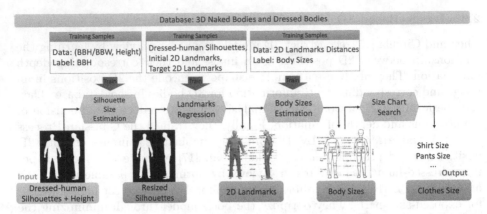

Fig. 1. *Overview.* We compute the bounding box of human contour in input silhouette and calculate the ratio BBH/BBW (i.e. the height of the bounding box divides the width of the bounding box). According to BBH/BBW and height information, we estimate BBH under our virtual camera configuration and resize silhouette. For both front and side silhouette, we regress the positions of 2D landmarks. 3D body sizes are estimated using corresponding 2D landmarks distances. Finally, clothes sizes are obtained through searching the size chart. We use a database of 3D naked and dressed bodies to construct training samples.

3.2   Silhouette Size Estimation

Camera configuration (intrinsic and extrinsic parameters) has an effect on the size and shape of the human silhouette. Therefore, most image-based methods [1,17] need camera calibration to recover 3D information from the silhouette. However, when the camera points approximately to the center of human, the direction of camera view is orthogonal to human plane and the distance between camera and human is relatively far, perspective projection has little effects on the shape of body contour. We set our virtual camera configuration and restrict the input of our method to satisfy these three conditions. We use height information as a clue to estimate the silhouette size under our virtual camera configuration.

We suppose a linear relationship between human height and silhouette size, and use training data to learn the relationship. The bounding box of body contour is computed, and we calculate the height of the bounding box (abbr. BBH) and the width of the bounding box (abbr. BBW). We also compute the height information of bodies in the training database. For silhouettes in the training database, we have their BBH and BBW values and compute the ratio between them (BBH-BBW- Ratio, abbr. HWR). Then we train a linear model (Ridge Regression [10]) with training samples whose data are (height, HWR) and labels are BBH. We also tried several other models to fit the training data and compare their results in Sect. 4.2.

3.3   2D Landmarks Regression

The locations of body landmarks we use are shown in Fig. 2 (a), which are related to the body size measurements. We estimate the positions of 2D landmarks for both front and side silhouettes using a regression method similar to [1].

Song et al. [1] regress 3D landmarks using a pair of silhouettes (front and side) with a boosting tree regression method. They construct training samples as front and side silhouettes, initial and target 3D landmarks, and learn the relationship between the appearance of silhouettes and 3D landmarks movements. They define the feature descriptor as the displacement from projected 2D landmarks and their nearest contour points. For projecting landmarks, they need to calibrate the camera.

We train two separate models for both front silhouette and side silhouette. Our training samples consist of front or side silhouette, initial and target 2D landmarks. We adopt the same boosting tree regression method to estimate 2D landmarks from the silhouettes. For more details of the regression method, please refer to Sect. 6 of [1].

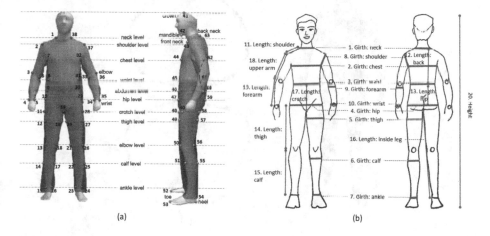

(a)   (b)

Fig. 2. *Landmarks and body sizes.* (a): the locations of 63 landmarks. Landmarks 1-39 are used for front silhouettes while landmarks 40-63 are designed for side silhouettes. (b): 20 body sizes. 10 of them are length information and the others are girth information of body.

3.4   Body Sizes Estimation

We use the measurements which are closely related to clothes size as our 3D body sizes (Fig. 2(b)), and estimate 3D body sizes from 2D landmarks. We first obtain 2D body sizes by computing the distances between related 2D landmarks. The correspondences between 2D body sizes and 2D landmarks are shown in table 1. Then we predict 3D body sizes using 2D body sizes with a linear regression model.

Table 1. The related landmarks for 2D body sizes

Size no	Related landmarks no	Size no	Related landmarks no
1	(1,38), (43, 63)	11	(1, 2), (37, 38)
2	(7, 32), (44, 62)	12	(1, 8), (31,38)
3	(8, 31), (45, 61)	13	(8, 10), (29, 31)
4	(10, 29), (47, 59)	14	(10, 13), (26, 29)
5	(12, 19), (20, 27), (49, 57)	15	(13, 15), (24, 26)
6	(14, 17), (22, 25), (51, 55)	16	(16, 39), (23, 39)
7	(15, 16), (23, 24)	17	(8, 39), (31, 39)
8	(2, 7), (32, 37)	18	(2, 3), (36, 37)
9	(3, 6), (33, 36)	19	(3, 4), (35, 36)
10	(4, 5), (34, 35)	20	(41, 54)

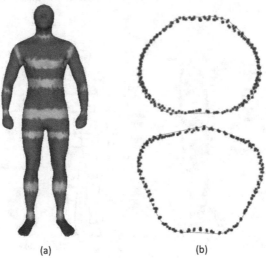

(a)   (b)

Fig. 3. *Girth calculation.* (a): related vertices for girth information. The related vertices are marked with pink color. (b): Two examples of girth calculation. Firstly, the related 3D vertices are projected to a plane. Then, we compute the convex-hull of 2D projected points. Girth information is the circumference of the convex-hull. (Color figure online)

2D distances (unit: pixel) between related 2D landmarks are computed as 2D body sizes. Our 3D body sizes are classified into length information and girth information. Length information is acquired by computing 3D distances between related 3D landmarks. The correspondences between length values and related 3D landmarks are similar to 2D situation (table 1). Each girth information of body is related to a group of vertices which are marked with pink color in Fig. 3 (a). These 3D vertices are projected to a plane and we compute the convex-hull of 2D projected points. We define the girth value as the circumference of the convex-hull. Figure 3(b) shows two examples of girth calculation.

We suppose a linear relationship between 2D sizes and 3D sizes, and use training data to train the regression model (ridge regression). 2D body sizes are prepared as the data of training samples, while 3D body sizes are used as the label of training samples. We train a separate model for each body size. We also try several other regression models to fit training data, and compare their results in Sect. 4.4.

3.5 Size Chart Searching

Figure 4 shows an example of men's apparel sizing for online shopping.[2] According to the measurements of neck, chest, sleeve, waist, hip and inseam, customers determine their clothes sizes. Our proposed body sizes contain these information and are consistent with the common size chart.

MEN'S APPAREL SIZING

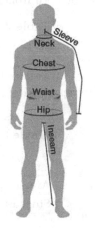

	S		M		L		XL	
	CM	INCHES	CM	INCHES	CM	INCHES	CM	INCHES
Neck	37	14.5	39	15.5	42	16.5	44	17.5
Chest	91-98	36-38.5	99-106	39-41.5	107-113	42-44.5	114-121	45-47.5
Sleeve	84	33	86.5	34	89	35	91.5	36
Waist	73-80	29-31.5	81-89	32-34.5	89-96	35-37.5	97-103	38-40.5
Hip	86-93	34-36.5	94-101	37-39.5	102-108	40-42.5	109-116	43-45.5
Inseam	77.5	30.5	79	31	81	32	82.5	32.5

Sizing refers to body measurements, not garment dimensions.
How to measure:
Neck: Around the fullest part of the neck, at the base
Chest: Around the chest, just under the arms and across the shoulder blades
Sleeve: From the center back of the neck, across the shoulder, and down the arm to the wrist
Waist: Around the narrowest part of the waist
Hip: Around the widest point of the hips
Inseam: From the crotch to the anklebone on the inside of the leg

Fig. 4. *An example of size chart.* An online shopping website uses this figure to illustrate the size chart for men's apparel.

4 Results

The hardware environment for our experiments is a 64-bit desktop with 32 GB RAM. The processor is Intel(R) Core(TM) i7-4790K CPU at 4.00 GHz. The whole procedure completes within 0.1 s. The prediction time-consumption of size regression is within $1e^{-4}$ second. 2D landmarks regression costs about $1.60e^{-2}$ second. We illustrate our testing data in Sect. 4.1. The whole procedure and each process of our method are evaluated in the following sections. We should mention that currently we use male bodies in 1 clothes type to validate our framework.

---

[2] https://blackdiamondequipment.com/en/size-chart-apparel-mens-f13.html.

4.1   Testing Data Illustration

We use the testing database of previous work [1] containing 637 pairs of 3D naked and dressed bodies, which are separate from training database. The resolution of testing silhouettes is 800×600. The average BBH (i.e., height of human bounding box) value of front silhouettes is 362.98 pixels and the average BBH value of side silhouettes is 372.26 pixels. We use testing data to evaluate each process of our pipeline and the whole procedure in the following sections.

4.2   Estimation Error of Silhouette Size

We compute BBH (i.e., height of human bounding box), HWR (i.e., BBH/BBW) and height values for testing data. With HWR and height values of testing data as input, we estimate BBH value with several regression models and compare the results with the ground truth. Tables 2 and 3 compare the estimation error for BBH value. The results show that ridge regression performs best for both front and side conditions.

Table 2. Estimation error for front silhouette size (unit: pixel)

	Ridge	SVR	Random forest	Gradient boosting
Average Error	1.58	3.36	2.22	1.81
Stdev Error	1.12	1.78	1.66	1.25

Table 3. Estimation error for side silhouette size (unit: pixel)

	Ridge	SVR	Random forest	Gradient boosting
Average Error	1.63	1.93	1.89	1.81
Stdev Error	1.18	1.70	1.63	1.35

4.3   Regression Error of 2D Landmarks

We project 3D dressed bodies and 3D landmarks of naked bodies in the testing database to dressed-human silhouettes and 2D landmarks with the same virtual camera. Given dressed-human silhouette, we regress 2D landmarks positions and compare them with the ground truth. The average landmarks regression error is 0.64 pixel for font silhouette and 0.57 pixel for side silhouette.

4.4   Estimation Error of Body Sizes

For testing data, we compute 2D body sizes and 3D body sizes. Then we use 2D body sizes to estimate 3D body sizes with several regression models, and compare the results with the ground truth. Table 4 illustrates the error of different regression models.

Table 4. Estimation error for body sizes (unit: centimeter)

	Ridge	SVR	Random forest	Gradient boosting
Average Error	0.42	1.03	0.46	0.42
Stdev Error	0.38	0.90	0.47	0.40

4.5 Overall Estimation Error of Body Sizes

In this section, we test the overall estimation error of 3D body sizes. For each testing data, we take dressed-human silhouettes and height information as input, and use 3D body sizes as the ground truth. Firstly, we estimate silhouette size with ridge regression method and resize silhouette. Secondly, we regress 2D landmarks from resized silhouette. Thirdly, based on estimated 2D landmarks, we compute 2D body sizes. Finally, 3D body sizes are acquired using 2D body sizes with ridge regression method. Figure 5 shows the average error for each one of 20 body sizes. With the same testing database, Song et al. [1] estimate chest/waist/hip girth and height. The results show that we can acquire comparative accuracy. We should mention that the time-consumption of [1] is within 4 s while ours is within 0.1 s. Our method is more efficient for clothes size suggestions for online shopping.

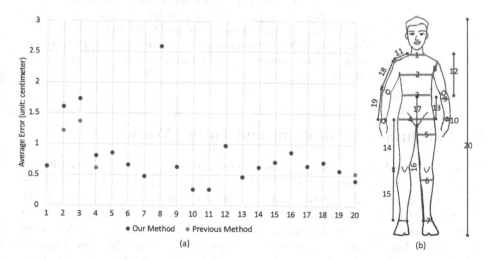

Fig. 5. *Average error for 20 body sizes.* (a): average error for 20 body sizes. The blue points show the error of our method while the red points illustrate the error of the previous method [1]. (b): the body size that each number stands for. (Color figure online)

4.6   Implementation Details

The configurations of regression methods for size estimation are shown in table 5. For 2D landmarks regression, the configuration is the same as [1] whose regression target is 3D landmarks.

Table 5. The configuration details for regression models

Regression method	Configuration
Ridge	(alpha = 1.0, fit_intercept = True, normalize = False, copy_X = True, max_iter = None, tol = 0.001, solver = 'auto', random_state = None)
SVR	(kernel = 'rbf', degree = 3, gamma = 'auto', coef0 = 0.0, tol = 0.001, C = 1.0, epsilon = 0.1, shrinking = True, cache_size = 200, verbose = False, max_iter = -1)
Random forest	(n_estimators = 10, criterion = 'mse', max_depth = None, min_samples_split = 2, min_samples_leaf = 1, min_weight_fraction_leaf = 0.0, max_features = 'auto', max_leaf_nodes = None, min_impurity_split = 1e-07, bootstrap = True, oob_score = False, n_jobs = 1, random_state = None, verbose = 0, warm_start = False)
Gradient boosting	(loss = 'ls', learning_rate = 0.1, n_estimators = 100, subsample = 1.0, criterion = 'friedman_mse', min_samples_split = 2, min_samples_leaf = 1, min_weight_fraction_leaf = 0.0, max_depth = 3, min_impurity_split = 1e-07, init = None, random_state = None, max_features = None, alpha = 0.9, verbose = 0, max_leaf_nodes = None, warm_start = False, presort = 'auto')

5   Conclusion, Limitations and Future Work

We adopt 20 body sizes which are closely related to clothes size, including length information and girth information of 3D body. We explore an automatic framework to efficiently estimate 3D body sizes from dressed-human silhouettes. We get rid of camera calibration through estimating the size of silhouette under known virtual camera configuration with human height information. We learn the relationship between the positions of 2D landmarks and the appearance of silhouette. Several regression models are tried to estimate 3D body sizes from 2D body sizes. We have compared several regression models and ridge regression is most suitable for our tasks. The whole procedure and each process of our framework are evaluated. Our method completes in less than 0.1 s and the average estimation error of body sizes is 0.824 cm. This satisfies the real-time and accuracy requirements for customers to shop clothes online.

We provide an effective and efficient solution for clothes size prediction when customers buy clothes online, but we still face some difficulties to overcome. It will be more convenient if we take natural photos instead of silhouettes as input without the limitation of clothes types. We validate our framework through male bodies and should extend our work to female situations.

Acknowledgements. The research is supported in part by NSFC (61572424) and the People Programme (Marie Curie Actions) of the European Unions Seventh Framework Programme FP7 (2007-2013) under REA grant agreement No. 612627-"AniNex". Min Tang is supported in part by NSFC (61572423) and Zhejiang Provincial NSFC (LZ16F020003).

References

1. Song, D., Tong, R., Chang, J., Yang, X., Tang, M., Zhang, J.J.: 3D body shapes estimation from dressed human silhouettes. Comput. Graph. Forum **35**(7), 147–156 (2016)
2. Zhu, S., Mok, P.Y.: Predicting realistic and precise human body models under clothing based on orthogonal-view photos. Procedia Manufact. **3**, 3812–3819 (2015)
3. Lin, Y.L., Wang, M.J.J.: Automatic feature extraction from front and side images. In: IEEE International Conference on Industrial Engineering and Engineering Management, IEEM 2008, pp. 1949–1953. IEEE (2008)
4. Nguyen, H.T.: Automatic anthropometric system development using machine learning. BRAIN Broad Res. Artif. Intell. Neurosci. **7**(3), 5–15 (2016)
5. Cheng, K.L., Tong, R.F., Tang, M., Qian, J.Y., Sarkis, M.: Parametric human body reconstruction based on sparse key points. IEEE Trans. Visual Comput. Graph. **22**(11), 2467–2479 (2016)
6. Dollar, P., Welinder, P., Perona, P.: Cascaded pose regression. In: 2010 IEEE Conference on Computer Vision and Pattern Recognition (CVPR), pp. 1078–1085 (2010)
7. Cao, X., Wei, Y., Wen, F., Sun, J.: Face alignment by explicit shape regression. Int. J. Comput. Vis. **107**(2, SI), 177–190 (2014)
8. Cao, C., Weng, Y., Lin, S., Zhou, K.: 3D shape regression for real-time facial animation. ACM Trans. Graph. **32**(4), 41:1–41:10 (2013)
9. Shao, H., Chen, S., Zhao, J., Cui, W., Yu, T.: Face recognition based on subset selection via metric learning on manifold. Front. Inf. Technol. Electron. Eng. **16**(12), 1046–1058 (2015)
10. Hoerl, A.E., Kennard, R.W.: Ridge regression: biased estimation for nonorthogonal problems. Technometrics **12**(1), 55–67 (1970)
11. Liaw, A., Wiener, M.: Classification and regression by randomForest. R news **2**(3), 18–22 (2002)
12. Friedman, J.H.: Greedy function approximation: a gradient boosting machine. Ann. Stat. **29**(5), 1189–1232 (2001)
13. Cortes, C., Vapnik, V.: Support-vector networks. Mach. Learn. **20**(3), 273–297 (1995)
14. Boser, B.E., Guyon, I.M., Vapnik, V.N.: A training algorithm for optimal margin classifiers. In: Proceedings of the Fifth Annual Workshop on Computational Learning Theory, pp. 144–152 (1992)
15. Chen, Y., Cipolla, R.: Learning shape priors for single view reconstruction. In: 2009 IEEE 12th International Conference on Computer Vision Workshops (ICCV Workshops), pp. 1425–1432. IEEE (2009)

16. Anguelov, D., Srinivasan, P., Koller, D., Thrun, S., Rodgers, J., Davis, J.: SCAPE: shape completion and animation of people. ACM Trans. Graph. **24**(3), 408–416 (2005)
17. Bălan, A.O., Black, M.J.: The naked truth: estimating body shape under clothing. In: Forsyth, D., Torr, P., Zisserman, A. (eds.) ECCV 2008. LNCS, vol. 5303, pp. 15–29. Springer, Heidelberg (2008). doi:10.1007/978-3-540-88688-4_2
18. Boisvert, J., Shu, C., Wuhrer, S., Xi, P.: Three-dimensional human shape inference from silhouettes: reconstruction and validation. Mach. Vis. Appl. **24**(1), 145–157 (2013)
19. Hasler, N., Stoll, C., Sunkel, M., Rosenhahn, B., Seidel, H.P.: A statistical model of human pose and body shape. Comput. Graph. Forum **28**(2), 337–346 (2009)

The Application of Motion Capture and 3D Skeleton Modeling in Virtual Fighting

Xinliang Wei[✉], Xiaolong Wan, Sihui Huang, and Wei Sun

Sun Yat-sen University, Guangzhou, China
weixinl@mail2.sysu.edu.cn

Abstract. With the rapid development of new technology, motion capture technology has been widely used in film and television animation, motion analysis, medical research and game design. Especially in the game design, we not only gain the real-time motion data, but also consider the motion data and three-dimensional model matching. In this paper, we propose a unified method for 3D skeleton modeling, so that the motion data and 3D model can be matched perfectly. We apply the method to the virtual fighting game to verify the effectiveness of the method. In this process, this paper also analyzes the influence of other factors and realistic motion data model, and puts forward the corresponding solutions, providing strong support for the development of virtual games.

Keywords: Motion capture · Virtual fighting · 3D skeleton modeling

1 Introduction

With the rapid development of new technology, motion capture technology has been widely used in film and television animation, motion analysis, medical research and game design. Especially in game design, we not only gain the real-time motion data, but also consider the motion data and 3D model matching [1].

In this paper, we design a virtual fighting game using motion capture devices. In the virtual fighting game, two players in different places can play virtual fighting in real time. Each player in the game can control his/her virtual character by means of motion capture devices. The game provides multiple battle scenes as well as virtual characters for players to choose. A player's motion data can be transmitted over the network to another player in real time.

But while developing the virtual fighting game, we found that the virtual character deformed and some joints twisted when our players were controlling their virtual characters by motion capture devices. What's more, the transmission time of motion data was high and the virtual scene could not run fluently.

Based on this, we propose a unified 3D skeleton modeling method to solve the problems of deformed body and twisted joints. In addition, we optimize the motion data so that the transmission time can be reduced.

© Springer International Publishing AG 2017
J. Chang et al. (Eds.): AniNex 2017, LNCS 10582, pp. 99–113, 2017.
https://doi.org/10.1007/978-3-319-69487-0_8

2   The Matching of Motion Data with 3D Model

In fact, the movement of the 3D skeleton model can bring about the human-body motion by controlling the 3D character models. With the help of mechanical dynamics, gravity and other physical factors, the simulations of human motion are more similar to real ones.

In terms of human movements' features, the joint of the 3D skeletal model revolves around the joint between the other two joints. Any acts of one joint may affect the other joints connected to it. Therefore, to make sure of the integrity of the model in each joint movement, it is necessary to ensure that the parent-bone node and the sub-bone node remains the original link [2]. When the motion capture data is assigned to the 3D human model and change its position and direction, the compliance of the joints' changes in position and direction are required to be kept.

There are two kinds of common 3D human body models. One is Standard mesh model. It designs each joint position for a unit to store the corresponding vertex, textures, materials, and transform matrices. The other is Skinning mesh model. It defines the skeleton of the model. Each skeleton in the human model has a set of corresponding vertices, and the motion of the model is mainly determined by the position and direction of the set of vertices [3].

As shown in Fig. 1, W stands for the world coordinate, and Joint0, Joint1 and Joint2 respectively represents 3 different joints. Each vertex in the diagram has its own local coordinate, and the coordinate of the skeletal node changes as the capture data is assigned to the 3D model. When the body moves, the motion capture data changes, and the changing data will adjust the translation and rotation of the coordinates of the nodes.

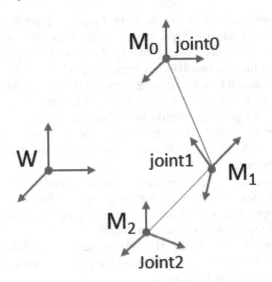

Fig. 1. The sketch map of skinning mesh transformation

Generally the translation of the 3D character model is represented by three-dimensional coordinates, that is, the coordinate positions of each joint point in three-dimensional space [4, 5]. Rotation can be expressed in terms of rotation matrix, Euler angle or four-element number. The following part will describe the process how the motion capture data changes the 3D model node coordinates.

From the perspective of hierarchical description, the position of each node in the global coordinate can be calculated by formula (1).

$$P_i^t(x, y, z) = M_{Root}^t R_{Root}^t M_1^t R_1^t \dots M_i^t R_i^t P_{init}^t(x, y, z) \tag{1}$$

Changes in motion capture data are actually reflected in the 3D model where the joint positions and rotations translate [6, 7]. Firstly, we calculate the position and rotation of parent node, and then calculate the position of each child node, as shown by formulas (2) and (3).

$$P_{Root}^t(x, y, z) = M_{Root}^t R_{Root}^t P_{Root}^{t-1}(x, y, z) \tag{2}$$

$$P_i^t(x, y, z) = M_i^t R_i^t P_i^t(x, y, z), i = 1, 2, 3 \dots \tag{3}$$

The process of motion capture data matching with 3D model is shown in Fig. 2.

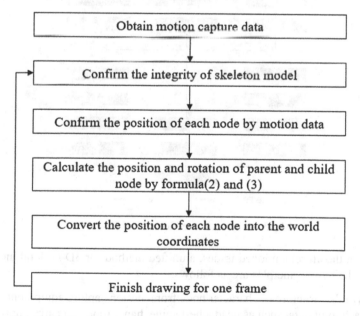

Fig. 2. The process of motion capture data matching with 3D model

The 3D skeleton models of different motion capture devices are not the same, which leads to the distortion of the 3D character model because the skeleton model does not match when applied to an arbitrary 3D human body model. Therefore, this paper also proposes a method of unified 3D skeleton modeling. According to different motion capture devices, we construct the skeleton model corresponding to the 3D models in the design. The constructed skeletal model can promote the matching between motion capture technology and the model.

2.1 Unified 3D Skeleton Modeling

In order to restore the gestures and facial expressions of moving objects in real terms, the integration of motion data with the model is also crucial besides the accuracy and real-time transmission of motion data.

At present, the 3D model of the film and television animation is produced according to the proportion of reality, so the motion data can be matched and fused with the 3D model, which also reduces the steps of adjustment in the fusion [8]. However, in most cases, such as game developing, the 3D models are impossible to bulid according to the proportion of each person's shape, which requires plenty of time, manpower and material resources to carry out (Figs. 3, 4 and 5).

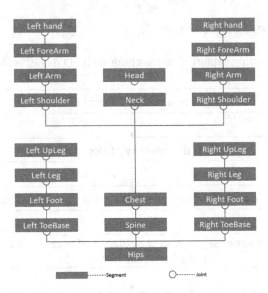

Fig. 3. Joint and bone hierarchical structure

Based on the aforementioned issues, a unified method for 3D skeletal modeling is proposed. The basic principles are as follows:

(1) Analyze the structure of character node from motion capture equipment, and classify each joint data, such as head, chest spine, hand, foot, and carry out proportion parameters $(W_1, W_2, W_3 \dots W_n)$ of each joint node by the structure of character node.

(2) Design the human hierarchical structure from the information of step 1.

(3) Define the joint coordinate system from the information of step 1 and 2.

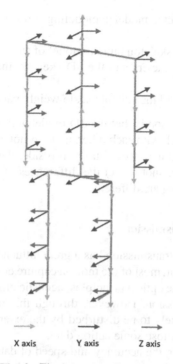

X axis   Y axis   Z axis

Fig. 4. The joint coordinate system

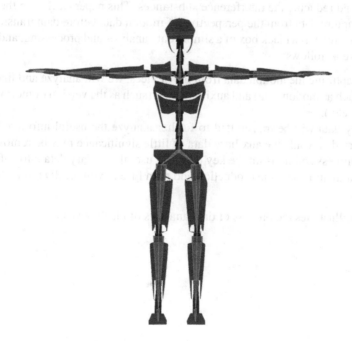

Fig. 5. The Final skeleton model

(4) Design the basic 3D skeleton model in modeling software from the joint coordinate system of step 3.
(5) Create a skin for the 3D skeleton human model of step 4.
(6) Adjust scale weight parameters and the 3D skeleton model to match the motion capture device.
(7) Repeat step 6 until we find the suitable scale weight parameters.

The advantage of this method is that the 3D model and motion capture data in the device can match and fuse well with each other, and it is not easy to cause the 3D model distortion due to individual differences. On the flip side, the 3D models are designed with a uniform size, which cannot reflect the differences of each individual, although the facial features and clothing are different.

2.2 Precise and Fast Transmission

The integrity of motion data transmission has a great influence on the representation of model authenticity. At present, most of the motion capture devices need to transmit data through cables, and others use optical principles, acoustic principles, wireless networks and other means of transmission. However, through this mode of transmission, the motion data will be more likely to be disturbed by the external interference, and then generate excess noise data or lose some action data.

For the sake of improving the accuracy and speed of data transmission in wireless mode of action, it is required to improve signal strength by means of increasing the bandwidth and reducing the interference substances. This paper carries on the analysis of motion capture data from the perspective of motion data before data transmission.

This paper reveals a black box of a simple data analysis and processing, and its basic principles are as follows:

(1) After capturing the motion data from the devices, we will analyze and find the key data (such as motion data) and auxiliary data (such as the version of motion capture device, etc.).
(2) The key data will be transmitted to further analyze the useful information in the auxiliary data while the auxiliary data of little significance may be removed.
(3) We compress and transmit the key data and useful auxiliary data into software for video animation or game production and then fuse it with the 3D motion character model.

Figure 6 illustrates the process of data analysis of black boxes.

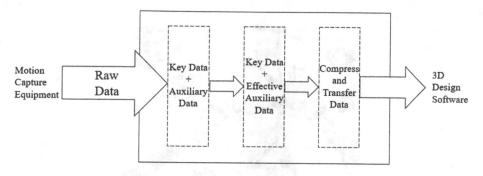

Fig. 6. The procedure of motion data analysis

3 Experimental Analysis and Result

3.1 Experimental Environment

The software and hardware used by the experiment are as follows.

The motion capture technology: Perception Neuron motion capture system.
The 3D modeling software: Maya, 3DMax.
Game developing platform: Unity 5.5.2.
Experimental platform: Intel i7-4790K CPU, 4.00 GHz, 16 GB RAM and Nvidia GeForce GTX980Ti.
Programming tools: Visual Studio 2017.
Figure 7 shows the Perception Neuron motion capture equipment.

3.2 Experimental Process

Unified 3D Skeleton Modeling. After the motion data analysis is completed by the motion capture system, we find the parameters in accordance with the corresponding proportion of each node in human body. Each motion capture device set different proportions, so it is necessary to initialize the design of the 3D model. In this paper, we take advantage of Maya and 3DMax for skeleton building. According to the skeletons provided by the software and the adjustment of the proportion of human bones, we ultimately determine the reasonable unified 3D character skeleton, as shown in Fig. 8. Here is a skeleton drawing that was designed during the process of skeleton adjustment.

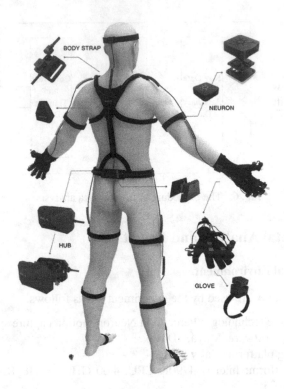

Fig. 7. The Perception Neuron motion capture equipment

Fig. 8. One of the 3D skeleton model by first adjustment

The above figures are just a part of the design pictures during adjustment process. We got Fig. 9 after 7 modifications from Fig. 8. In this process, it appeared different levels of distortion when the designed skeleton was applied to the model given the motion data. The main reason why it happened is that the prescribed proportion of skeleton model in motion capture system is inconsistent with the skeleton we designed.

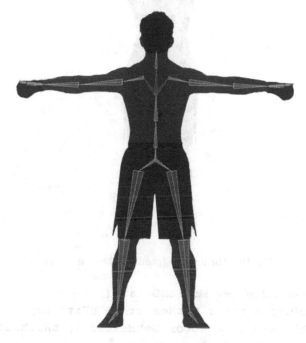

Fig. 9. One of the 3D skeleton model by seventh adjustment

After the tenth adjustment, the 3D character skeleton of the motion capture system was finally determined and applied to the character model, as shown in Fig. 10.

Precise and Fast Transmission. Based on the research of the Perception Neuron motion capture system, the key data and effective auxiliary data are analyzed in the 3D model.

Key data: motion data.
Effective auxiliary data: data of bWithDisp and bWithReference.

We carry out the package transmission of key data and effective auxiliary data. Besides, we deal with some repeatedly invalid auxiliary data by means of initialization assignment and the absence of transmission after the key data reach the 3D scene, as shown in Figs. 11 and 12.

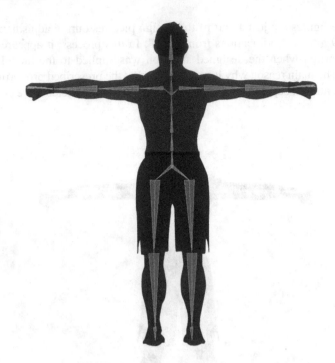

Fig. 10. The final designed 3D skeleton model

```
MotionDatas md = new MotionDatas () {
    bWithDisp = actor.GetHeader ().bWithDisp,
    bWithReference = actor.GetHeader ().bWithReference,
    Datas = actor.GetData ()
};
```

Fig. 11. The package transmission of key data and effective auxiliary data

```
NeuronActor actor = new NeuronActor(1);
actor.SetData(motionData.Datas);
BvhDataHeader header = new BvhDataHeader();
header.Token1 = 0xDDFF;
header.DataVersion = new DataVersion() { BuildNumb = 1, Revision = 1, Minor = 0, Major = 0 };
header.DataCount = 59;
header.bWithDisp = motionData.bWithDisp;
header.bWithReference = motionData.bWithReference;
header.AvatarIndex = 0;
header.AvatarName = "healthy mall";
header.FrameIndex = 0;
header.Reserved = 0;
header.Reserved1 = 0;
header.Reserved2 = 0;
header.Token2 = 0xEEFF;
actor.SetHeader(header);
```

Fig. 12. The direct initialization of duplicate auxiliary data

This greatly reduces the amount of data in the network transmission process. In addition, without considering the details of the fingers, the number of hand sensors can be decreased from 11 to 1 while ensuring data integrity.

3.3   Experimental Analysis

Unified 3D Skeleton Modeling. In the experiment of unified 3D skeleton modeling, we use the same 3D character model, input the same motion capture data, and apply different 3D skeletons. The results are shown as follows.

In this experiment, we input the same motion capture data into these two 3D models. From Fig. 13, we can find out that there is obvious distortion and stretch in the joint and the two legs of the left 3D character model while the right 3D character has good performance.

Fig. 13. The left one is the original skeleton model and the right one is the skeleton we design by our method

Data Transmission Time In order to eliminate interference from other factors, most of the strong magnetic materials have been removed in the experimental environment, and the wireless network has been adjusted to the optimum state. In the experiment, the transmission time of raw data and processed data is compared. In addition, the transmission time of glove detail data before and after deletion is also compared. The comparison is as follows.

From Table 1, we can find the original data transmission time is 0.5 s. The 3D scene cannot run fluently. The optimized data transmission time is 0.07 s, which is better than the original data transmission time.

Table 1. The comparison of original and optimized data transmission time

Serial number	Experimental item	Delay/s
1	The original data transmission time	0.5
2	The optimized data transmission time	0.07

From Table 2, the transmission time of glove detail data before deletion is 0.07 s. After removing 20 sensor nodes on the hands and preserving only 2 sensor nodes at the back of the hands, the data transmission time is 0.01 s.

Table 2. The transmission time of glove detail data before and after deletion

Serial number	Experimental item	Delay/s
1	The glove detail data before deletion	0.07
2	The glove detail data after deletion	0.01

The Virtual Fighting. Now we apply our 3D character models to the virtual fighting game, and optimize the motion data transmission time. The virtual fighting game includes several modules such as Main Menu Modules, Players Selection Modules, Scenes Selection Modules and Fighting Scenes Modules. These modules are shown as follows (Figs. 14, 15, 16 and 17).

Fig. 14. The main menu picture

Fig. 15. The scene select picture

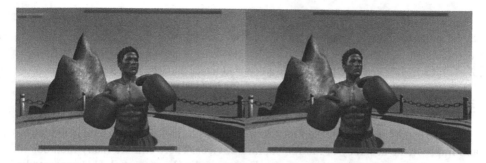

Fig. 16. The fighting scene picture of one player

Fig. 17. The fighting scene picture of the other player

3.4 Comparative Analysis

This paper proposed a unified 3D skeleton modeling method to solve the problems of deformed body and twisted joints. In order to improve the accuracy and speed of movement of data transmission, we designed a black box to analyze the motion data.

There are so many studies discussing the human modeling for motion capture. Tao et al. [9] designed an anatomic virtual human model and proposed a method of real-time reconstruction of human motion for the MMocap system. One of the contributions of their study is the human model, which is a compact representation of the movement. Another contribution of their study is the kinematic equation, which is based on quaternions. The experiments have shown that it can reconstruct the postures of human motion with good fidelity and low latency.

Li et al. [10] presented a human motion model and animation for a micro-sensor motion capture system. This method is based on biomechanics. The joints of human body are categorized according to the motion characteristics. Motion parameters estimated from sensor data are used to control the movement of human skeleton model and the deformation of skin model, and consequently reconstruct the human body motion in real-time animation. The experiments have shown that the proposed model is suitable for sensor data-driven virtual human in real time animation.

The comparison of modeling methods and real-time performance are shown as follows (Table 3).

Table 3. The comparison of modeling methods

Serial number	Paper number	Experimental method
1	This paper	A unified 3D skeleton modeling method
2	Tao et al. [9]	An articulated human model which is an anatomic skeleton human model
3	Li et al. [10]	This method is based on biomechanics

Those papers above are presenting different methods to achieve 3D human modeling and improve the accuracy of motion capture devices. There still are many methods to improve the accuracy of motion capture. For example, Haratian et al. [11] presented a signal processing approach and Young [12] took a use of body model constraints. Although our method is different, we all achieved the goal of 3D human modeling and accuracy improvement (Table 4).

Table 4. The comparison of improving accuracy methods

Serial number	Paper number	Experimental method
1	This paper	Optimized the motion data by removing some auxiliary data
2	Tao et al. [9]	Build a software platform MMocap 3D which is an easy-to-use graphical user interface
3	Li et al. [10]	Consequently reconstruct the human body motion in real-time animation

4   Conclusion

In this paper, through the application of motion capture technology in virtual fighting, the problems related to the matching of motion capture data and 3D model are found, and a unified modeling method of 3D skeleton model is proposed. In addition, in order to improve the accuracy and speed of movement of data transmission, we designed a black box to analyze the motion data. Without compromising the integrity of the data, we improved motion data transmission speed.

The above two methods all achieve the ideal effect in the virtual fighting application, and then we verify the validity and feasibility of the two methods. Nevertheless, there are still some limitations to be improved in the experimental design, such as:

(1) The analysis of motion capture data is still in a relatively simple stage, and it should be combined with some coding rules to analyze, which will achieve better results [13].
(2) Unified modeling is not the best solution for different individuals, but on this basis, we can find a further adaptive method of motion capture data and 3D model data fusion process [14].

In this paper, the research is still at the primary stage, there are still a lot of problems for improvement. We hope this paper can provide a strong support for motion capture technology applied in film and television animation, game production, and research on virtual human-computer interaction.

References

1. Wang, X., Zhu, X., Zhao, J., Xu, H.: The research of real time motion capture technology in film and television animation. Microcomput. Appl. **3**, 16–17 (2014)
2. Cai, Z.: Research on human computer interaction design based on motion capture. Digital Technol. Appl. **3**, 80 (2014)
3. Ji, Q., Pan, Z., Li, X.: Application of virtual reality in sports simulation. J. Comput. Aided Design Comput. Graph. **11**, 1333–1338 (2003)
4. Zhang, T., Wang, X.: Application of motion capture technology in sports. Electron. Test **24**, 103–104 (2015)
5. Yao, X.: Modeling and motion simulation of virtual human based on motion capture data Computer. Simulation **06**, 225–229 (2010)
6. Chan, J.C.P., Leung, H., Tang, J.K.T., Taku, K.: A virtual reality dance training system using motion capture technology. IEEE Trans. Learn. Technol. **4**(2), 187–195 (2011)
7. Liu, B., Li, Y., Zhou, D.: The application of motion capture system and virtual simulation software in virtual maintenance. In: International Conference on Quality, Reliability, Risk, Maintenance, and Safety Engineering, pp. 1986–1988 (2013)
8. Chen, S., Ning, T., Wang, K.: Motion control of virtual human based on optical motion capture in immersive virtual maintenance system. In: International Conference on Virtual Reality and Visualization, pp. 52–56. IEEE (2011)
9. Tao, G., Sun, S., Huang, S., Huang, Z., Wu, J.: Human modeling and real-time motion reconstruction for micro-sensor motion capture. In: IEEE International Conference on Virtual Environments Human-Computer Interfaces and Measurement Systems, pp. 1–5. IEEE (2011)
10. Li, G., Wu, Z., Meng, X.: Modeling of human body for animation by micro-sensor motion capture. In: International Symposium on Knowledge Acquisition and Modeling, pp. 98–101. IEEE (2009)
11. Haratian, R., Twycross-Lewis, R., Timotijevic, T., Phillips, C.: Toward flexibility in sensor placement for motion capture systems: a signal processing approach. IEEE Sens. J. **14**(3), 701–709 (2014)
12. Young, A.D.: Use of body model constraints to improve accuracy of inertial motion capture. In: International Conference on Body Sensor Networks, pp. 180–186. IEEE (2010)
13. Wang, H., Tu, C.: Encoding and retrieval of motion capture data based on Hash learning. J. Comput. Aided Design Comput. Graph. **12**, 2151–2158 (2016)
14. Liang, F., Zhang, Z., Li, X., Tong, Z.: Recognition of human lower limb movements during human motion capture. J. Comput. Aided Design Comput. Graph. **12**, 2419–2427 (2015)

Replacement of Facial Parts in Images

Jiang Du[1], Yanjing Wu[2], Dan Song[1], Ruofeng Tong[1(✉)], and Min Tang[1]

[1] State Key Lab of CAD&CG, Zhejiang University, Hangzhou 310027, China
trf@zju.edu.cn
[2] The Third Affiliated Hospital, Zhejiang Chinese Medicine University, Hangzhou, China

Abstract. It is interesting to edit facial appearance in images to create a desirable facial shape of persons. In this paper, we propose a novel method to modify facial appearance by replacing facial parts between arbitrarily paired images. To this end, our method consists of face segmentation, face reconstruction, mesh deformation and image editing. Given one source and one target image, the target image is first segmented into the front facial region and background image. Secondly, 3D facial models and relevant scene parameters are estimated from both images. Thirdly, the target facial part is replaced with the selected source part on the 3D mesh. Then, the new replaced 3D face is rendered into a facial image. Finally, the new facial image is generated by seamlessly blending the rendered image and background image. The main advantage of this method is that we transfer facial geometric information between images using 3D model, which can deal with arbitrarily paired images with the different facial viewpoint. We present several experimental results to show the effectiveness of our method and comparison with those existing methods to demonstrate that our method is more advantageous and flexible in terms of practical applications.

Keywords: Facial parts replacement · Mesh deformation · Face reconstruction

1 Introduction

The human face has always been one of the most important aspects in human interaction and communication, because it plays a great role in making people distinguishable and giving people visible impression. As the use of huge digital images in the current multimedia era, facial images have become the most common digital avatar that might have higher status than the real face in our daily life, such as pasting facial images on resumes or some application forms. Furthermore, this advanced digital representation can enable many impossible things into reality in the digital world, which brings in many potential applications for various fields. For example, in medical beauty, it will be very helpful to provide a vivid preview of client's ideal facial image before plastic surgery [1]. In forensics, it is significant to compose the suspect's facial image according to the description of victims and witnesses [2]. In entertainment, it is interesting to show personal or friends' funny facial images. In privacy preservation, it is necessary to protect people's facial images from the public online system such as Google Street View [3]. These applications are all based on the great advantage of the facial images that users can

© Springer International Publishing AG 2017
J. Chang et al. (Eds.): AniNex 2017, LNCS 10582, pp. 114–129, 2017.
https://doi.org/10.1007/978-3-319-69487-0_9

arbitrarily edit their faces to create a new facial appearance. Thus, it is meaningful to develop facial image editing methods for the users to conveniently edit facial images.

In recent years, there exist some methods which might help users to edit facial images at least to some extent. Blanz et al. proposed a face swapping method to replace a face in a target image with a face in a source image for virtual try-on of hairstyles [4]. Afterwards, some face swapping methods were proposed for de-identification [5], transfiguring user's portraits [6, 7], and face perception [8]. Liao et al. proposed a face beautifying method by enhancing the symmetry and proportion of user's face in the image [9]. Zhao et al. changed the weight of the face in the images [10]. Researchers also developed face composing methods to create a new facial image by combining selected facial part images [1, 2, 11]. Recently, the field of facial performance applied face reanimating methods to transfer facial expression from a source image to a face in a target image while preserving the identity of the target person [12–14]. However, these existing methods are inadequate to satisfy the whole demand of the facial image editing. For example, before taking the facial micro-cosmetic surgery, users usually want to see a preview of the local edited facial image like the region of eyes or nose. A flexible solution is to edit facial parts in images. Thus, we focus on developing facial parts replacement method to effectively replace facial parts between images.

Though previous methods can replace entire face between images under some precedent conditions, the replacement of facial parts between images confronts greater challenge than previous face swapping methods. For instance, replacement of facial parts between two images can be easily completed when both images have the faces with the same viewpoint, illumination, and size [8], while this situation is rarely possible. Bitouk et al. [5] also demonstrated that different illuminations and viewpoints made this task even more difficult and might lead to abnormal facial images. In addition, the replacement of facial parts with different sizes in images easily results in weird facial images. For example, a small facial part substitutes a big one in a target image [1]. Furthermore, the face is a visually sensitive object, thus very small flaws can affect people's sensory effects. Thus, the replaced results must be surely normal faces except for entertaining demands.

In this paper, we propose a novel method to replace the facial parts in a target image with the ones from a source image. Our proposed method consists of face segmentation, face reconstruction, mesh deformation and image editing. The combination of these four parts can effectively alleviate the difficulties stressed above. Furthermore, we especially tailor mesh deformation to the need of facial parts replacement which can automatically identify facial parts and replace them between the 3D facial meshes, and this tailored algorithm can also eliminate redundant user's involvement. Our method takes one source and one target image as input and generates a new target image with the selected facial part from the source image. Firstly, the target image is segmented into a front facial region and a background image based on face segmentation method [8]. Secondly, from both images, we estimate 3D facial models and relevant scene parameters including facial orientation, position and camera parameters based on the Basel Face Model (BFM) [15]. Thirdly, the target facial part is replaced with the selected source part using mesh deformation [16]. In this stage, to satisfy the need of facial parts replacement on the 3D mesh, we introduce a template model which can automatically identify the facial parts, and we also devise a tailored alignment algorithm which can automatically align the selected facial part to target facial mesh. Then, the new replaced 3D face is rendered into a facial image using the scene parameters obtained in the second stage. Finally, the new image is generated by seamlessly blending the rendered facial image and the background image.

The main contributions of this paper are summarized in three aspects. Firstly, we provide a novel facial image editing tool to replace facial parts between images based on current state-of-the-art technologies in the computer graphics area. Secondly, for the proposed facial parts replacement, we devise an automatic facial parts identification and an alignment algorithm which can simplify the process of the user's interaction. Thirdly, unlike most existing methods for entire facial replacement between images, we edit the facial image using 3D meshes which contain more geometric information than 2D images. Furthermore, we edit the facial geometric information on 3D meshes, which reduces the impact on the texture as opposed to the methods using 2D images.

The rest of this paper is organized as follows. In Sect. 2, we review related work regarding facial image editing. Section 3 describes the facial parts replacement method and details of the tailored algorithm for the desired purpose. Section 4 demonstrates the rendered results of this work to show the effectiveness of our method. In Sect. 5, we conclude this work and give possible future extensions.

2   Related Work

Almost all facial image editing techniques derive from the combination of image processing [17] and face recognition [18] which are two popular research fields. However, the scope of these two fields is so large that they are beyond the scope of this paper. Thus, we focus mainly on the problem of facial image editing which can result in the modification of facial appearance. As a result, we review the most relevant work such as face swapping, face composing and face reanimating.

Face swapping. Blanz et al. proposed a method to swap faces based on the Morphable Model of 3D faces [4]. The use of 3D face model is a good solution to the limitation of different viewpoints between images. The reconstructed face can be consistently aligned and illuminated with the face in the target image, which enables the face to be easily rendered into the target scene. Bitouk et al. [5] solved the limitation of facial viewpoint and illumination by constructing a large face database including various facial poses, image resolution and image blur. Then, the candidate images to be replaced are selected by matching the corresponding criteria as similar as possible to the input. Ira [6] upgraded this work by directly and automatically searching candidate images from the Internet, which eliminated the expense of building the face database. Other recent face swapping methods adopted current advanced technologies including face detection, face segmentation and face reconstruction [8], which improves the robustness of previous works and produces excellent results. However, their methods only allow the entire face to be replaced, which is not flexible enough for some practical applications. Our proposed facial parts replacement can modify the facial appearance with finer granularity such as the region of eyes or nose.

Face composing. In the digital forensics [2], it is common to synthesize the suspect's facial image by composing the facial part images from a large database. The images of facial parts are almost frontal faces. Forensic artists can select the most similar image according to the description of the victims and witnesses. Then, these parts are placed in the corresponding position of a template facial image, which results in a slightly abstract facial image [2, 11, 19]. For non-professional requirements, Chou et al. [1] replaced facial parts based on 2D images. Users selected the facial parts from the source image. Then the proposed algorithm automatically aligned the selected parts to the target image and replaced the original region by Poisson image editing. However, this method lacks the mechanism of filtering candidate images like Bitouk [5] and Ira [6], which leads to that their method can only deal with the frontal facial images. Thus, our proposed method applies 3D face models to alleviate the limitation of facial viewpoint, which can be suitable for more applications.

Face reanimating. The method for reanimating faces was proposed as far back as 2003 by Blanz et al. [20]. Afterward, this method was extended into fully automatic techniques for video facial reenactment or digital avatar performance [12, 14]. These methods are also called facial expression transfer. Benefiting from the excellent representation of 3D face parametric model [15, 21, 22], facial expression can be easily controlled by a set of expression parameters. When transferring the expression between images, Vlasic et al. [21] transferred the parameters of source facial image to the target image. To preserve personalized information in each actor's expression, Thies et al. [12] used a sub-space deformation transfer technique as opposed to direct transfer. However, these technologies focus on expression for facial performance [23, 24]. Facial expression transfer seems very similar to our proposed method of facial part replacement, since both methods transfer the shape of the source image to the target. Nevertheless, the replacement of facial parts results in the change of personal identity which is invariant for each individual and difficult to isolate like facial expressions [25]. Thus, it is difficult to transfer the facial parts by transferring the facial parameters. In this paper, to distinguish between the shape of facial expression and identity, we only call the shape of identity as facial shape. Furthermore, editing facial shape can create new identity, which motivates us to develop a new method to replace facial parts between images for more potential applications.

3   Method

In this section, we describe how our replacement method is achieved through current state-of-the-art technologies including face segmentation, 3D face reconstruction, 3D mesh deformation and image editing. We start by giving an overview of our method.

3.1   Overview of Method

Figure 1 summarizes our facial part replacement method. In Fig. 1, we take the replacement of eyes part between images as an example. When replacing a facial part from a source image $\mathbf{I}_S$ to a target image $\mathbf{I}_T$, our method firstly segments the target image into a facial region and background image (Sect. 3.2). Then, we reconstruct the 3D facial model and estimate scene parameters which are described in Sect. 3.3. Thirdly, we describe how to replace the selected facial parts by mesh deformation (Sect. 3.4). Finally, the replaced face is rendered and blended with the background image (Sect. 3.5).

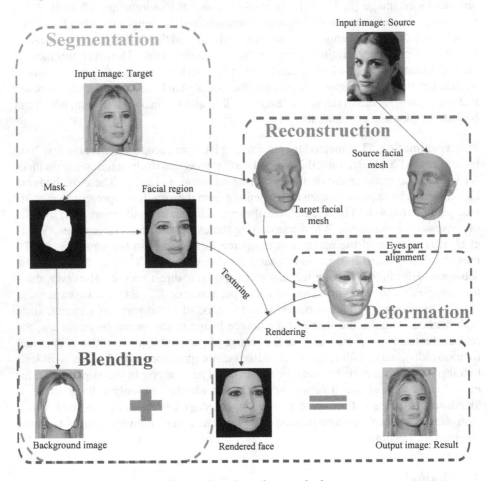

Fig. 1. Overview of our method.

3.2 Face Segmentation

To preserve all local characteristics of the target face, our method firstly segments the target image into a facial region and background image. The facial region is applied to extract the real visible texture and the background image is applied for the final blending.

We use the recent state-of-the-art, deep method [8] for face segmentation which is shown to work well on unconstrained images. Moreover, it also works well on segmenting the visible region of faces from occlusions. They trained a standard fully convolutional network (FCN) which used the FCN-8 s-VGG architecture. Please refer to [8] for more details on the FCN. Figure 2 shows two examples of segmentation to demonstrate that this method can deal with the facial images with different viewpoint very well and successfully split the facial region from the image. These excellent results are very helpful for the extraction of facial texture by off-the-shelf extracting method [4, 22].

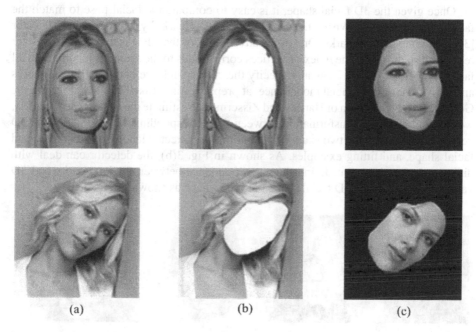

(a)   (b)   (c)

Fig. 2. Examples of Segmentation results, (a) input images, (2) segmented background images, (3) facial regions.

3.3   Face Reconstruction

To alleviate the limitation of different facial viewpoint in images, inspired by previous work [4, 26, 27], we explicitly reconstruct 3D facial shapes from both images. We use the popular Basel Face Model (BFM) [15] to represent 3D faces. More specifically, a 3D facial shape S with texture T is defined by combining the following independent generative models:

$$S = \bar{s} + \sum_{i=1}^{m} \alpha_i \cdot s_i, \qquad T = \bar{t} + \sum_{i=1}^{m} \beta_i \cdot t_i. \tag{1}$$

Here, vector $\bar{s}$ and $\bar{t}$ are the mean facial shape and texture of aligned 3D scans in the Basel Faces collection, respectively. Vector s_i and t_i are the principle components computed by Principal Component Analysis (PCA) from 3D scans. α and β are subject-specific 99D parameter vectors estimated separately for each facial image. From a given set of model parameters α and β, we can compute a colorized 3D face model.

To reconstruct 3D face shapes from a single image, we need to compute the parameters α and β. Unlike previous methods [4, 7, 27, 28] to solve an energy equation for fitting the pixels of the image, we adopt the deep network proposed by Tran et al. [29] to regress the parameters α and β which are 99D parameters for shape and texture separately.

Once given the 3D facial shape, it is easy to compute the facial pose to match the face in the input image. We use the detected facial landmarks by an off-the-shelf detector [30] including 68 landmarks. One of the advantages of the BFM is that the vertices are registered so that the same index of vertices corresponds to the same 2D landmark in all faces. Therefore, we can manually specify the correspondence between 2D landmarks and 3D vertices on the facial model once, at preprocessing. Like Huber et al., using the Gold Standard Algorithm of Hartley and Zisserman to estimate the pose of the face [31], we can find an affine transformation between the corresponding 2D landmarks and 3D vertices. Figure 3 shows two examples including the detected landmarks, reconstructed facial shape, and fitting examples. As shown in Fig. 3(b), the detector can deal with different facial viewpoint. Using the correspondence between 2D landmarks and 3D vertices, we can fit the 3D facial shape onto the image as shown in Fig. 3(d).

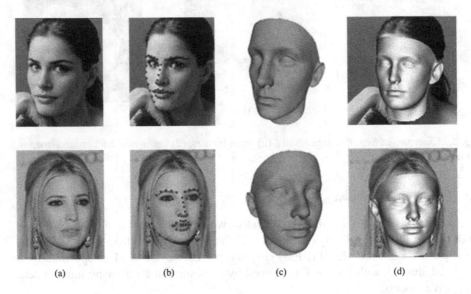

(a)   (b)   (c)   (d)

Fig. 3. Examples of facial landmarks detection, reconstruction and fitting the image, (a) input images, (b) the detected landmarks, (c) the reconstructed 3D facial shape, (d) examples of fitting image with 3D facial shape.

3.4 Mesh Deformation

To replace the facial parts in the target face with the corresponding parts of the source, we need some preparations to help facial parts replacement. Firstly, it is necessary to define the region of each facial part on the 3D facial model, which can help to establish the correspondence of facial parts between different faces and can also define the region of deformation. Thus, we introduce a template facial model which is manually specified several desirable regions on it. Benefiting from the BFM facial model which has the same number of vertices and faces and the same topology, the specifying process only needs to be done once. Figure 4(a) shows our facial template model. Figure 4(b) shows different segmented regions with different colors. The region of eyes is colored with blue, eyebrows with purple, nose with yellow, mouth with red and the green area denotes the transitional region for deformation. Therefore, each part of the template model can automatically correspond to the facial parts between different face. When users select a facial part like nose or mouth, our method will automatically turn on subsequent processing which is the alignment algorithm described in the following content.

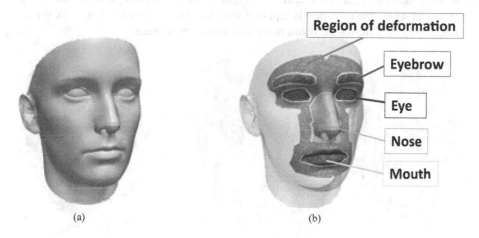

(a)   (b)

Fig. 4. Example of template model, (a) the facial template model, (b) different regions of facial parts with different color. (Color figure online)

Since selected facial parts are from different images, they have the different viewpoint. It is necessary to align them to the target face. Similar to computing the affine transformation between 2D landmarks and 3D vertices, it is easy to compute the rigid transformation between each pair of facial parts when the two sets of corresponding points are given [32]. Here, we need to slightly adjust the method for our purpose. We seek a rotation matrix R, a translation vector t, and a scale s such that

$$(R, t, s) = arm\,min_{R,t,s} \sum_{i=1}^{n} \omega_i \left\| s(Rp_i + t) - q_i \right\|^2 + \mu \left| c_p - c_q \right|^2 \qquad (2)$$

Here, $P = \{p_1, p_2, \dots, p_n\}$ and $Q = \{q_1, q, \dots, q_n\}$ are two sets of corresponding points on source and target facial meshes respectively. The second item restrains that the centers of two corresponding facial parts are as close as possible. Because the central position of facial parts is originally the most appropriate location of the target face, it is necessary to restrain the center of the new part to be the same as the original one. For the scale s, we try to compute a suitable size for the new part. Because there is a case where a selected facial part is smaller than the target one, this may lead to an abnormal replacement. Before the user makes the final decision, we can take this suitable scale as a candidate. Moreover, we also provide an optional adjustment for scale s to $\rho \cdot s$ ($0.8 \leq \rho \leq 1.2$).

After alignment, the selected facial part can be replaced with the source part by mesh deformation method. An obvious choice is to apply a drag-and-drop-pasting method [33–35]. However, these methods usually lead to subsequent cumbersome processing, because these methods change the topology of the original model including the number of vertices and faces. To complete facial parts replacement, we adopt a more suitable method to deform the facial part of the target to the selected part. The deformation can form the Laplacian energies which leads to a biharmonic equation with region boundary condition proposed by Jacobson et al. [16]. Figure 5 shows an example of our facial part replacement where the nose part is replaced with the source shown in Fig. 5(b), the red region. Figure 5(c) shows the result has a new facial appearance.

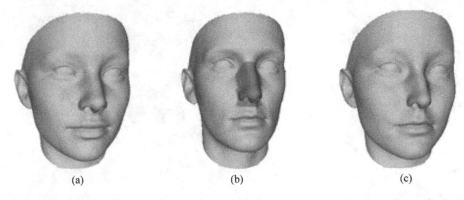

(a)   (b)   (c)

Fig. 5. An example of our facial part replacement, (a) the target model, (b) the source model with selected nose part (red region), (c) the replaced result with source's nose. (Color figure online)

3.5 Face Blending

After obtaining the deformed 3D face model as mentioned above (Sect. 3.4), our method can compose the final image with the new facial appearance by blending between the new rendered facial image and the background image. Figure 6 shows a blending example.

Though the BFM provides the linear combination of textures, it cannot reproduce high-quality facial appearance [4]. Therefore, we use the segmented facial region to render replaced facial appearance like previous methods [4, 12]. The scene parameters of the target obtained from face reconstruction (Sect. 3.3) are also used to render the new 3D face into an image shown in Fig. 6(b). Finally, the rendered face is blended-in with the background image using an off the shelf method [36].

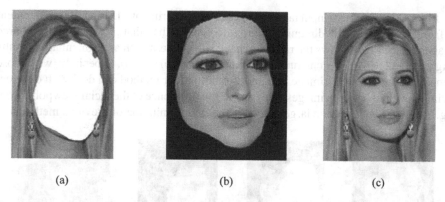

Fig. 6. An example of final blend, (a) background image, (b) rendered facial image, (c) blending result.

4   Experiments

Our experiments are implemented on an Inter Core i7-4790 4.00 GHz machine with 32 GB memory and the Windows 10 operating system. We use the segmentation Caffe model [8] for face segmentation, the BFM model [15] for facial reconstruction and libigl [37] for the mesh deformation. In this section, we show several results of replacement and the results of each sub-process which demonstrates that the final excellent results are inseparable from the help of each sub-process. We also provide comparisons against previous facial appearance processing methods

Figure 7 shows two input source images in our experiments. During the replacement of facial parts, our method only requires the geometric information of the source image. Thus, Fig. 7 also provides the reconstructed 3D facial model. Both of these two persons have salient facial parts like McKellen's nose and Parsons' eyes. We use Ian McKellen's nose and Jim Parsons' eyes to replace the corresponding parts in the target images.

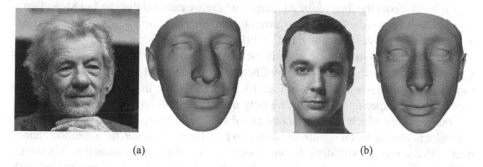

Fig. 7. Input source images, (a) Ian McKellen's image and the reconstructed 3D facial model, (b) Jim Parsons' image and the reconstructed 3D facial model.

Figure 8(a) gives two input target images in our experiments. During the replacement of facial parts, our method requires more information than that provided by the source images. Thus, Fig. 8 shows the results of each sub-process such as segmentation results (Fig. 8(b) and (c)) and reconstructed 3D facial model (Fig. 8(d)). Especially, we choose Benedict Cumberbatch's image to demonstrate that our method can deal with different facial viewpoint between images. We can see the difference of the facial viewpoint from Fig. 8(a) and Fig. 7 is quite large, which is the main limitation of previous methods.

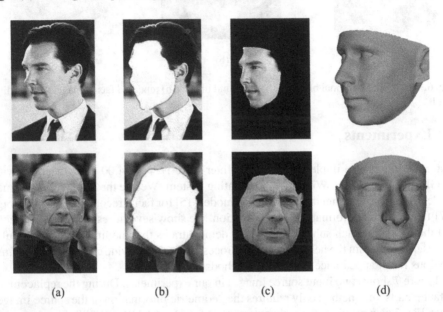

(a)   (b)   (c)   (d)

Fig. 8. Input target images and the results of each sub-process, (a) Cumberbatch's image and Bruce Willis' image, (b) background images, (c) facial region images, (d) the reconstructed 3D facial model.

Figure 9 shows the final replaced images where we can find that the Ian McKellen's nose and Jim Parsons' eyes are transferred to Benedict Cumberbatch and Bruce Willis. The new facial images are shown in Fig. 9(b) and (c).

To further demonstrate the effectiveness of our method, we compare the results generated by our method with those by Chou et al.'s face-off [1] and Bitouk et al.'s face swapping [5] methods as shown in Fig. 10. Since the input image of their methods is required to be a specific viewpoint, we only use images that are suitable for both theirs and our methods, which take the frontal facial viewpoint as input. Chou et al.'s method is similar to ours and their results are shown in Fig. 10(c). However, their method cannot deal with the images with different viewpoint like the Benedict Cumberbatch's image in Fig. 9. Bitouk et al.'s method is to replace the entire face between two images with similar viewpoints and the results are shown in Fig. 10(d). The comparisons can also demonstrate that our facial parts replacement is more advantageous and flexible in terms of practical applications, because users can see the vivid preview of their changed facial appearance on some local region.

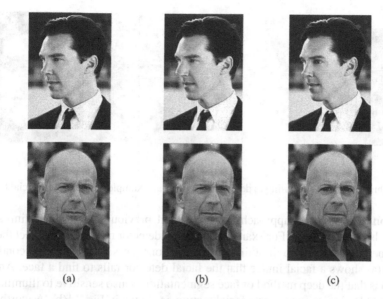

Fig. 9. Results of our facial parts replacement, (a) original images, (b) results with new nose part, (c) results with new eyes part.

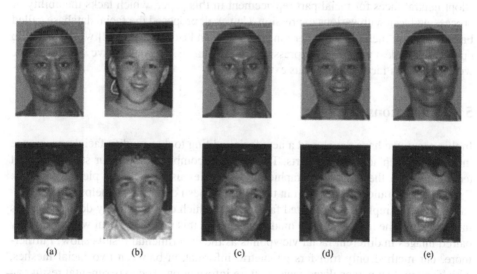

Fig. 10. Comparisons with previous methods, (a) target images, (b) source images, (c) replaced nose and eyes part separately by Chou et al. [1], (d) replaced entire face by Bitouk et al. [5], (e) replaced nose and eyes part separately by our method.

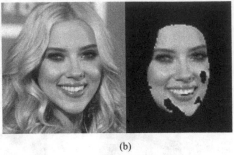

(a)   (b)

Fig. 11. Our limitations, (a) failing to detect the face, (b) an example of incomplete facial texture.

Limitation. Because our approach adopts several previous works, their limitations might be also our obstacles. For example, the facial detector might fail to detect the face from some images due to illumination, occlusions or some unknown condition. Figure 11(a) shows a facial image that the facial detector fails to find a face. Another limitation is that the deep method of face segmentation is also sensitive to illumination, which might lead to an incomplete facial texture as shown in Fig. 11(b). A worthwhile solution is to use the segmentation of 3D mesh [38] reconstructed from image to guide the segmentation of the facial region in the image. The third limitation is that we only adopt neutral faces for facial part replacement in this paper, which lacks the ability of processing faces with various expression. Cao et al. proposed the facial database called Facewarehouse including a wider range of faces and expressions [22] which can help our method to deal with facial expressions in the images. Thus, we leave it to our future work to process faces with various expressions.

5   Conclusions

In this paper, we have developed a new facial editing tool to modify facial appearance in images by replacing facial parts. The effective combination of four state-of-the-art technologies in the computer graphics area enables us to generate pleasing results. Especially, the tailored algorithm in the stage of mesh deformation helps to automatically align and replace the selected facial parts, which can effectively decrease user's involvement. The use of 3D face model can enable this method to deal with arbitrarily paired images in different facial viewpoints as the experimental results show. Furthermore, our method only transfers geometric information between two facial meshes, which can protect personalized facial texture information. The experimental result can demonstrate that our method can effectively generate pleasing results. The comparison with those existing methods demonstrates that our method is more advantageous and flexible in terms of practical applications.

In the future, we will not only address the aforementioned issues but also strive for more potential applications. For example, plastic-beauty based face replacement method is guided by real soft tissue deformation [39] for virtual surgery. Furthermore, it is interesting to build a web platform for more users to experience the facial image editing.

Acknowledgements. The research is supported in part by NSFC (61572424) and the People Programme (Marie Curie Actions) of the European Union's Seventh Framework Programme FP7 (2007–2013) under REA grant agreement No. 612627-"AniNex". Min Tang is supported in part by NSFC (61572423) and Zhejiang Provincial NSFC (LZ16F020003).

References

1. Chou, J.K., Yang, C.K., Gong, S.D.: Face-off: automatic alteration of facial features. Multimedia Tools Appl. **56**(3), 569–596 (2012)
2. Klum, S., Han, H., Jain, A.K., Klara, B.: Sketch based face recognition: Forensic vs. Composite sketches. In: 2013 International Conference on Biometrics (ICB), pp. 1–8. IEEE, Madrid, Spain (2013)
3. Google Street View. http://maps.google.com/help/maps/streetview
4. Blanz, V., Scherbaum, K., Vetter, T., Seidel, H.P.: Exchanging faces in images. Comput. Graph. Forum **23**(3), 669–676 (2004)
5. Bitouk, D., Kumar, N., Dhillon, S., Belhumeur, P., Nayar, S.K.: Face Swapping: automatically replacing faces in photographs. ACM Trans. Graph. (TOG) **27**(3), 39:1–39:8 (2008)
6. Kemelmacher-Shlizerman, I.: Transfiguring portraits. ACM Trans. Graph. (TOG) **35**(4), 94:1–94:8 (2016)
7. Afifi, M., Hussain, K.F., Ibrahim, H.M., Omar, N.M., Video face replacement system using a modified Poisson blending technique. In: 2014 International Symposium on Intelligent Signal Processing and Communication Systems (ISPACS), pp. 205–210. IEEE, Kuching, Malaysia (2014)
8. Nirkin, Y., Masi, I., Tran, A. T, Hassner, T., Medioni, G.: On Face Segmentation, Face Swapping, and Face Perception. arXiv preprint arXiv:1704.06729, (2017)
9. Liao, Q., Jin, X., Zeng, W.: Enhancing the symmetry and proportion of 3D face geometry. IEEE Trans. Visual Comput. Graph. **18**(10), 1704–1716 (2012)
10. Zhao, H., Jin, X., Huang, X., Chai, M., Zhou, K.: Parametric weight-change reshaping for portrait images. IEEE Comput. Graph. Appl. **36** (2016)
11. Best-Rowden, L., Han, H., Otto, C., Klare, B.F., Jain, A.K.: Unconstrained face recognition: identifying a person of interest from a media collection. IEEE Trans. Inf. Forensics Secur. **9**(12), 2144–2157 (2014)
12. Thies, J., Zollhofer, M., Stamminger, M., Theobalt, C., Niebner, M.: Face2Face: real-time face capture and reenactment of RGB videos. In: Proceedings of the IEEE Conference on Computer Vision and Pattern Recognition, pp. 2387–2395. IEEE, Las Vegas, NV, USA (2016)
13. Cao, C., Weng, Y., Lin, S., Zhou, K.: 3D shape regression for real-time facial animation. ACM Trans. Graph. (TOG) **32**(4), 41:1–41:10 (2013)
14. Li, H., Yu, J., Ye, Y., Bregler, C.: Realtime facial animation with on-the-fly correctives. ACM Trans. Graph. (TOG) **32**(4), 42:1–42:10 (2013)
15. Paysan, P., Knothe, R., Amberg, B.: A 3D face model for pose and illumination invariant face recognition. In: 6th IEEE International Conference on Advanced Video and Signal Based Surveillance (AVSS 2009), pp. 296–301. IEEE, Genova, Italy (2009)
16. Jacobson, A., Tosun, E., Sorkine, O.: Mixed finite elements for variational surface modeling. Comput. Graph. Forum **29**(5), 1565–1574 (2010)
17. Wang, H., Cao, J., Liu, X., Wang, J., Fan, T., Hu, J.: Least-squares images for edge-preserving smoothing. Comput. Visual Media **1**(1), 27–35 (2015)

18. Shao, H., Chen, S., Zhao, J., Cui, W., Yu, T.: Face recognition based on subset selection via metric learning on manifold. Front. Inf. Technol. Electron. Eng. **16**(12), 1046–1058 (2015)
19. Oikawa, M.A., Dias, Z., de Rezende Rocha, A., Goldenstein, S.: Manifold learning and spectral clustering for image phylogeny forests. IEEE Trans. Inf. Forensics Secur. **11**(1), 5–18 (2016)
20. Blanz, V., Basso, C., Poggio, T., Vetter, T.: Reanimating faces in images and video. Comput. Graph. Forum **22**(3), 641–650 (2003)
21. Vlasic, D., Brand, M., Pfister, H., Popovic, J.: Face transfer with multilinear models. ACM Trans. Graph. (TOG) **24**(3), 426–433 (2005)
22. Cao, C., Weng, Y., Zhou, S., Tong, Y., Zhou, K.: FaceWarehouse: a 3D facial expression database for visual computing. IEEE Trans. Visual Comput. Graph. **20**(3), 413–425 (2014)
23. Cao, C., Wu, H., Weng, Y., Shao, T., Zhou, K.: Real-time facial animation with image-based dynamic avatars. ACM Trans. Graph. (TOG) **35**(4), 1–12 (2016)
24. Saito, S., Li, T., Li, H.: Real-time facial segmentation and performance capture from RGB input. In: Leibe, B., Matas, J., Sebe, N., Welling, M. (eds.) ECCV 2016. LNCS, vol. 9912, pp. 244–261. Springer, Cham (2016). doi:10.1007/978-3-319-46484-8_15
25. Blanz, V., Vetter, T.: A morphable model for the synthesis of 3D faces. In: Proceedings of the 26th Annual Conference on Computer Graphics and Interactive Techniques, pp. 187–194. ACM Press/Addison-Wesley Publishing Co., New York, USA (1999)
26. Lin, Y., Wang, S., Lin Q., Tang, F.: Face swapping under large pose variations: a 3D model based approach. In: IEEE International Conference on Multimedia and Expo (ICME), pp. 333–338. IEEE, Melbourne, VIC, Australia (2012)
27. Song, H., Lv, J., Liu, H., Zhao, Q.: A face replacement system based on 3D face model. In: Deng, Z., Li, H. (eds.) Proceedings of the 2015 Chinese Intelligent Automation Conference. LNEE, vol. 336, pp. 237–246. Springer, Heidelberg (2015). doi:10.1007/978-3-662-46469-4_25
28. Lin, Y., Lin, Q., Tang, F., Wang, S.: Face replacement with large-pose differences. In: 20th ACM International Conference on Multimedia, pp. 1249–1250. ACM, Nara, Japan (2012)
29. Tran, A.T., Hassner, T., Masi, I., Medioni, G.: Regressing robust and discriminative 3D morphable models with a very deep neural network. arXiv preprint arXiv:1612.04904 (2017)
30. Kazemi, V., Sullivan, J.: One millisecond face alignment with an ensemble of regression trees. In: Proceedings of the IEEE Conference on Computer Vision and Pattern Recognition, pp. 1867–1874. IEEE, Columbus, OH, USA (2014)
31. Huber, P., Hu, G., Tena, R., Mortazavian, P., Koppen W.P., Christmas, W., Ratsch, M., Kittler, J.: A multiresolution 3D Morphable Face Model and fitting framework. In: 11th International Joint Conference on Computer Vision, Imaging and Computer Graphics Theory and Applications, pp. 1–8 (2016)
32. Sorkine, O.: Least-squares rigid motion using svd. Tech. Notes **120**(3), 52 (2009)
33. Takayama, K., Schmidt, R., Singh, K., Igarashi, T., Boubekeur, T., Sorkine, O.: GeoBrush: interactive mesh geometry cloning. Comput. Graph. Forum **30**(2), 613–622 (2011)
34. Yu, Y., Zhou, K., Xu, D., Shi, X., Bao, H., Guo, B., Shum, H.-Y.: Mesh editing with poisson-based gradient field manipulation. ACM Trans. Graph. (TOG) **23**(3), 644–651 (2004)
35. Schmidt, R., Singh, K.: Drag, drop, and clone: an interactive interface for surface composition. Technical Report CSRG-611, Department of Computer Science, University of Toronto (2010)
36. Perez, P., Gangnet, M., Blake, A.: Poisson image editing. ACM Trans. Graph. (TOG) **22**(3), 313–318 (2003)
37. Libigl. http://libigl.github.io/libigl/. Accessed 2016

38. Zhao, J., Tang, M., Tong, R.: Mesh segmentation for parallel decompression on GPU. In: Hu, S.-M., Martin, R.R. (eds.) CVM 2012. LNCS, vol. 7633, pp. 83–90. Springer, Heidelberg (2012). doi:10.1007/978-3-642-34263-9_11
39. Tang, X., Guo, J., Li, P., Lv, J.: A surgical simulation system for predicting facial soft tissue deformation. Comput. Visual Media **2**(2), 163–171 (2016)

User Centered Design and Modeling

Automatic Data-Driven Room Design Generation

Yuan Liang[1], Song-Hai Zhang[1(✉)], and Ralph Robert Martin[2]

[1] TNList, Tsinghua University, Beijing, China
liangyua14@mails.tsinghua.edu.cn, shz@tsinghua.edu.cn
[2] School of Computer Science and Informatics, Cardiff University, Cardiff, UK
ralph@cs.cf.ac.uk

Abstract. In this work, we address a novel and practical problem of automatically generating a room design from given room function and basic geometry, which can be described as picking appropriate objects from a given database, and placing the objects with a group of predefined criteria. We formulate both object selection and placement problems as probabilistic models. The object selection is first formulated as a supervised generative model, to take room function into consideration. Object placement problem is then formulated as a Bayesian model, where parameters are inferred with Maximizing a Posteriori (MAP) objective. By introducing a solver based on Markov Chain Monte Carlo (MCMC), the placement problem is solved efficiently.

Keywords: Automatic layout · Probabilistic model · Constrained optimization

1 Introduction

With the rapid growth of entertainment application in desktop computers, content generation is becoming an important problem in such applications. For applications such as virtual reality and computer games, an important problem is generating indoor environments for them to interact with, which raises the room design problem. With the help of modern commercial CAD tools [1–3] or independently developed toolchains, professional designers or even architects can design rooms with different levels of details. However, these tools usually require a considerable number of interactions for object selection and placement in these rooms. Existing works have shown success in reducing the number of interactions in such designs, which saves designers' effort in the content generation, and the designers only have to offer some insight into the tool with a reduced number of interactions.

However, modern entertainment applications often employ an open world (namely sandbox) design pattern, which requires procedural and automatic content generation in contents. As a result, a fully automatic room design algorithm that works with little supervision and no interaction is required in aforementioned virtual reality and computer game applications.

© Springer International Publishing AG 2017
J. Chang et al. (Eds.): AniNex 2017, LNCS 10582, pp. 133–148, 2017.
https://doi.org/10.1007/978-3-319-69487-0_10

Major challenges in the fully automatic room design include (1) automatically deciding which objects are to be placed and (2) designing a group of criteria on how to place objects in the generated room to integrate both aesthetics and interactivity. The key idea behind selecting objects to be placed in the room is to measure how objects are related to room functions, which is difficult as the relationship between objects and room functions does not follow traditional relation patterns such as one-to-one or one-to-many, but appears to be a fuzzy relationship, where an object type can be used for utilizing several room functions, and a room function also requires several groups objects to be placed. Placing the objects in the room is a non-trivial problem, as a good placement requires not only tidiness in the aspect of aesthetics, but also interactivity in the aspect of usability. Accordingly, learning-based or rule-based criteria are needed to address the requirements. However, existing methods only take semantic information into consideration, ignoring how the placements fit a given room.

To overcome these challenges, we developed a fully automatic algorithm generating room designs. The algorithm takes room geometry, placements of doors or windows, and a set of keywords with weights describing room functions as input. It then generates which objects to be placed in the room, as well as how they are placed. In this algorithm, a generative model is introduced to select models with the supervision of room functions. Specifically, a variant of topic model, which is a common method in natural language processing, is proposed to model the hidden relationships between room functions and objects. We have also proposed a group of criteria based on our training database and our interview with professional interior designers. A user study shows that rooms designed by our algorithm are more preferred than those designed by non-professionals without much caution in the benchmark database.

Our work has made the following technical contributions:

- Applying topic models in mining relationships between objects and room functions.
- A group of criteria in object placement optimization and a corresponding solver with a Bayesian framework.

1.1   Interactive Room Design and Automatic Placement

To reduce the number of interactions in room design, contextual modeling [4], which tries to evaluate if a model and its placement fit its context, is proposed in interactive room design. Different routines for interaction are then proposed, to facilitate these interactive systems with different design requirements. Typical interactions include: Finding a proper placement for a user-selected model [4], retrieving a model and finding a proper orientation with a user selected placement [5], synthesizing a scene with a group of selected examples [6], suggesting objects for adding different levels of details to scenes [7], using freehand sketch drawings for co-retrieval and co-placement [8], or using natural language as scene description [9]. All of the methods achieve a certain level of success, however requires humans' basic idea, insight, and expertise to be converted as interaction, which makes it unsuitable for open world applications.

Fully automatic approaches are proposed to solve the problem in open world. Typical methods [10,11] define criteria representing the "goodness" of a layout, and generates a layout with a given set of objects. As these methods require the set of objects to be given as input, the approaches still require input based on empirical object selection, and the massive input limits the usage of those approaches.

Existing work in open world synthesis [12], which is the closest work to ours, uses a generative model for getting the set of objects. It succeeded in synthesizing a fixed category of scenes, e.g. coffee shops at various scales and geometry. It uses a hand-craft and hard-coded generative model for generating a single category of indoor scenes with fixed types of objects, but fails to model the diversity of different categories of scenes. Our work is different from open world synthesis in the following aspects: (1) Generation of objects and placements are split into separate steps, to simplify the model and cut the original time consumption of thousands of seconds. (2) Our generative model for objects is learned from training data, which models object selection based on room functions free from category-wise specific empirical rules. (3) General rule-based criteria on layouts, based on interviews with designers are used in our work, to help us get better layouts.

The remainder of this paper is organized as follows. An introduction to our general data-driven pipeline and our methodology in data collection is shown in Sect. 2. Section 3 gives our formulation and solution to the generative model applied by object selection. Section 4 proposes the Bayesian framework in object placement and the group of criteria applied, and a solver based on MCMC is then discussed in Sect. 5. Section 6 demonstrates our experimental results. The conclusion and further discussion on this work are then shown in Sect. 7.

2   Overview

2.1   Pipeline

Figure 1 gives an overview of the pipeline of our algorithm. Based on the existing method [12], we split object selection and placement into independent steps. Both steps are initialized with ensemble training processes, to model both the relationships between objects and room functions and the context relativity.

While both steps can be executed independently, (e.g. Manually select objects and use only the object placement step to generate the layout of the room), we execute both steps in a cascading sequence, to build a fully automatic pipeline with a cascade generator.

The object selection algorithm applies a generative model, which is trained with supervision of labeled room functions, to find the hidden relationship

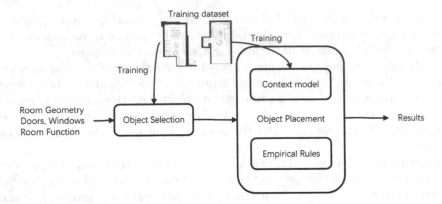

Fig. 1. Algorithm pipeline. Our data-driven algorithm suggests objects to be selected and their placements, based on the room geometry, placements of doors and windows, as well as the room function.

between room functions and individual objects. As a result, a set of objects, with randomness (which is supplied by random variables in the generative model) is provided to the forthcoming placement step.

The object placement algorithm combines a group of criteria, including the context relativity and empirical criteria proposed by designers we interviewed. The criteria are then combined into a Bayesian model, which can be solved with random programming.

2.2   Data Collection and Annotation

Existing works in 3D modeling and synthesizing have released an adequate number of indoor scenes. SUN3D [13] and Stanford Scene Dataset [6] are representatives among them. However they both have some drawbacks incorporating our learning task. SUN3D contains rooms collected with RGB-D sensors, but only a few number of rooms are provided with semantic labels. Stanford scene dataset includes rooms designed by users and it has supported many works on context modeling, however as we interviewed the professional designers, they have some drawbacks in design: (1) A large proportion of the rooms are designed carelessly, as they include either layouts either too sparse or too dense (Fig. 2(a) and (b)), which may cause the resulting scene to be too sparse or dense consequently by context matching. (2) Most of the scenes are provided without a door or window (Fig. 2(c) and (d)), which makes it hard to model context relativity between objects and windows or doors.

To overcome such drawbacks, we built our own datasets with Autodesk Revit [2] BIM (Building Information Management) projects (Fig. 3(a)) provided by the designers, which includes 6 houses with 37 realistic rooms. We also added user-designed rooms extracted from a PC Game, the Sims 4 [14] (Fig. 3(b)),

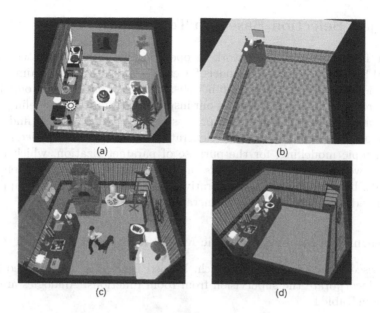

Fig. 2. Typical low-quality cases in Stanford Scene Dataset. (a) Too dense layout. (b) Too sparse layout. (c) (d) Rooms without doors or windows.

where users design their houses with both aesthetics and usability considerations and update them to the workshop for online sharing. We included 60 lots and 945 rooms with multiple functions from the game. Both data sources have provided rich metadata, with semantic categories of objects. We labeled function surfaces (e.g. a TV is functional from its front, and a square table is functional from all of its 4 orthogonal orientations) and movability (e.g. a chair is easy to move and a bed is hard to) for each category. We also label each room based on its functions (e.g. kitchen, public gym, etc.), here multiple functional labels on a single room are also supported, to model special cases such as integrated kitchens.

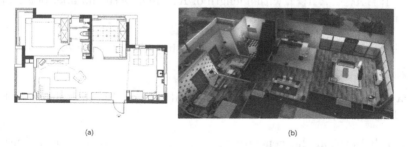

Fig. 3. Typical cases in our database. (a) BIM projects provided by professional indoor designers. (b) User-generated lots in the Sims 4.

3   Object Selection Based on Topic Model

Different from aforementioned work in open world synthesis [12] which used empirical hard-code generative models for each scene category, we aim to use a single general model for all room functions, which is trained from our dataset and free from empirical rules. We get our inspiration from topic modeling in bag-of-words model in natural language processing [15], which aims to find hidden topics among words and documents. Generative models [16] are applied in recent works in topic modelling, for the purpose of parameterization, which fits our work very well, as it not only models the hidden relationships between topics and words, but also models the generative process in a probabilistic approach, which provides randomness to our generation.

3.1   Learning a Supervised Topic Model for Model Selection

A supervised topic modeling approach, labeled LDA [17], is employed in our work, to incorporate the supervision from room functions. Analogies are made as shown in Table 1.

Table 1. Analogies we made between labeled LDA [17] and our model.

Concept in Labeled LDA	Concept in our work	Symbol
Document	Room	$D = \{d_1, d_2, \ldots\}$
Labels of a document	Functions of a room	$\Lambda^{(d)} = [\Lambda_1^{(d)}, \Lambda_2^{(d)}, \ldots \Lambda_K^{(d)}]^T$
Topic distribution of a document	Function distribution of a room	$\theta^{(d)} = [\theta_1^{(d)}, \theta_2^{(d)}, \ldots, \theta_K^{(d)}]^T$
Words in a document	Objects in a room	$w^{(d)} = \{w_1^{(d)}, w_2^{(d)}, \ldots w_{N_d}^{(d)}\}$

For each training room in $D = \{d_1, d_2, \ldots\}$, it is represented by a tuple d with a list of objects $w^{(d)} = \{w_1^{(d)}, w_2^{(d)}, \ldots, w_{N_d}^{(d)}\}$ and a function existence vector $\Lambda^{(d)} = [\Lambda_1^{(d)}, \Lambda_2^{(d)}, \ldots \Lambda_K^{(d)}]$, with a length of K, which is the number of all unique functions, where

$$l_i^{(d)} = \begin{cases} 1, i\text{-th unique function is included in room } d. \\ 0, \text{otherwise} \end{cases} \tag{1}$$

Then a detailed plate notation for the generative model is thus shown in Fig. 4 with following steps:

1. For each function Λ_k, generate $\phi_k = [\phi_{k,1}, \phi_{k,2}, \ldots, \phi_{k,V}]^T$ using Dirichlet prior $\phi_k \sim \text{Dirichlet}(\cdot|\beta)$, which represents how objects are to be generated under this function.
2. For each room d,

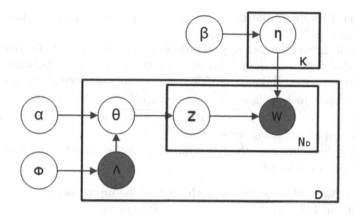

Fig. 4. Plate notation of our generative model.

(a) For each function in the room, generate $\Lambda_k^{(d)} \sim \text{Bernoulli}(\cdot|\phi_k)$, where ϕ_k denotes the prior probability for each function, to generate function existence of each room.

(b) For each function in the room, generate $\theta_k^{(d)}$ with Dirichlet prior integrated with function existence $\theta_k^{(d)} \sim \text{Dirichlet}(\cdot|\alpha)\Lambda_k^{(d)}$, which denotes the distribution of each function in the room, constrained by the function existence.

(c) For each object $w_i^{(d)}$ in the room:

    i. Generate a function $z_w^{(d)}$ with prior possibility of $\text{Multinomial}(\cdot|\theta_k^{(d)})$, which is the function that the object is generated from.

    ii. Generate an object w_i with prior possibility of $\text{Multinomial}(\cdot|\phi_{z_w^{(d)}})$, which generates the object with the guidance of the function.

Note that the label existence indicators $\Lambda_k^{(d)}$ are observed variables in the model, the model has the same structure as the original LDA [16]. Thus it can be solved with the same solver based on collapsed Gibbs sampling [18].

3.2 Randomness-Aware Objects Selection

With the help of the generative model, the relationship between room functions and objects are modeled. As a result, we can simply apply a generative model to select a group of objects with a given distribution of functions $\theta^{(d)}$. However the generative model has introduced too much randomness into model selection in our experiments, for example, it often selects too many chairs pairing a single dining table. Accordingly, we introduced a randomness-aware method, to control the randomness of object selection with a simple parameter.

As shown in the generative model, it has an expectation of $E(n_w^{(d)}) = N_d\phi\theta^{(d)}$ and uncertainty $\sigma(n_w^{(d)}) = \sqrt{N_d(\phi\theta^{(d)}) \circ (1 - \phi\theta^{(d)})}$ for selecting $n_w^{(d)}$ instances of object w, as all the N_d objects are generated independently. Here $\circ$ denotes the Hadamard product, and ϕ denotes the matrix formed by all the ϕ_k in the generative model.

To control the randomness of generating objects, we instead of generating N_d objects as shown in the original model, we generate tN_d objects, where t is the controlling factor for randomness. After the sampling process, we add a post-processing step, which assigns $n_w^{(d)} := \text{round}(n_w^{(d)}/t)$. The method reduces the uncertainty to $\sigma(n_w^{(d)}) = \sqrt{N_d(\phi\theta^{(d)}) \circ (1 - \phi\theta^{(d)})/t}$ while keeping the expectation. In our implementation, we set $t = 1.75$.

The final algorithm uses the following steps for an input room d and distribution of room functions $\theta^{(d)}$:

1. Generate $N_d \sim S\text{Gaussian}(\mu, \sigma)$, where S is the input room:
2. For each i in $1, 2, \ldots, tN_d$:
   (a) Sample a function $z_w^{(d)}$, with prior possibility of $\text{Multinomial}(\cdot|\theta_k^{(d)})$.
   (b) Sample an object w_i with prior possibility of $\text{Multinomial}(\cdot|\phi_{z_w^{(d)}})$.
3. For each object w which is sampled with $n_w^{(d)}$ instances, keep $\text{round}(n_w^{(d)}/t)$ instances and discard others.

4   Bayesian Framework on Object Placement

As discussed earlier, a satisfying placement of all objects selected must satisfy criteria not only on aesthetics to generate visually pleasing objects, but also usability, to allow users of the open world interact with the objects placed. This section will discuss how the criteria are incorporated and introduce the criteria added to the system.

4.1   Bayesian Formulation

To incorporate several desired criteria, including aesthetics, usability as well as context relativity, the object placement problem is formulated with a Bayesian framework. Then we can infer the Maximum a Posteriori (MAP) solution of state variables, thus to get an optimal solution. Here we model $\mathbf{x} = \{x_i\} = \{(p_i, r_i, o_i)\}$, (where p_i, r_i are the position and orientation of i-th object) given the observation $\mathbf{z}$, which is a tuple including the shape of the room, the selected objects and the set of fixed objects (doors and windows). An optimal solution can thus be written as :

$$\hat{\mathbf{x}} = \arg\max_{\mathbf{x}} P(\mathbf{x}|\mathbf{z}) = \arg\max_{\mathbf{x}} P(\mathbf{z}|\mathbf{x})P(\mathbf{x}) \tag{2}$$

As shown in the equation, the criteria are split into two parts: a likelihood model, noted as $P(\mathbf{z}|\mathbf{x})$, measures the quality of the placement described by $\mathbf{x}$, and a prior model $P(\mathbf{x})$, measures the availability of a placement.

4.2   Likelihood Model

Much like existing works [10], we proposed some simple hand-craft rules according to suggestions by professional designers. To make the algorithm usable in open world cases, the criteria should be light-weighted in computation, to support faster optimization.

We model the likelihood as an exponential distribution:

$$P(\mathbf{z}|\mathbf{x}) \propto \exp(\lambda_a C_a + \lambda_u C_u + \lambda_s C_s + \lambda_f C_f) \tag{3}$$

Here C_a, C_u, C_s, C_f are criteria for object alignment, placement uniformity, free space and functionality.

The criteria are defined as following:

Object alignment. Real-world human as well as designers tend to align objects together: desks in aligned rows in offices, bed and bedside cabinet against wall, etc. As a result, we added an object alignment term,

$$C_a = \sum_i \sum_{j \neq i} C_a(x_i, x_j), \text{where}$$

$$C_a(x_i, x_j) = \begin{cases} 0, \text{bounding boxes of object } i \text{ and } j \text{ are not parallel} \\ (\epsilon_a + d_a(x_i, x_j)^2)^{-1}, \text{otherwise} \end{cases} \tag{4}$$

Here $d_u(x_i, x_j)$ is the distance between nearest parallel pair of surfaces in the bounding boxes of object i and object j. We only involve bounding boxes surfaces perpendicular to the ground in the computation of the criterion.

Placement uniformity, which tends to distribute objects in the room, to make the placement balanced. Inspired by the repulsive term in force-directed graph drawing [19], we simply encourage objects to be placed far from each other:

$$C_u = \sum_i \sum_{j \neq i} (1 + \exp(w_u(-\|p_i - p_j\| + \epsilon_u))) \tag{5}$$

Note this criterion also pushes objects that should be placed in close proximity (e.g. tables and chairs) away from each other, it should be balanced by relativity in the prior model.

Free space. A good placement should leave enough space for user activities or for new objects to be further placed. This term is defined as the area of the maximum axis-aligned rectangle in $\Omega_{\text{free}} = \Omega_{\text{room}} - \cap_i \Omega_i$, where Ω_{room} denotes the area of the room and Ω_i denotes the projected area from the i-th object to the floor.

Functionality. To guarantee that the users can interact with objects in the room, some import functional surfaces are defined to each category, to make sure that the surfaces not to be covered. As a result, we define

$$C_f = \sum_i \bar{U}_{ij} \tag{6}$$

Here U_{ij} denotes the usability of j-th functional surface of i-th object, which is set to 1 if the surface is not obstructed, or $1 - m_i$ if the surface is obstructed by an object i with a movability of m_i.

4.3 Prior Model

We define the prior model as:

$$P(\mathbf{x}) = P(x_1, x_2, \dots, x_n) = (P(x_1, x_2, \dots, x_n)^n)^{\frac{1}{n}}$$

$$= \left(\prod_i \left(P(x_i) P(x_1, x_2, \dots x_{i-1}, x_{i+1}, \dots x_n | x_i) \right) \right)^{\frac{1}{n}}$$

$$\approx \left(\prod_i \left(P(x_i) \prod_{j \neq i} P(x_j | x_i) \right) \right)^{\frac{1}{n}} \tag{7}$$

$$= \left(\prod_i \left(P(p_i) P(r_i) \prod_{j \neq i} P(x_j | x_i) \right) \right)^{\frac{1}{n}}$$

Here to avoid any bias to be introduced, we set $P(p_i)$ as a uniform distribution on anywhere the placement is available, such as tables on the floor, paintings on the wall, etc. $P(r_i)$ is set to 1 given it is placed orthogonally and 0.02 given it is placed diagonally, to encourage an orthogonal layout, which is a most common layout pattern in indoor design. For fixed objects such as doors or windows, we set $P(x) = 1$ if it is placed exactly on the fixed place, and 0 otherwise.

The rest of the equation denotes the context relativity learned from the input dataset. A massive number of works [20] utilized methods such as graph-based models for modeling the context relativity. However, to save the computation cost for the evaluation, we use only binary relationships $P(x_j | x_i)$ here. Here we model $P(x_j | x_i) = P(x_j | x_i, w_i, w_j)$, where w_i, w_j are semantic categories of objects i and j. We also include fixed objects in the room such as walls, windows and doors in the set $\{x_1, x_2, \dots, x_n\}$ in the context model. The model is thus fitted with a Gaussian mixture model, where the number of mixtures is determined with the Elbow method [21].

5 MCMC-Based Solver

We employed Markov Chain Monte Carlo, which is a widely used solver for high-dimensional and non-convex optimization for object placement. It attempts to find the $\mathbf{x}$ in the state space with maximum likelihood of a distribution $\pi(\mathbf{x})$, which is the MAP $P(\mathbf{x}|\mathbf{z})$ in our case. Its basic strategy is to explore the state space of $\mathbf{x}$ with a Markov chain mechanism, which generates a sequence $\mathbf{x}^1, \mathbf{x}^2 \dots$ to get to a stationary distribution of $\mathbf{x}^k$, which converges to $\arg\max_{\mathbf{x}^k} \pi(\mathbf{x}^k)$.

Our solver is based on Metropolis-Hastings (MH) algorithm, which uses a proposal function $q(\mathbf{x}|\mathbf{x}^k)$ to sample a candidate $\mathbf{x}^*$ with a given $\mathbf{x}^k$. The efficiency of a Metropolis-Hastings-based algorithm is largely depends on how the proposal function $q(\mathbf{x}|\mathbf{x}^k)$ is designed.

5.1 Formulation of the Proposal Function

To make the MCMC converge quickly to an optimal value and avoid sticking at local optimum, we design the proposal function as a mixture of (1) a local proposal function q_l which fine-tunes the solver state, and a global proposal function q_g to discover the whole state space to overcome the obstacle of local maxima. The final proposal function is thus defined as:

$$q(\mathbf{x}|\mathbf{x}^k) = \lambda_l q_l(\mathbf{x}|\mathbf{x}^k) + \lambda_g q_g(\mathbf{x}|\mathbf{x}^k) \tag{8}$$

Each time we sample a candidate $\mathbf{x}^*$, we only try to apply a linear transform to a subset of objects, to simplify the evaluation and sampling of the proposal functions. We try to select the objects to be moved with neighborhood information, accordingly we take the following steps for choosing the objects to be moved:

1. Select a random object w from all the objects in the room, with equal possibilities.
2. Sample $K \sim \text{Poisson}(1)$ to determine how many extra objects are involved in the proposal.
3. Sample K nearest neighbours that share the same positional constraints with object w, e.g. both a painting and a mirror share the positional constraint that they can only be placed on the wall.

With these steps, we selected a local neighborhood from the scene, where we note the indexes of the selected objects as $i_1, i_2, \ldots, i_{K+1}$.

5.2 Local and Global Proposals

To search in the space locally, we randomly choose $q_l(\mathbf{x}|\mathbf{x}^k)$ as one of the following each time we try to sample $\mathbf{x}^*$:

Translation proposal, which is defined based on random-ray sampling [22]:

1. Sample a random unit vector e as the orient of transition. Sample a random group of $u_1, u_2 \ldots u_S$ under a uniform distribution. A set of transition vectors is thus generated as $t_s = e u_s$. For each object i_k selected, we set $p_{i_k,s} = p_{i_k,s}^k + t_s$. The candidate set $\{\mathbf{x}_s\}$ is thus generated.
2. Sample a $\mathbf{x}^*$ from the candidate set, with a probability proportional to $\pi(\mathbf{x}_s)$ for each $\mathbf{x}_s$ in the candidate set.
3. Compute the Metropolis ratio to decide whether to accept this sample.

Rotation proposal, which is sampled with the orientation prior $P(r_i)$. It samples to rotate all the selected objects with a multiplier of $45°$.

The global proposal tries to adjust the current state with a strong disturbance. Here we randomly choose $q_g(\mathbf{x}|\mathbf{x}^k)$ as one of the following each time we try to sample $\mathbf{x}^*$:

Translation proposal, which is defined similar to that in the local proposal, however the transition vector is sampled with a uniform distribution over a regular grid, to allow long movements of the objects selected.

Swap proposal, which randomly selects another set of objects $j_1, j_2, \ldots, j_{K+1}$, and we pairwise swap the placements of objects i_k and j_k.

Suspension proposal, which is only available for objects hanging on walls. It takes the objects off the wall and hang them onto another random wall with random placement.

With these proposals, a single MCMC chain can converge within 10 s in most cases. With a parallel multi-chain optimization, the time consumed can be cut to 4 s with 8 parallel threads.

6   Results

In this section, we show the effectiveness of our algorithm. The effectiveness is shown in two aspects: (1) It can generate diverse room designs with different keywords on functions. With different weighting on room functions, the room can emphasize different functions. (2) The layouts generated is visually pleasing comparing to existing datasets designed by amateur users.

6.1   Generating Diverse Room Designs

Our layout can generate diverse room designs with diverse keywords. To show the effectiveness of our algorithm under various detail level of labeling, we labeled each room in the training dataset with the following two function sets:

- Function set A that uses rough descriptive words, such as kitchen, bathroom, etc.
- Function set B that uses detailed activity-centric words, such as chatting, watch TV, etc.

It is obvious that labeling the dataset with function set B requires more effort than function set A.

With function set A, our algorithm can generate some well-formed results, Fig. 5 shows the results generated by our algorithm with functions "restroom", "meeting room", "bedroom", as well as mixed functions "dining room" and "kitchen". The results show that the algorithm is effective in generating room designs. However some details on object placement are still not satisfying enough. For example, placing the towel rack in Fig. 5(a) near the shower might be a better solution.

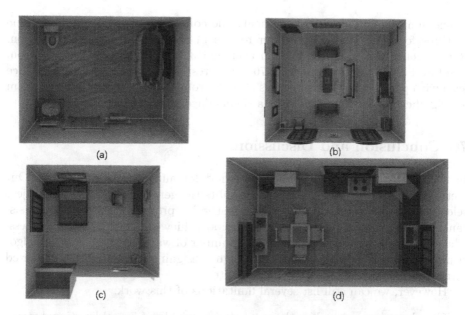

Fig. 5. The results generated with function (a) "restroom", (b) "meeting room", (c) "bedroom", as well as (d) mixed functions "dining room" and "kitchen".

Given a more detailed function set B, we can generate diverge room design with different weights of different functions, which can help developers to generate a variety of random rooms with different objects placed in the room. Figure 6 shows the rooms generated with different weights of different functions.

6.2   Comparison to Existing Room Design Dataset

We compared room designs generated by our algorithm with Stanford Scene Dataset, which was synthesized by amateur users. We sampled 15 rooms from the Stanford Scene Dataset. For each room, we labeled its functions and generated a room with the same set functions. 7 volunteers are invited to rate each pair of

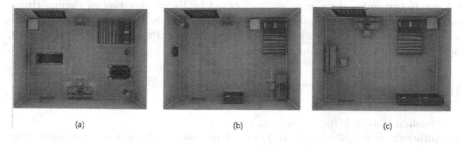

Fig. 6. The results generated with different weights over a combination of functions. Layout on the left side has a higher weight on room function "relaxation", while layout on the right side has higher weight on room function "study".

rooms in a 5-point Likert scale. To make the comparison fair, we used the same textures for floors and walls to our results in these rooms in our evaluation. Rooms generated by our algorithm averaged 3.35, while rooms selected from Stanford Scene Dataset averaged 2.70 in this test. We analyzed user's preference level with paired t-test, and it shows that the rooms generated by our algorithm are significantly more preferred, at a significance level of $p < 0.05$.

7   Conclusion and Discussion

In this work, we developed a novel method for automatic room design. Our method uses a cascade generator, which splits the generative process into object selection and placement. A data-driven method is proposed, and with the assistance of some empirical criteria, the method achieves a certain level of access. The system can also be augmented in a number of ways, such as replacing algorithm for each step with interactive design, designing a room with some fixed furniture that have already been placed, etc.

However, we can still list several limitations of this work:

- The algorithm only solves the room design problems in unidirectional steps. Even if we discovered an object cannot be placed with a satisfying layout in a room, the method does not try to modify the selected object set, which causes unsatisfactory layouts in some cases. In future work, we plan to utilize a joint model to solve the problems.
- Generative model generates each object independently, which does not take relationship among the objects into consideration, causing some strange combinations of the objects in some cases, such as "sofa and dining table" with given labels of "chatting and dining". It could be solved by introducing an extra topic hierarchy in the topic model [23].
- The empirical criteria are defined with empirical suggestions by professional designers, however the criteria lacks support in the absence of a quantitative study. Convolutional network [24], which is a powerful tool in image-based visual task, can also be used as a criterion, comparing these techniques would be interesting.

Acknowledgments. This work was supported by Research Grant of Beijing Higher Institution Engineering Research Center and the People Programme (Marie Curie Actions) of the European Union's Seventh Framework Programme FP7/2007-2013/ under REA grant agreement n° [612627].

References

1. Sketchup (2017). http://www.sketchup.com
2. Autodesk revit (2017). https://www.autodesk.com/products/revit-family/over view
3. Archicad (2017). http://www.graphisoft.com/archicad/

4. Fisher, M., Hanrahan, P.: Context-based search for 3d models. ACM Transactions on Graphics (TOG) **29**(4), 182 (2010)
5. Savva, M., Chang, A.X., Agrawala, M.: Scenesuggest: Context-driven 3D scene design. arXiv preprint arXiv:1703.00061 (2017)
6. Fisher, M., Ritchie, D., Savva, M., Funkhouser, T., Hanrahan, P.: Example-based synthesis of 3D object arrangements. ACM Trans. Graphics (TOG) **30**(4), 135 (2012)
7. Yu, L.F., Yeung, S.K., Terzopoulos, D.: The clutterpalette: an interactive tool for detailing indoor scenes. IEEE Trans. Visual Comput. Graphics **22**(2), 1138–1148 (2016)
8. Xu, K., Chen, K., Fu, H., Sun, W.L., Hu, S.M.: Sketch2Scene: Sketch-based co-retrieval and co-placement of 3D models. ACM Trans. Graphics (TOG) **32**(4), 123 (2013)
9. Chang, A.X., Eric, M., Savva, M., Manning, C.D.: SceneSeer: 3D scene design with natural language. arXiv preprint arXiv:1703.00050 (2017)
10. Merrell, P., Schkufza, E., Li, Z., Agrawala, M., Koltun, V.: Interactive furniture layout using interior design guidelines. ACM Trans. Graphics (TOG) **30**(4), 87 (2011)
11. Yu, L.F., Yeung, S.K., Tang, C.K., Terzopoulos, D., Chan, T.F., Osher, S.J.: Make it home: automatic optimization of furniture arrangement. ACM Trans. Graphics (TOG) **30**(4), 86 (2011)
12. Yeh, Y.T., Yang, L., Watson, M., Goodman, N.D., Hanrahan, P.: Synthesizing open worlds with constraints using locally annealed reversible jump mcmc. ACM Trans. Graphics (TOG) **31**(4), 56 (2012)
13. Xiao, J., Owens, A., Torralba, A.: SUN3D: A database of big spaces reconstructed using SfM and object labels. In: Proceedings of the IEEE International Conference on Computer Vision, pp. 1625–1632 (2013)
14. The sims 4 (2017). https://www.thesims.com/
15. Papadimitriou, C.H., Tamaki, H., Raghavan, P., Vempala, S.: Latent semantic indexing: a probabilistic analysis. In: Proceedings of the seventeenth ACM SIGACT-SIGMOD-SIGART Symposium on Principles of Database Systems, pp. 159–168. ACM (1998)
16. Blei, D.M., Ng, A.Y., Jordan, M.I.: Latent Dirichlet allocation. J. Mach. Learn. Res. **3**(Jan), 993–1022 (2003)
17. Ramage, D., Hall, D., Nallapati, R., Manning, C.D.: Labeled LDA: a supervised topic model for credit attribution in multi-labeled corpora. In: Proceedings of the 2009 Conference on Empirical Methods in Natural Language Processing, vol. 1, pp. 248–256. Association for Computational Linguistics (2009)
18. Liu, J.S.: The collapsed gibbs sampler in Bayesian computations with applications to a gene regulation problem. J. Am. Stat. Assoc. **89**(427), 958–966 (1994)
19. Fruchterman, T.M., Reingold, E.M.: Graph drawing by force-directed placement. Softw. Pract. Experience **21**(11), 1129–1164 (1991)
20. Fisher, M., Savva, M., Hanrahan, P.: Characterizing structural relationships in scenes using graph kernels. ACM Trans. Graphics (TOG) **30**(4), 34 (2011)
21. Caliński, T., Harabasz, J.: A dendrite method for cluster analysis. Commun. Stat. Theory Methods **3**(1), 1–27 (1974)
22. Liu, J.S., Liang, F., Wong, W.H.: The multiple-try method and local optimization in metropolis sampling. J. Am. Stat. Assoc. **95**(449), 121–134 (2000)

23. Griffiths, D., Tenenbaum, M.: Hierarchical topic models and the nested chinese restaurant process. Adv. Neural Inform. Process. Syst. **16**, 17 (2004)
24. Krizhevsky, A., Sutskever, I., Hinton, G.E.: ImageNet classification with deep convolutional neural networks. In: Advances in neural information processing systems, pp. 1097–1105 (2012)

An Efficient Learning-Based Bilateral Texture Filter for Structure Preserving

Zhe Zhang[1,2]($\boxtimes$) and Panpan Xu[1,2]

[1] State Key Laboratory of Computer Science, Institute of Software,
Chinese Academy of Sciences, Beijing, China
zhangzhe@ios.ac.cn
[2] University of Chinese Academy of Sciences, Beijing, China

Abstract. Images generally contain rich visual information that can be decomposed into edges and textures. Particularly, human beings are more sensitive to edge information. However, it is difficult to separate edges from textures since they are tough to be differentiated by computers. In this paper, we provide a novel learning-based bilateral filter to effectively remove textures from the image. Firstly, edge features are extracted as the guidance image through structured forests learning method. Then the guidance image with very rough edge features needs to be optimized. Finally, the joint bilateral filter is applied to produce the filtered result according to the input image and the optimized guidance image. Comparing with some previous approaches, our method is simpler and faster, as well as more effective in preserving edge structures and removing textures.

Keywords: Bilateral filter · Texture smoothing · Structure preserving

1 Introduction

Images usually have edges and textures, which carry rich information in regard to human perception. According to psychology, edges can capture the structures which are the principal information for human visual perception. Therefore, the structure-preserving filtering is widely used to smooth photographic images while preserving significant edges. Many applications choose to use it because of its simplicity, adaptability and extensibility. The applications include image segmentation, object recognition, detail enhancement and so on. Therefore separating edges from textures plays an important role in computer vision and computational photography.

Recently, many researchers have developed a variety of methods in filtering textures while preserving edge structures. Many of the existing texture filtering methods [1–3] are based on local filtering which relies on pixel gradients to distinguish edges and textures because the gradient methods are intuitive and simple to use. However, they are often ill-equipped to separate edges from textures due to that there is no explicit measurement to differentiate the two.

© Springer International Publishing AG 2017
J. Chang et al. (Eds.): AniNex 2017, LNCS 10582, pp. 149–158, 2017.
https://doi.org/10.1007/978-3-319-69487-0_11

On the other hand, the optimization-based [4,5], and patch-based approaches [6] are also employed, which are specifically designed to deal with textures and thus perform well in terms of texture removal. However, almost all the methods above have additional level of complexity and sophistication, which makes them hard to implement and accelerate.

In this paper, we present a novel and efficient learning-based method for structure preserving. Our contributions are in the following:

- We extract edge features using structured forests learning strategy which is proposed by [7], then enhancing edge features and removing noises using a non-linear equation, whose result is to be used as a weighted image that balances the structure preserving and texture removal.
- Two filters of different sizes are applied to produce blurry images with various levels. The larger filter is used to remove textures while the smaller filter is used to preserve structures. Final guidance image is produced by interpolating the two blurry images using the weighted image mentioned above.

2   Related Work

Structure preserving filter is an important filter which can remove textures of an image while preserving its structures, so lots of methods are developed based on different strategies. However, the goal of all the methods is similar that is to preserve structures. Average-based methods and optimization-based methods are the two major categories in structure preserving filters. Recently, the patch-based method is proposed. We will briefly discuss these relevant studies in this section.

2.1   Average-Based Filter

The average-based filter is also called local filtering [8] due to the fact that it considers the local variation of pixels. Each pixel's value of the output image is computed by the weighted average of its neighborhood. So how to compute the weight of pixels is the essential problem. Average-based filters include bilateral filter [9,10], guided filter [11], geodesic filter [12], etc. These methods obtain different types of affinity between neighboring pixel pairs by contrasting color difference.

Bilateral filter is one of the most widely used non-linear, edge preserving operators for image smoothing and decomposition. It convolves a filter of weights with each grid cell and its neighbours in an image. However, these average-based filters cannot handle texture images since their scale of color variation may not be small.

Moreover, several methods use a guidance image within the joint bilateral filter to preserve edges, our approach is similar to this concept. However, we do not use the traditional methods such as $mRTV$ that is proposed by [2], but taking advantage of learning strategy to generate the guidance image.

2.2 Optimization-Based Filter

Many robust optimization-based approaches have also been developed, such as total variation [13] and L_0 gradient minimization [4]. Optimization-based approaches generally use global optimization. First, it needs to design an energy function, which consists of two terms: the data term and the smoothness term. The data term is used to measure the similarity between input and output images. The smoothness term is used to remove noises or textures. Second, it needs to find out the best solution according to the energy function. Therefore, designing the energy function and solving it are the essential part in optimization-based filter methods.

2.3 Patch-Based Filter

Recently, several patch-based approaches were proposed. Karacan et al. [6] proposed a patch-based texture removal algorithm that uses the similarity measures based on a region covariance descriptor. Comparing with the conventional pixel-based methods, it uses patches to enable a more accurate description and identification of texture features, leading to a better performance in structure preserving. However, the path-based method can make some edges jagged due to path shift. Instead of patch shift, our method uses two filters of different sizes to preserve small structures.

3 Learning-Based Bilateral Texture Filter

Our method is simple, fast and effective which we will introduce in detail in the following sections. Section 3.1 introduces our algorithm. Section 3.2 illustrates how to generate modified edge features. Section 3.3 describes how to apply the joint bilateral filter to produce the output image.

Algorithm 1. Learning-based Bilateral Texture Filter

1: **Input:** image I, filter size c, k $(c < k)$, iteration number n_{iter}
2: **Output:** image J
3: $S \leftarrow$ Structured Forests method
4: $W \leftarrow$ Apply non-linear equation (Eq. 1) to each pixel of S
5: **for** $t = 0$ to $n_{iter} - 1$ **do**
6:     $B_0 \leftarrow$ Uniform blurring of I (filter size c×c)
7:     $B_1 \leftarrow$ Uniform blurring of I (filter size k×k)
8:     $G \leftarrow (1 - W) \circ B_0 + W \circ B_1$ ($\circ$ is the element-wise multiplication)
9:     $J \leftarrow$ Joint bilateral filter (Input I, guidance image G)
10:     $I \leftarrow J$
11: **end for**

3.1 Algorithm Overview

Our algorithm steps are as follows: Given an image I, the first step is using the Structured Forests (SF) method [7] to create an edge feature image S. Then a non-linear equation (Eq. 1) is applied to S to generate a weighted image W that can remove most of the noises and preserve structures. Next, we use two filters to produce different level of blurry images, which are described at line 6 to 7 in Algorithm 1. Optimized guidance image G is calculated through blending the two blurry images taking advantage of W. Finally, output image J is obtained by the joint bilateral filter using G as the guidance image. J is assigned to I as an input image for next iteration.

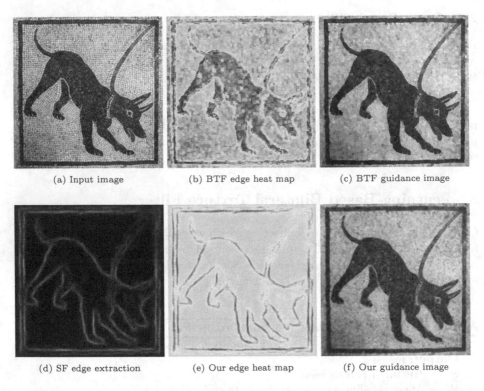

(a) Input image   (b) BTF edge heat map   (c) BTF guidance image

(d) SF edge extraction   (e) Our edge heat map   (f) Our guidance image

Fig. 1. We compare our method with BTF [2]. (a) is the input image. (d) is the edge extraction by the SF method [7]. (b) and (e) are edge heat map images for visualization. (c) and (f) are the BTF guidance image and our guidance image respectively.

3.2 Optimized Structured Forests Guidance Image

We use the Structured Forests learning method [7] to generate the approximate edge features as shown in Fig. 1(d). As we can see, the image has many noises and the edge is not very clear. So we use the non-linear equation to enhance edges and remove noises. We are inspired by [2], in this paper, the authors use the non-linear equation to enhance the features and reduce the noises. We slightly modified the equation and it performs well in our method. The equation is defined as:

$$W = 2 \left(\frac{1}{1 + \exp(-\alpha S)} - 0.5 \right) \tag{1}$$

In Eq. (1), S is the edge features produced by the Structured Forests method. W is the result. α is the parameter which controls the edge enhancement, the larger α is, the more significant the effect of edge strengthening is. Through many experiments, we found $\alpha = 0.02$ is acceptable for all images.

In order to compare the edge extraction with the previous method, we convert W to a heat map image which is shown in Fig. 1(e). We compare our heat map image with BTF [2] in Fig. 1(b). The BTF method does not remove textures well and the edges are not clear, while our method produces much clear structure image that can generate a better guidance image, which is shown in Fig. 1(f).

3.3 Joint Bilateral Filter

Bilateral filter is the most fundamental edge preserving operator which can smooth image and reduce noises. It calculates the pixel value of an output image using the weighted average of nearby pixels in the input image, which is defined as:

$$J_p = \frac{1}{k_p} \sum_{q \in \Omega_p} f(\|q - p\|) g(\|I_q - I_p\|) I_q \tag{2}$$

In Eq. (2), I is input image, J is output image, p, q are pixel indices and Ω_p is a patch centered at p. The output J_p at pixel p is a weighted average of I_q in the patch Ω_p. The spatial kernel f and the range kernel g are typically Gaussian functions, they are defined as Eqs. (3) and (4),

$$f(\|q - p\|) = \exp \left(-\frac{(x_q - x_p)^2 + (y_q - y_p)^2}{2\sigma_s^2} \right) \tag{3}$$

$$g(\|I_q - I_p\|) = \exp \left(-\frac{\|I_q - I_p\|^2}{2\sigma_r^2} \right) \tag{4}$$

where x and y represent the position of the pixel. The closer the Euclidean distance between p and q, the greater the weight of q is; the more similar the colors are, the greater the weight of q is. k_p is a normalization term written as:

$$k_p = \sum_{q \in \Omega_p} f(\|q - p\|) g(\|I_q - I_p\|) \tag{5}$$

This non-linear weighting equation (Eq. 2) enables bilateral filter to blur small-scale intensity variations while preserving edges. However, the bilateral filter cannot deal with the texture images where their scale of color variation may be large. Therefore, we substitute the guidance image $G_q - G_p$ for the input image $I_q - I_p$ in range filter g. The joint bilateral filter is written as follows:

$$J_p = \frac{1}{k_p} \sum_{q \in \Omega_p} f(\|q - p\|)g(\|G_q - G_p\|)I_q \tag{6}$$

This is a texture-filtering variant of Eq. (2), and it depends heavily on the design of G, which is also called guidance image in the context of joint bilateral filtering [14]. The guidance image G is yielded by line 8 of Algorithm 1, which has an important effect on the filtered result. Because our guidance image is generated by two images of different level of blur using W as the weighted value, small structures are preserved and textures are smoothed well, as shown in Fig. 1(f). If pixels of textures in the guidance image are similar, they will be smoothed away due to a large weight in range filter $g(\|G_q - G_p\|)$. Therefore, our guidance image makes a great contribution in distinguishing structures and textures.

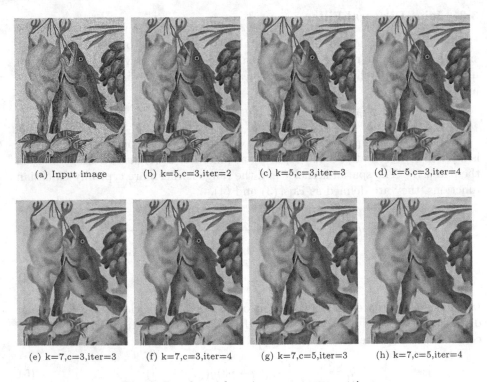

(a) Input image   (b) k=5,c=3,iter=2   (c) k=5,c=3,iter=3   (d) k=5,c=3,iter=4

(e) k=7,c=3,iter=3   (f) k=7,c=3,iter=4   (g) k=7,c=5,iter=3   (h) k=7,c=5,iter=4

Fig. 2. Results with various parameter setting

4   Results and Comparisons

4.1   Parameter Setting

Our method mainly has three parameters, which are the larger filter size k, the smaller filter size c, and the iteration number n. The larger filter size k is related to the texture size that we want to remove. However, with the larger size k, the structure is blurred more easily. The smaller filter size c determines how small the scale of structure is to be preserved. Another parameter is n. When n is too large, image is over smoothed, when n is too small, image may be not smoothed enough. In our experiments, the flattened image is respectable and the computational time is acceptable with $k = 5$ or 7, $c = 3$ and $n = 2$ or 3. Figure 2 shows the different effect with various parameters.

The joint bilateral filter is set as the same as the original method of Cho et al. [2], σ_r is set to $0.05 \times \sqrt{c}$, c is the number of channels, σ_s is set to $k - 1$, where k is the larger filter size.

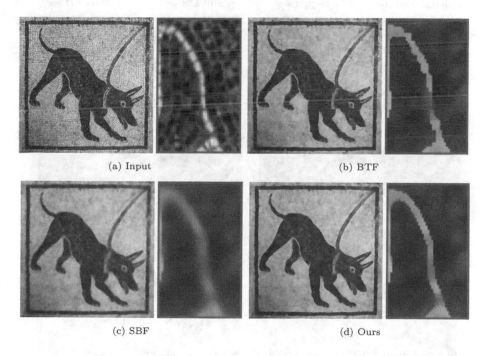

    (a) Input   (b) BTF

    (c) SBF   (d) Ours

Fig. 3. Compare our method with BTF [2] and SBF [3]

4.2   Comparison

To evaluate the performance of our method, we implemented some previous state-of-art methods for comparison, including BTF [2] and SBF [3], as shown in Fig. 3. Figure 3(b), this image is produced by BTF, which has some jagged

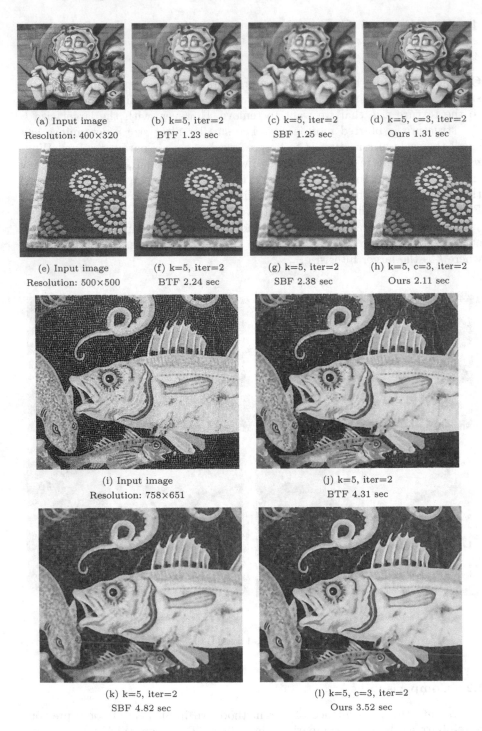

(a) Input image
Resolution: 400×320

(b) k=5, iter=2
BTF 1.23 sec

(c) k=5, iter=2
SBF 1.25 sec

(d) k=5, c=3, iter=2
Ours 1.31 sec

(e) Input image
Resolution: 500×500

(f) k=5, iter=2
BTF 2.24 sec

(g) k=5, iter=2
SBF 2.38 sec

(h) k=5, c=3, iter=2
Ours 2.11 sec

(i) Input image
Resolution: 758×651

(j) k=5, iter=2
BTF 4.31 sec

(k) k=5, iter=2
SBF 4.82 sec

(l) k=5, c=3, iter=2
Ours 3.52 sec

Fig. 4. Compare our method with BTF [2] and SBF [3] in quality and efficiency

edges and the textures are not removed well. Figure 3(c) is generated by SBF, which is blurry in edges and it is hard to distinguish between edges and textures. Figure 3(d) shows our result, which is more clear in edge preserving.

In order to compare our efficiency with the previous method. We test all the methods on a machine with Intel Core I7 2.2 GHz CPU and 16G RAM. The comparative result is shown in Fig. 4. We found that when the input image has low resolution, the time cost of our method is similar to the other two, as shown in Fig. 4(a)–(d). Moreover, when the input image has medium or high resolution, our method is faster than other two methods, which is shown in Fig. 4(e)–(l). This is because we produce the optimized edge features at first, and it does not need to be modified in the iterations, while other methods calculate different a guidance image in each iteration. When the dimension of the input image becomes larger, it would cost more time.

5   Conclusion and Future Work

In this paper, we proposed a learning-based bilateral texture filter to remove texture patterns and preserve structures. Our method is simple and fast, as well as effective. The major contributions are two-fold: On the one hand, we applied the SF method to produce learning-based edge structure image as the guidance image in joint bilateral filter. The SF method is very time efficient in iteration due to the fact that the algorithm is real-time and only needs to run once. On the other hand, we take advantage of two filters of different sizes to remove textures and preserve edges. The size of the filters could be set to various values by users according to different input images to achieve better performance.

Future work includes improving the learning method such as using convolutional neural network, which can understand the semantic meanings of the images and extract different level of feature maps better, to produce better edge features. In addition, we will focus on reducing the parameter settings to decrease user intervention, for example, the filter size can be set automatically according to edge feature extraction.

Acknowledgements. We would like to thank the anonymous reviewers for their valuable comments. We would also like to thank the People Programme (Marie Curie Actions) of the European Union's Seventh Framework Programme FP7/2007-2013/ under REA grant agreement n° [612627] for their support.

References

1. Paris, S., Hasinoff, S., Kautz, J.: Local laplacian filters. ACM Trans. Graph. **30**, 1 (2011)
2. Cho, H., Lee, H., Kang, H., Lee, S.: Bilateral texture filtering. ACM Trans. Graph. **33**, 1–8 (2014)
3. Lin, T., Way, D., Shih, Z., Tai, W., Chang, C.: An efficient structure-aware bilateral texture filtering for image smoothing. Comput. Graph. Forum **35**, 57–66 (2016)

4. Xu, L., Lu, C., Xu, Y., Jia, J.: Image smoothing via L0 gradient minimization. ACM Trans. Graph. **30**, 1 (2011)
5. Xu, L., Yan, Q., Xia, Y., Jia, J.: Structure extraction from texture via relative total variation. ACM Trans. Graph. **31**, 1 (2012)
6. Karacan, L., Erdem, E., Erdem, A.: Structure-preserving image smoothing via region covariances. ACM Trans. Graph. **32**, 1–11 (2013)
7. Dollar, P., Zitnick, C.: Structured forests for fast edge detection. In: 2013 IEEE International Conference on Computer Vision (2013)
8. Kass, M., Solomon, J.: Smoothed local histogram filters. ACM Trans. Graph. **29**, 1 (2010)
9. Yang, Q., Tan, K.-H., Ahuja, N.: Real-time O(1) bilateral filtering. In: 2009 IEEE Conference on Computer Vision and Pattern Recognition (2009)
10. Yang, Q.: Recursive bilateral filtering. In: Fitzgibbon, A., Lazebnik, S., Perona, P., Sato, Y., Schmid, C. (eds.) ECCV 2012. LNCS, vol. 7572, pp. 399–413. Springer, Heidelberg (2012). doi:10.1007/978-3-642-33718-5_29
11. He, K., Sun, J., Tang, X.: Guided image filtering. In: Daniilidis, K., Maragos, P., Paragios, N. (eds.) ECCV 2010. LNCS, vol. 6311, pp. 1–14. Springer, Heidelberg (2010). doi:10.1007/978-3-642-15549-9_1
12. Gastal, E., Oliveira, M.: Domain transform for edge-aware image and video processing. ACM Trans. Graph. **30**, 1 (2011)
13. Rudin, L., Osher, S., Fatemi, E.: Nonlinear total variation based noise removal algorithms. Physica D Nonlinear Phenomena **60**, 259–268 (1992)
14. Petschnigg, G., Szeliski, R., Agrawala, M., Cohen, M., Hoppe, H., Toyama, K.: Digital photography with flash and no-flash image pairs. ACM Trans. Graph **23**, 664 (2004)

A Novel Multi-touch Approach for 3D Object Free Manipulation

Jiechang Guo[1], Yigang Wang[1(✉)], Peng Du[1], and Lingyun Yu[1,2]

[1] Hangzhou Dianzi University, Hangzhou 310018, China
yigang.wang@hdu.edu.cn
[2] Center for Medical Imaging North East Netherlands,
University of Groningen, University Medical Center Groningen,
Hanzeplein 1, 9713 GZ Groningen, Netherlands

Abstract. In the field of scientific visualization, 3D manipulation is a fundamental task for many different scientific datasets, such as particle data in physics and astronomy, fluid data in aerography, and structured data in medical science. Current researches show that large multi-touch interactive displays serve as a promising device providing numerous significant advantages for displaying and manipulating scientific data. Those benefits of direct-touch devices motivate us to use touch-based interaction techniques to explore scientific 3D data. However, manipulating object in 3D space via 2D touch input devices is challenging for precise control. Therefore, we present a novel multi-touch approach for manipulating structured objects in 3D visualization space, based on multi-touch gestures and an extra axis for the assistance. Our method supports 7-DOF manipulations. Moreover, with the help from the extra axis and depth hints, users can have better control of the interactions. We report on a user study to make comparisons between our method and standard mouse-based 2D interface. We show in this work that touch-based interactive displays can be more effective when applied to complex problems if the interactive visualizations and interactions are designed appropriately.

Keywords: Direct-touch interaction · 3D manipulation · Multi-touch gesture

1 Introduction

Scientific visualization focuses on the comprehension of many different scientific datasets, such as particle data in physics and astronomy, fluid data in aerography, and structured data in medical science. By effectively exploring and interacting with data, scientists can understand, clarify, and gain insight from their dataset. Large multi-touch interactive displays have become commonplace in our daily life as a promising device, as it provides numerous significant advantages for displaying and manipulating scientific data. For instance, the large size and high-resolution screen for visualizing scientific data [1], the extra input bandwidth provided by multi-points [2] and the somesthetic perception feedback that offers users the sense of control of their data [3]. There is also great potential for direct-touch interaction to promote the process of scientific visualization, as it can meet the need of direct manipulation on the data rather

© Springer International Publishing AG 2017
J. Chang et al. (Eds.): AniNex 2017, LNCS 10582, pp. 159–172, 2017.
https://doi.org/10.1007/978-3-319-69487-0_12

than being restricted to traditional indirect mouse/keyboard-based interaction in desktop environments. Those benefits of direct-touch devices motivate us to take full advantage of them to build a more intuitive touch interaction of scientific 3D data.

3D manipulation is the fundamental task for scientific visualization. Unlike the touch interaction of 2D data, interacting with 3D data in a virtual 3D world using a 2D multi-touch display is a tough and challenging task that demands an instinctive mapping from 2D touch input to 3D manipulation. For positioning tasks, the absence of depth information makes it complicated for users to translate the object along the depth direction. For orienting tasks, it is even harder for users to determine the rotation angles respectively for each of the three axes let alone defining the rotation center in a 3D space. Conventionally, 2D interfaces such as mouse typically uses 3D widgets or combinations of mouse and keyboard to manipulate the 3D models. However, these interactions are indirect. Besides, 3D widgets in system control mode is not suggested for the touch-based large screen since it is difficult for users to reach the menu or buttons on a large screen. In contrast, multi-touch devices provide the possibilities to accomplish different exploration tasks by multi-touch gestures. Most of the previous works [2, 4, 5] introduced the basic interactions of 3D manipulation, but to place and orient a 3D object correctly is still difficult.

Previous works have proven that the touch interaction facilitates precise control over 3D particle space [3]. In this work, we focus on the interactions of the structured 3D model, which have even higher requirements in terms of the precision of the manipulations. We present a novel multi-touch approach for positioning and orienting structured models in 3D visualization spaces, which combines multi-touch gestures and an additional assistant axis. Our method supports 7-DOF manipulation (translation along the x-/y-/z-axis, rotation around x-/y-/z-axis, and uniform zoom), two free rotation modes (trackball rotation and rotation around user-defined center), and viewpoint control to view and manipulate 3D models from different viewpoints. We evaluate our method by a user study, with a controlled experiment of eight independent interaction tasks and one complex integrated task.

2   Related Work

The sense of touch is significant in human-computer interaction (HCI) for its somesthetic capabilities [6]. Thus, enabling touch interaction with scientific visualization is essential. Interaction in scientific visualization is unique in HCI domains for complex analysis tasks and datasets [7]. The challenge of touch interaction in scientific visualization is defining an instinctive mapping from 2D touch input to 3D manipulation [1].

Several researchers and tool developers have addressed this challenge of 2D-to-3D mapping, and their work gave us some inspiration. Based on the de facto standard technique RST for manipulating 2D data [8], Screen-space technique extended it into 3D manipulation which controls the 6 DOF in an integral way with three or more fingers [9]. We have benefited a lot from this technique. The Z-technique [4] for performing depth positioning by adding another finger can be considered as a baseline for designing intuitive 3D position interactions. Other techniques like the Sticky tools designed full 6-DOF interactions by dividing the DOFs of 3D manipulation tasks [10].

Depth-Separated Screen Space (DS3) [11] extended the concept of separation DOFs which consisted of the Z-technique [4] to control translation and Screen-space technique to control rotation. Studies like Sticky Tools [10] and DS3 [11] pointed out that by separating the degrees of freedom, the RST technique can perform better, from which we derived our work. Besides, the work of Mendes [12] inspires us to provide unconstrained viewing angles for interactions which most researches did not involve in. Eden, a professional multi-touch tool, was designed for constructing virtual organic environments that used conjoined touch instead of single touch to differentiate interactions [5]. Yu et al. [3] proposed a frame-based touch interaction for manipulating astronomy particle data in 7-DOF, with the assistant of the frame they allowed full 7-DOF manipulations using one or dual touch input. FI3D focused on the scientific exploration of particle data in astronomy and supported the manipulation of the data as a whole rather than specific objects in the scene. When there are multiple structured 3D models in the scene, the interactions of FI3D will be inappropriate. We learned from the lessons of the mentioned works and made improvements.

3 Proposed Approach

3.1 Design Goals

To overcome the challenges presented above, we developed a number of supplementary goals so as to help us design better interactions for users to manipulate the 3D structured model. We designed our method to:

G1: support all 7-DOF for 3D manipulations,
G2: provide constrained manipulations as well as free manipulations,
G3: enable users to define rotation center in 3D space,
G4: provide extra depth hints for precise manipulations,
G5: provide unconstrained viewing angles for interactions,
G6: design sophisticated interactions without influencing the usability of the basic interactions,
G7: ensure a smooth switch between different types of interactions,
G8: construct clear and intuitive gestures, and
G9: be more effective than standard 2D interface when applied to complex problems.

In the following subsection, we state the method we use to achieve the above goals. We discuss how instinctive mappings from 2D input to 3D manipulations have been developed and introduce the user controlled axis tool and gestures that are designed for interacting with the 3D model.

3.2 Interactions Design for 3D Model Manipulation

Our method supports eleven operations for interacting with the 3D model, and these operations are realized by a user controlled axis tool and a set of elaborately designed gestures. Figure 1 shows a screenshot of rotating the object about the x-axis. Note that we use the shadow to provide depth hint (G4).

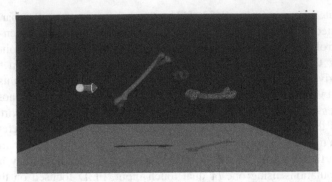

Fig. 1. Screenshot of rotating the object about x-axis.

User Controlled Axis Tool. We provide an additional user controlled axis for the following three reasons:

1. To avoid the use of system control mode metaphors, the axis appears only when users trigger it by dedicated gestures.
2. We are able to construct a set of intuitive and uniform gestures for the interactions based on the tool (G6, G7, G8).
3. Unlike the extra frame in FI3D [3], having an axis next to the object is a better choice since it is easy to reach and understand for manipulation.

Gestures Design. Based on the use of axis tool, aseries of multi-touch gestures are built, using up to four touch points to complete the 11 different interactions. Meanwhile, the advanced interaction was designed without influencing the usability of the basic interaction (G6). We divide the gestures into four types including translation,

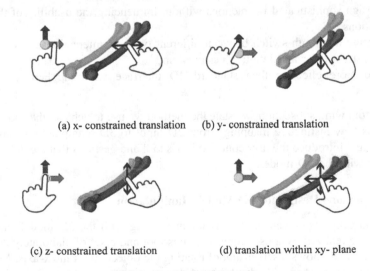

(a) x- constrained translation   (b) y- constrained translation

(c) z- constrained translation   (d) translation within xy- plane

Fig. 2. Translation interaction.

rotation, scaling and viewpoint controlling. The gestures can be manipulated smoothly and users can switch between different types of gestures on the fly to realize different operations (G7).

Translation. For translation, the axis tool is triggered when one finger touches the model. After that users can move the object directly within the plane parallel to the view plane (Fig. 2d). In this condition, the model is "sticking" with the finger so as to perform a precise movement. By adding one more finger from the other hand to pick x-/y-/z-axis on the axis tool, the model will be moved separately in the three directions (Fig. 2).

Rotation. We design three types of interactions for orienting the model including constrained rotation, trackball rotation, and rotation around user-defined center.

For constrained rotation, after triggering the axis tool by two adjacent touches on the screen, users can add one touch point on the axis tool to a specific axis that the model is expected to rotate around (Fig. 3). By dragging two touches on the screen, users perform trackball rotation (Fig. 4a).

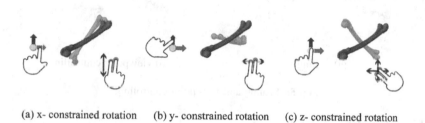

(a) x- constrained rotation   (b) y- constrained rotation   (c) z- constrained rotation

Fig. 3. x-/y-/z-constrained rotation interaction

Additionally, we provide users the ability to rotate the model around a user-defined center (Fig. 4b). After triggering the rotation interaction by two touches on the screen, users can add two more touches to define the rotation center. The 2D location of the rotate center is defined at the first intersecting point on the object corresponding to ray-casting of the middle point of the two adjacent touches. By moving fingers up and down, users can adjust the rotation center in the depth direction. The rotation center is shown as a small red ball (Fig. 4b).

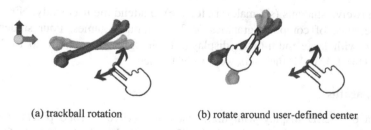

(a) trackball rotation   (b) rotate around user-defined center

Fig. 4. Free rotation interaction (Color figure online)

Scale. For uniform scaling task (Fig. 5a), we choose the standard split-close and split-apart gestures from two hands to support large scale. We map the changes of distance between two touch points to the scale factor. With increasing distance, the object is enlarged, and vice versa.

Viewpoint Control. We provide unconstrained viewing angles for interactions so as to enable users to view and manipulate models from different angles (G5). This is important for the task of positioning and orienting an object relative to another. Since we manipulate 3D objects in the object coordinate system, changing the position of the camera will cause a problem when users want to align objects based on viewpoint changing. In order to realize viewpoint control as well as manipulate the object from different angles correctly, we decided to rotate the scene itself instead of changing the position of the camera. Users can swipe three fingers on the screen to view the models from different angles (Fig. 5b).

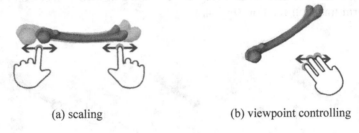

(a) scaling   (b) viewpoint controlling

Fig. 5. Scaling and viewpoint controlling

4   User Study

A proven fact is that distinct input modalities such as mouse, keyboard and multi-touch display, each has its unique properties of benefits and disadvantages relying on the different application fields and the given interaction tasks [13]. To take an important step towards a better comprehension of pros and cons of these interaction techniques when dealing with structured 3D model, we report on a user study to compare our method with the standard mouse-based 2D interface. Meanwhile, we evaluate our method by users' performance and preference, particularly for our goals G8 and G9.

4.1   Participants

We invite twelve students (six male, six female) to attend the user study. Nine of them have experience of computer graphics or 3D computer games. Four students have experience with large multi-touch displays. Their ages varies from 20 to 25 (M = 21.538, SD = 1.45). All the users were right-handed.

4.2   Apparatus

We use a 65″ LED display with high resolution (1920 * 1080 pixels) and a G5 Multi-touch screen overlaying the display from PQLab, which supports 50+ touch points detectable simultaneously.

For standard 2D interface, we chose a 450 dpi average speed mouse and keyboard as interaction devices as shown in Table 1 instead of using widgets so that we can avoid computing the extra time and distance for mouse to reach the menus or buttons. The examples of setups for the experiments are shown above (Fig. 6). For touch interactions, users stood in front of the large display, while a table was placed in front of the screen for mouse/keyboard interactions condition. The application ran under Windows 10.

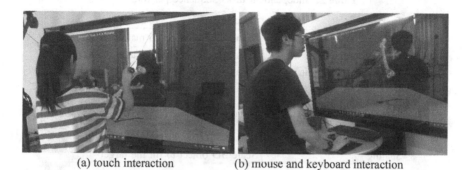

      (a) touch interaction   (b) mouse and keyboard interaction

Fig. 6. Example setup of touch and mouse/keyboard interaction.

Table 1. 3D manipulation of mouse and keyboard

Task	Mapping event
x-/y-translation	Left button drag
z-translation	Left button down + scroll up and down
x-/y-/z-constrained rotation	Key {x|y|z} down + right button drag
Trackball free rotation	Right button drag
Rotation around user-defined center	Define center: key {c} down + left button down + scroll up and down rotate: right button drag
Scaling	Scroll up and down
Viewpoint controlling	Key {left|right} down

4.3   Tasks

We tested eight tasks of independent basic manipulations and one complex integrated task of positioning and orienting one model according to another. The independent tasks test the performance of our interactions method separately with exact task instructions for 3D manipulation, while the complex integrated task requires users to think and make decisions on specific interactions they would like to use to translate and rotate the 3D object to the target location.

The eight independent tasks are the basic components of the integrated task. We tested three interaction techniques, translation, rotation, and scale. There were two translation tasks, one for translating on the x-/y-plane and the other for translating in 3D space. We tested constrained rotation and free rotation separately within a total of five rotation interactions. Table 2 below shows the description of each task.

Table 2. Independent tasks sequence per round

	Task	Description
1	x-/y-translation	Translate 3D object to match the target
2	x-/y-/z-translation	Translate 3D object to match the target
3	x-constrained rotation	Rotate 3D object to match the target
4	y-constrained rotation	Rotate 3D object to match the target
5	z-constrained rotation	Rotate 3D object to match the target
6	Trackball free rotation	Rotate 3D object to match the target
7	Defining center free rotation	Rotate 3D object to match the target
8	Scaling	Scale 3D object to fill the target

We asked users to position and orient a bone relative to a gray wireframe bone which indicates the target model as precisely and quickly as possible. We gave instructions of each task on the top of the viewport to guide users to perform corresponding interaction (Fig. 7). We calculated whether the bone has matched the desired position when the users' fingers left the screen or the mouse button was released, the task would be stopped automatically if matched. Participants were allowed to give up the task.

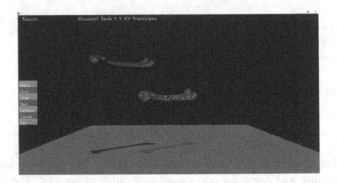

Fig. 7. Independent tasks setting.

For the integrated tasks, users were asked to position and orient the bone relative to the other without instructions. The bone is placed in a random place with a random orientation. To match the models, several interactions may need to be taken. The viewpoint control interaction was enabled during this task for users to view the scene and manipulate the object from different angles. In this condition, users needed to make decisions on which interactions they would like to use to match the models. They could use the eleven types of interactions we provided to complete the task.

4.4 Design

We used a repeated-measures design for the independent tasks with two input devices (multi-touch display, mouse/keyboard). Each user should complete tests separately for the two devices, half of the users tested mouse first while the other half tested multi-touch display first.

For the eight independent tasks, each user performed four rounds of tests, four times on each task and input devices. The tasks were always shown in the same sequence (Table 2). For each of the translation tasks, the target wireframe bone was placed in the middle of the screen, and the position of the manipulated bone was placed on 4 different starting positions varied by a Latin square. For rotation tasks, the bone and target bone were placed in the middle of the scene with two different rotation directions varied between rounds using the Latin square. For zoom tasks, the bone and target bone were placed on four unique positions with two different zoom factors. The first two rounds were considered as practice rounds which we do not consider them for the final analysis of the data.

In total, we have 12 users × 2 input devices × 8 tasks × 4 times × 4 rounds = 3072 interactions for the independent tasks. We first introduced the interaction mappings for each input devices to users before they began the test. Between the independent tasks of each input devices, we asked users to fulfill a questionnaire to give the subjective evaluation of the usability of the input device, including the degree of difficulty to complete each task and the memory difficulty for each interaction mappings on a seven-point Likert scale. After finishing all the independent tasks, users had to express their preference for the two input devices and their reasons.

For complex integrated tasks, there was no time limitation. We measure the errors between the models. Meanwhile, we record users' interactions and subjective assessment such as preference.

Eventually, when all tasks finished, users were asked to describe their overall feelings without consideration of the tasks, including their favors for the input devices, preference for constrained or free manipulation, and evaluation for the depth hints we provided by rendering model shadows and viewpoint controlling interaction. In addition, we collected their previous experiences of computer graphics, 3D game, and multi-touch large display. We also communicated with each user for advice and inspiration on our future work.

5 Results

We report the results of user study from three parts, the independent tasks' results, the complex integrated task results, and users' overall preference. In this section, we analyze the result and discuss our lessons learned.

5.1   Independent Tasks

We compared the average completion time for each task and each input device and present the results in Table 3. The task of x-/y-translation shows no obvious difference between mouse and touch. In contrast, mouse showed a significant difference when dealing with the task of z translation. The results for rotation showed a significant difference. For the tasks of constrained rotation, the mouse was much faster than touch. However, for tasks related to free rotation, the touch outperformed mouse, especially when dealing with rotate around user-defined center tasks. Mouse was faster when dealing with scale tasks.

Table 3. Task completion time of independent tasks.

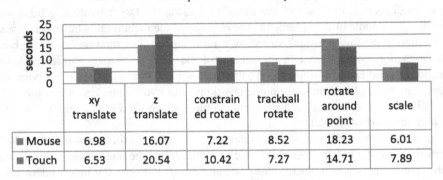

	xy translate	z translate	constrain ed rotate	trackball rotate	rotate around point	scale
▪ Mouse	6.98	16.07	7.22	8.52	18.23	6.01
▪ Touch	6.53	20.54	10.42	7.27	14.71	7.89

From the questionnaire, users were asked to compare the two interactions of the input devices according to the difficulty of completing each task, the ease of remembering for each interaction on a 7-point Likert scale, the results are shown in Table 4. Overall, both interaction techniques rated high, we think we achieved our goal G8 and G9.

Table 4. The scores for each interaction.

Interaction	Mouse	Touch
x-/y-translation	6.91	6.83
z-translation	6.12	6.12
Constrained rotation	6.33	5.91
Trackball free rotation	6.25	6.25
Defining center rotation	4.87	5.58
Scaling	6.83	6.62

5.2   Complex Integrated Tasks

The position bias is defined as the ratio of the length of position deviation to the length of the actual path [11]. The result of position bias showed a significant difference between mouse and touch input devices. The position bias for mouse condition is

1.19% and 0.73% for touch. The rotation bias is described by the Tait-Bryan angle as shown in Table 5. This time, the mouse and touch show no significant difference. The total rotation bias for mouse condition is 6.15° and for touch is 5.54°. As the result, the manipulation is more accurate in touch condition.

Table 5. Rotation bias

Tait-Bryan angle	Mouse	Touch
Yaw	0.98	0.07
Pitch	0.56	0.28
Roll	4.61	5.07

The number of interactions users took to complete the tasks is 1963. For mouse condition, the average interactions number is 67 times and for touch condition, the average interactions number is 80 times. The switching between different interactions is smoother in the touch condition than mouse, with 1.16 s for touch and 1.32 s for mouse. Given this result, the goal G7 was achieved. We specifically count up the interaction times for free rotations and constrained rotations. As expected, we found that users preferred free rotation than constrained rotation for they took 412 times with 20.98% of the total for free rotation interactions and only 174 times with 8.86% of the total for constrained rotation interactions. What's more, the times of viewpoint control interaction is 440 times with 22.41% of the total interactions.

5.3 Overall Preferences

After completing all independent tasks with each input devices, we asked users to describe their preference when dealing with the time-limited independent tasks. Half of the users preferred mouse and keyboard interactions because they are familiar with mouse (3×), the speed of mouse is faster (2×) and less body movement (1×). While the other half preferred touch for the interactions are more intuitive (3×), the somesthetic feedback (2×) and the sense of immersive (1×).

After the more complex integrated task some users changed their mind. At this time, 83.3% users preferred touch interactions. The reasons were that they had more control over their model (4×), the transitions between different interactions were smoother (2×), more interesting (1×), more immersive (1×) and more intuitive (2×). Out of the two users who preferred mouse, they insisted that the mouse is more fast and precious.

After finishing all tasks, users were asked to report their overall preference. All users preferred touch interaction without considering other factors because it is more interesting. For constrained and free manipulations, 70% preferred free manipulations. The scores for the depth hints we provided by casting the shadows of models and the viewpoint controlling is 6.21, indicating that they thought the depth hints were quite useful.

6 Discuss and Lessons Learned

Touch and mouse input devices show no significant effect of x-/y-translation tasks. While for z-translation tasks, the reason might be that the scroll wheel of mouse is much faster and more accurate than moving touch points.

For constrained rotation tasks, the fact that touch outperformed mouse largely due to the hardware. Unlike pressure sensitive touch screen or capacitive touch screen, PQlab's multi-touch screen detects the touch points by infrared ray, some extra touch points are inevitably detected when users' fingers are close to the screen, which makes some failures on the gesture recognition process. When doing repetitive movements on the multi-touch display, it was difficult for users to move their fingers smoothly due to the friction force. From those result, we can learn that we should use at most two fingers from each hand for frequent interactions to reduce the friction. Besides, during the movement, the two-touches we use to control rotation were often detected as one touch point unless the users were intentionally careful to keep these gestures. We can learn from this that the two-touches are not suitable for frequently-used interactions. Instead, a conjoined touches gesture combined with two fingers together may solve this problem, which needs to be recognized technically. For the trackball rotation tasks, we think the reason for touch's slender lead is the same as x-y-translation tasks. While for tasks of rotation around the user-defined center, touch was faster than mouse. We conjecture that the interaction can be performed with a single multi-touch gesture, but needs three steps to perform with mouse and keyboard due to the limited input bandwidth of mouse, which is time-consuming. This result gives expression to the advantages of multi-touch interaction for the extra input bandwidth. As a user reported, we restrained the movement too much and the rotation is only triggered when the movement of two-near-touches is exactly vertical or horizontal. We believe that there is still room for the progress of the rotation interactions.

Due to the same reason as z-translation tasks, scale tasks for mouse was faster than touch for the scroll wheel was faster and precious. It is difficult to achieve fine adjustment. But as users reported, the scale on touch display is more intuitive and the increment is smoother.

The results of the complex integrated task reveal that the manipulation is more accurate in touch condition than mouse. We speculate that is because users were more concentrated on the models in touch condition. They did not need to spend extra effort on the keyboard. Thus, we think the touch interaction is suitable for tasks in which the precise manipulations are required. Besides, the touch interaction was more attractive than normal mouse interaction so that users would like to spend more time on the task. The switching between different interactions was smoother in touch condition. Therefore, we think we designed the interaction appropriately. According to our statistics, unsurprisingly most of the users preferred the free manipulation. The reasons might be that the free manipulation is more intuitive and this interaction offers users more freedom. The frequent use of viewpoint control interaction strongly demonstrated that providing unconstrained viewing angles for interactions is essential for 3D manipulations via 2D input and output devices.

7 Conclusion

In this paper, we presented a novel multi-touch approach for 3D object free manipulation. Our method is combined with a user-controlled axis tool and a set of elaborately designed multi-touch gestures. The method supports eleven operations for interacting with the 3D model in 7-DOF (goals G1, G2). We designed an advanced interaction for defining rotation center in 3D space (G3), which existing methods did not support. With the axis tool, gestures were designed in a simple and uniform way (G6). The switching between gestures can be on the fly (G7). Besides, we support 3D manipulations with unconstrained viewing angles, which provide users extra depth hints (G4, G5). We reported on a user study comparing our method with standard mouse and keyboard interactions. The results showed that our method was competitive when dealing with complex integrated tasks (G9). According to users report, the gestures are easy to learn and remember (G8). In the future, we would like to address the issues presented in the Lesson Learned section and design better multi-touch interactions for 3D manipulation.

Acknowledgements. We would like to thank Chenling Tang, Minda Chen and all the user study participants for their invaluable input. This work was supported by National Natural Science Foundation of China (Grant No. 61502132, No. 61502130) and Key Laboratory of Complex Systems Modeling and Simulation, Ministry of Education.

References

1. Isenberg, T.: Position paper: touch interaction in scientific visualization. In: Proceedings of the Workshop on Data Exploration on Interactive Surfaces—DEXIS, pp. 24–27 (2011)
2. Martinet, A., Casiez, G., Grisoni, L.: The effect of DOF separation in 3D manipulation tasks with multi-touch displays. In: Proceedings of VRST10 ACM Symposium on Virtual Reality Software & Technology, pp. 111–118 (2010)
3. Yu, L., Svetachov, P., Isenberg, P., Everts, M.H., Isenberg, T.: FI3D: direct-touch interaction for the exploration of 3D scientific visualization spaces. IEEE Trans. Vis. Comput. Graph. **16**(6), 1613–1622 (2010)
4. Martinet, A., Casiez, G., Grisoni, L.: The design and evaluation of 3D positioning techniques for multi-touch displays. 3D User Interfaces **30**, 115–118 (2010)
5. Kin, K., Miller, T., Bollensdorff, B., Derose, T., Hartmann, B., Agrawala, M.: Eden: a professional multitouch tool for constructing virtual organic environments. In: Proceedings of the SIGCHI Conference on Human Factors in Computing Systems, pp. 1343–1352 (2011)
6. Roblesdelatorre, G.: The importance of the sense of touch in virtual and real environments. IEEE Multimed. **13**(3), 24–30 (2006)
7. Keefe, D.F.: Integrating visualization and interaction research to improve scientific workflows. IEEE Comput. Graph. Appl. **30**(2), 8–13 (2010)
8. Hancock, M.S., Vernier, F.D., Wigdor, D., Carpendale, S.: Rotation and translation mechanisms for tabletop interaction. In: IEEE International Workshop on Horizontal Interactive Human-Computer Systems, Tabletop IEEE, p. 8 (2006)
9. Reisman, J.L., Davidson, P.L., Han, J.Y.: A screen-space formulation for 2D and 3D direct manipulation. In: ACM Symposium on User Interface Software and Technology, Victoria, DBLP, pp. 69–78 (2009)

10. Hancock, M., Cate, T.T., Carpendale, S.: Sticky tools: full 6DOF force-based interaction for multi-touch tables. In: ACM International Conference on Interactive Tabletops and Surfaces, pp. 133–140 (2009)
11. Martinet, A., Casiez, G., Grisoni, L.: Integrality and separability of multitouch interaction techniques in 3D manipulation tasks. IEEE Trans. Vis. Comput. Graph. **18**(3), 369–380 (2012)
12. Mendes, D., Ferreira, A.: Evaluation of 3D object manipulation on multi-touch surfaces using unconstrained viewing angles. In: Campos, P., Graham, N., Jorge, J., Nunes, N., Palanque, P., Winckler, M. (eds.) INTERACT 2011. LNCS, vol. 6949, pp. 523–526. Springer, Heidelberg (2011). doi:10.1007/978-3-642-23768-3_73
13. Besançon, L., Issartel, P., Ammi, M., Isenberg, T.: Usability comparison of mouse, touch and tangible inputs for 3D data manipulation (2016)

Sunken Relief Generation from a Single Image

Liying Yang[1], Tingting Li[1], Meili Wang[1(✉)], and Shihui Guo[2]

[1] Northwest A&F University, Xianyang, Shaanxi, China
wml@nwsuaf.edu.cn
[2] Xiamen University, Xiamen, China

Abstract. Sunken relief is an art form whereby the depicted shapes are sunk into a given flat plane with a shallow overall depth. In this paper, we propose a sunken relief generation algorithm based on a single image. Our method starts from a single image. First, we smoothen the image with morphological operations such as opening and closing operations and extract the feature lines by comparing the values of adjacent pixels. Then we apply unsharp masking to sharpen the feature lines. After that, we focus on local information enhancement and smoothing to obtain an image that with little burrs and jaggies. Differential operations are necessary to produce the perceptive relief effect. Finally, we construct the sunken relief surface by triangularization, by which two-dimensional information is transformed into a three-dimensional model. The results demonstrate that our method is simple and efficient.

Keywords: Sunken relief · Unsharp masking (USM) · Triangularization

1 Introduction

As a sculpture art, relief is widely used in a variety of items for signs, narratives, decorations and other purposes since ancient periods. In the modern industrial production, relief also has a broad applications, such as in producing nameplates, coins, or architectural decorations. Relief can be categorized into high relief, low relief (or bas relief), and sunken relief according to its depth structure. Digital high- and low relief generation has been widely investigated [1–5]. However, for the sunken relief, there remains much to be explored. Most studies [6–9] took three-dimensional (3D) models as inputs and extracted feature lines first. Then, the final sunken relief was generated by engraving the feature lines into a flat plane. Although satisfactory results can be obtained from a simple 3D model (Figs. 1(a), (b)), the algorithm process is complex. Especially, if the 3D model is complex, the generated sunken relief is less clear than that generated from a simple 3D model (Fig. 1(c)). Two-dimensional (2D) images are easier to obtain than 3D models. Therefore, Wang et al. [10] proposed an image-based algorithm that adopted gradient operations to convert an image into a relief, and then solved a Poisson equation to construct the depth information. Wu et al. [3] presented a low relief generation approach using a 2D image of a human face. First an image of low relief was generated from the input image. Then the shape-from-shading technique was applied to determine the 3D shape of the final low relief. Zeng et al. [11] also proposed a low relief generation algorithm based on a single image. They extracted feature lines,

J. Chang et al. (Eds.): AniNex 2017, LNCS 10582, pp. 173–185, 2017.
https://doi.org/10.1007/978-3-319-69487-0_13

then generated and enhanced a base surface using both intensity and gradient information. They also introduced a feedback process to prevent depth errors which arose during the enhancement process. All these three methods generated 3D low relief based on an image and obtained clear results. However, all of these techniques focused on low relief generation and did not consider sunken relief generation.

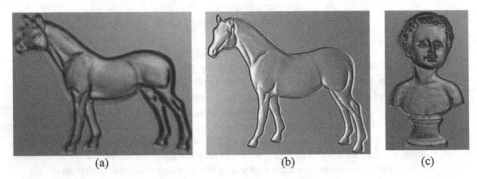

(a)   (b)   (c)

Fig. 1. Sunken relief of a horse model by (a) Wang et al. [8] and (b) Zhang et al. [9]; (c) Sunken relief of a complex model by Wang et al. [8].

Lines are fundamental elements in the art of painting and relief, and they can effectively convey both shape and material information. Lines also play an important role in human perception. In recent years, in the field of non-photorealistic rendering, depicting shapes using feature lines has become a popular topic [9]. The number of types of feature lines has continued to increase. The methods of extracting feature lines have also been continually innovated and improved. In reliefs, feature lines are divided into several main categories, including contours, creases, and suggestive contours [12–14].

As a form of sculpture, sunken relief is mainly generated by carving the relief into a smooth plane. Most studies focus on adopting complex algorithms to generate smooth curved surfaces whose depth varies within a limited range [7]. However, if only the feature lines are engraved into the plane, we can easily generate a sunken relief [7]. Despite this, few researchers were aware of the importance of feature lines for relief sculptures until Wang et al. [7] proposed an innovative method based on line-drawings. On the basis of this study, Wang et al. [8] and Zhang et al. [9] further investigated line drawings and relief generation from a 3D mesh.

In this paper, we propose a simple and efficient image-based sunken relief generation method based on extraction of feature lines from 2D images. First, some image pre-processing methods are applied to smooth the image. Then, feature lines are extracted by comparing adjacent pixel values. There are significant differences in pixel values between the feature lines and the interior zone. Third, unsharp masking (USM) and differential operations are used to enhance the features and produce a relief effect. Finally, 3D relief models are constructed by a triangulated mesh, in which the pixel values are considered as depth information.

2 Related Works

Methods to extract feature lines can be roughly classified into two categories: object-space and image-space approaches [15]. Object-space algorithms extract feature lines directly on 3D surfaces by seeking out points whose radial curvature is zero. Such approaches are more complex than image-space algorithms, which extract feature lines from images by image processing after rendering [16]. Saito et al. [17] developed a line-drawing method using 2D image processing operations instead of line tracking to extract silhouettes, creases and other lines.

Owing to the limited dynamic range, the influence of the light, and the image device restrictions, the quality of the image will be degraded during the acquisition process. Therefore much information in the original image cannot be recognized by human eyes. Image sharpening is an image enhancement method that uses various mathematical methods and transformations to improve image contrast and sharpness, to highlight objects in the image. USM originates from traditional photographic technology. It is an image edge sharpening algorithm which is based on image convolution. The principle of USM is to exaggerate the lighter-darker contrast between the two sides of an edge for the sake of enhancing the visual definition of the image [18].

The principle of the classic linear USM is that first the original image is smoothed by a linear high-pass filter and then multiplied by a scale factor [10]. The result of this is added to the original image to obtain the enhanced image. Mitra et al. [19] proposed a non-linear operator which can be approximated as a local mean weight high-pass filter and can reduce noise. Ramponi et al. [20] developed a cubic USM, which multiplies the Laplacian operator by an edge-square filter operator. This technology only enhances the image detail of the local luminance changed region. Lee et al. [21] introduced an operator based on the sequence statistics Laplacian algorithm. The output of this operator is proportional to the difference between local mean and local median. Thus, it can remove the Gaussian white noise effectively.

3 System Overview

First, the matrix of the 2D image is obtained, and processed by image processing techniques such as morphological expansion, opening and closing operations and mean filtering. Then we extract the feature lines and remove splashes in the feature line image. After that, USM technology is used to sharpen and enhance the contours and detail information. We define the feature lines as those that are engraved to enhance local details. Processing is necessary to smooth the feature lines. The sunken relief image is generated by a differential operation. Finally, the 3D relief is generated by triangularization. The framework is shown in Fig. 2.

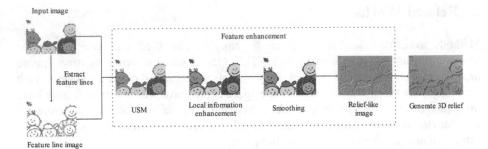

Fig. 2. Framework of our algorithm.

4   Feature Line Extraction and Feature Enhancement

4.1   Feature Line Extraction

Feature lines are based on the source 2D image. As with any edge-detection algorithm that operates in a continuous domain, a threshold parameter is necessary to adjust quality of the results. Thus, we extract feature lines from the original image through threshold detection.

The general idea is to compare the pixel value of the currently selected point with pixel values of adjacent points. If a difference above the threshold value exists, we consider that this selected point belongs to the boundary of the area; otherwise, the point does not. As shown in Fig. 3, the red point is defined as the selected point and the eight green points are the adjacent points. If the difference between the pixel value of the red point and that of any of the green points is greater than the pre-set threshold, this point is extracted as part of a feature line.

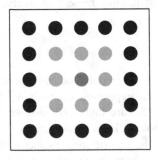

Fig. 3. Threshold detection.

To simplify the program code, considering that boundary pixels of the image have little effect on the final results of the feature line image, we neglect all the points lying on the image border; that is, the first and last rows and the first and last columns of the gray matrix are ignored when scanning the whole image row by row and column by column. Thus, we can ensure that there are always 8-neighbors for every test point and fewer constraint conditions need to be considered.

The algorithm of threshold detection for feature line extraction is as follows. Convert RGB values of the input image to grayscale values by forming a weighted sum of R, G, and B components. Obtain the gray matrix $I(i,j)$ where i represents a row and j represents a column of the matrix.

A linear transformation S is performed on $I(i,j)$ with the purpose of conveniently determining the range of differences among the pixel values and easily detecting the target point. In general, a sine function is selected with a range of $[0, 1]$ multiplied by a constant m so that the range is changed to $[0, m]$. The corresponding transformation is as follows:

$$S(I(i,j)) = m * \sin(I(i,j)) \tag{1}$$

Set t as the threshold. Scan the image row by row, and compare the selected point with its 8-neighbors. If there exists one difference that is bigger than the threshold, this point will be set to black (the pixel value is zero) and selected to be a part of the feature lines. Otherwise, it is not on the feature lines and will be set to white (the pixel value is 255). The determining condition is as follows:

$$I(i,j) - I(a,b) > t \tag{2}$$

where a represents the line number of neighbors which can be taken as $i - 1$ and $i + 1$, and b represents the column number of the neighbors which can be taken as $j - 1$ and $j + 1$.

The threshold is of great importance for the quality of the feature line image. When t is small, the extracted feature lines convey many details. As the value of t increases, the feature line image contains less details and line fractures increase. However, the line becomes thinner and burrs decrease. Therefore a suitable threshold results in a feature line image with many details but few line fractures. Repeated experiments we have performed show that good results can be achieved when the threshold is in the range of 0.3 to 2.5. Figure 4 shows feature line images for three different thresholds. A threshold of 0.25 results in a detailed image but with many burrs, whereas a threshold of 3.0 results in an image with many fractures. A threshold of 1.1 results in a relatively better image.

Fig. 4. Feature line images created by our algorithm using thresholds of (a) 0.25, (b) 1.1, and (c) 3.0.

Although a suitable threshold can improve the quality of feature line image, there still exists noise or blurriness in image; therefore, image processing is necessary before extracting feature lines. We smoothen the image using morphological opening and closing operations, and then apply a median filter. After extracting the feature lines, there are still some false edges in the feature line image affecting the accuracy of the extraction. Therefore, we remove these points by setting the pixel value to 255 when the point's pixel value is zero and all its 8-neighbors greater than zero. The condition is as follows:

$$I(i,j) == 0 \ \&\& \ I(a,b) > 0 \tag{3}$$

As a result, an image composed of black and white lines is obtained, which is a more effective feature lines image.

4.2 Feature Enhancement

After obtaining the feature lines image, we can directly generate a relief-like image; however, it contains a lot of breaks (see Fig. 5). To overcome this, we apply some image processing to the input image to sharpen the feature lines and to enhance the final relief quality (see Fig. 9).

Fig. 5. Relief images with breaks.

Unsharp Masking. USM is a commonly used technique which is used to sharpen the edges of an image [22]. By using USM, the contrast of the edge details can be quickly adjusted. A bright line and a dark line are generated on the two sides of any edges to make the image more distinct [18]. In this paper, we used the classic linear USM because it is simple and the enhancement effect is relatively good [10].

First the image is smoothed. We apply the neighborhood average method which adds the gray value of one pixel in the original image to the gray value of the pixel adjacent to it and then the average is calculated by dividing by 16. In this process, a template is needed. We defined a Gaussian template denoted by W which is a 3×3 matrix. The template can be seen as follows:

$$W = \begin{array}{ccc} 1 & 2 & 1 \\ 2 & 4 & 2 \\ 1 & 2 & 1 \end{array} \tag{4}$$

To obtain the average in the next step, we unitize it as follows:

$$W_u = \frac{1}{16} * W \tag{5}$$

Every pixel in the original image is multiplied by the corresponding value of the template. The process is as follows:

$$\begin{aligned}
g(i,j) &= W_u(1,1) * f(i-1,j-1) + W_u(1,2) * f(i-1,j) + W_u(1,3) * f(i-1,j+i) + \\
&\quad W_u(2,1) * f(i,j-1) + W_u(2,2) * f(i,j) + W_u(2,3) * f(i,j+1) + \\
&\quad W_u(3,1) * f(i+1,j-1) + W_u(3,2) * f(i+1,j) + W_u(3,3) * f(i+1,j+1)
\end{aligned} \tag{6}$$

where $f(\cdot, \cdot)$ is the gray value of the original image.

Because the smoothed image is the low frequency part of the image, to obtain the high frequency part, we subtract it from the original. Then the high frequency part is multiplied by a factor and added back to the original. This process is expressed as follows:

$$G(i,j) = f(i,j) + k(f(i,j) - g(i,j)) \tag{7}$$

where $g(i,j)$ is the smoothed version which obtained by Eq. 6, and k is the factor representing the amount of enhancement. We set $k = 5$ according to repeated experiments [10].

The image after USM is seen in Fig. 6, and we can see from the enlarged hat that the borders of objects in the image are sharper.

Fig. 6. Results of the unsharp masking.

Local Information Enhancement and Smoothing. After USM, the border is sharper, but the obtained image quality is poor (see Fig. 6). Therefore, we apply local information enhancement processing for a better effect. In this process, we define the points whose pixel value is 0 as the domain of definition to process the original image because pixel value of the point in the feature line is 0.

In principle, the original image is scanned row by row and changes are made to points on the feature lines if there are differences between that point and its neighbors. We set the pixel value difference to 64 because there can be a distinction generally when it is 64. For example, in Fig. 7, supposing o is the point on the feature line, we first traverse points of the image in directions of $\overrightarrow{ab}$ and $\overrightarrow{ad}$. If there is a case that $a < c$ and $|a - c| \geq 64$ (i.e., a is darker than c), we modify it to satisfy $|a - c| < 64$ by increasing the value of a and reducing the value of c. Then we set o to zero. The same work is done in directions of $\overrightarrow{da}$ and $\overrightarrow{dc}$.

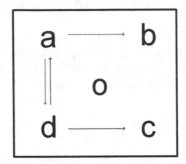

Fig. 7. Local information enhancement.

The result is that a black line is added to lighter parts. As shown in Fig. 8(a), a black line warps the contour line and through the differential operation, this black line will be transformed into a sunken curve. But the black line is rough, so we use Gaussian smoothing to smooth it. As seen in Fig. 8(b), burrs and jaggies are reduced.

(a)   (b)

Fig. 8. Images showing (a) the result of local information enhancement in which a black line warps the contour line and (b) the result of Gaussian smoothing with less burrs and jaggies than (a).

Differential Operation. Generating the sunken effect is a key step for digital sunken relief generation. Considering the image processing, we can obtain the relief effect from it. The convex or concave effect showed in many images is obtained by implementing a differential operation. A differential operation is a process in which the present value is subtracted from the next value (forward difference, see Eq. 8) or the previous value is subtracted from the present value (backward difference, see Eq. 9). These two differential operations can generate a concave effect.

$$\Delta f(x) = f(x+1) - f(x) \tag{8}$$

$$\nabla f(x) = f(x) - f(x-1) \tag{9}$$

In this paper, we apply the differential operation to obtain the perceptive sunken relief. We use a linear spatial filtering function, whose principle is convolution, to achieve the differential operation. However, for most images, low-frequency components often occupy the dominant position; that is, the images are based on low frequency components. Therefore, most results are small or even zero and thus the overall color tend to be black. To obtain better visual effects that the color is close to the lime color, we plus a direct component in such a result, that is, to increase a pixel value constant to ensure a certain gray level. The process is as follows:

$$F(i,j) = 0.5 + \sum_{k,l} G(i-k, j-l)h(k,l) \tag{10}$$

where $h(k,l)$ is the convolution kernel defined as $h = \begin{matrix} 1 & 0 \\ 0 & -1 \end{matrix}$, k and l represent rows and columns of $h(k,l)$ respectively and the constant 0.5 is the direct component. The result is seen in Fig. 9.

Fig. 9. Sunken relief of children.

5   Sunken Relief Generation and Comparisons

5.1   Triangularization

A triangulated mesh is adopted to construct 3D relief models after obtaining the required image information from the 2D image processing. For a simple implementation, the i

and j components of each vertex position correspond to the location of their counterpart in the line image F. Accordingly, connectives of 3D vertexes at each pixel constitute the triangular mesh.

$$z = F(i,j) - os \tag{11}$$

where $F(i,j)$ is the image pixel value, which corresponds to depth z, os is the offset value. This leads to a sculpture in which the background is mapped to a zero-level and each line is carved deeper into the material. Figure 10 shows the result of triangularization.

Fig. 10. 3D triangularization result of the children image.

5.2   Comparisons

Our algorithm mainly uses image processing to construct a 3D sunken relief from a 2D image. We implemented the algorithm in Matlab. All experiments were tested on a 3.20 GHz Intel CPU with 8 GB RAM assisted by a NVIDIA GeForce GTX 750 graphics card.

Compared with the object-based method, one important advantage of our method is that it does not require costly computation and can be easily implemented in graphics hardware. Table 1 shows the computation time of our algorithm for four images. From Table 1, we can see that our method is more efficient.

Table 1. Time cost of our algorithm for three different images.

Name (faces)	Time cost (seconds)				
	Feature line extraction	Feature enhancement	Triangularization	Total	Average time for each 10,000 faces
Bust (557106)	0.089	0.703	13.560	14.352	0.253
Children (804420)	0.089	0.537	19.613	20.239	
Horse (839808)	0.114	0.533	20.419	21.066	

Experimental results verify that the proposed method is effective for generating a sunken relief from a single 2D image. For complex images, our method can better maintain detail information. Figures 11 and 12 compare images produced by our method with those produced using the method of Wang et al. [8]. Any image can be processed to generate 3D sunken relief; therefore, development of industrial production for sunken relief can be greatly promoted. However, for images with intensive lines, our method needs to be further improved.

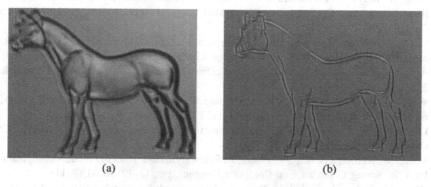

    (a)   (b)

Fig. 11. Sunken relief of a horse by (a) Wang et al. [8] and (b) our method.

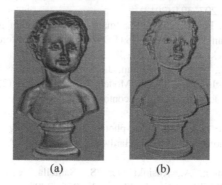

    (a)   (b)

Fig. 12. Sunken relief of a bust by (a) Wang et al. [8] and (b) our method.

6   Conclusions and Future Work

In this paper, we proposed a simple and effective method to generate sunken relief from a single image focused on feature lines. We adopted some image pre-processing to smooth the original image and improve the quality of the image obtained by feature line extraction. Local information enhancement and differential operation were applied to enhance feature information. We obtained a smooth and distinct relief-like image. Finally, a triangulated mesh was applied to construct 3D relief models through triangularization. However, all lines have the same engraving depth. In future work, we will consider introducing relief stylization which will make sunken relief more natural.

Acknowledgments. This work was funded by the National Natural Science Foundation of China (61402374). We thank all reviewers for editing the English of this manuscript.

References

1. Cignoni, P., Montani, C., Scopigno, R.: Computer-assisted generation of bas-and high-reliefs. J. Graph. Tools **2**(3), 15–28 (1997)
2. Song, W., Belyaev, A., Seidel, H.P.: Automatic generation of bas-reliefs from 3D shapes. In: IEEE International Conference on Shape Modeling and Applications, pp. 211–214. IEEE Computer Society (2007)
3. Wu, J., Martin, R., Rosin, P., Sun, X., Langbein, F., Lai, Y., Marshall, A., Liu, Y.: Making bas-reliefs from photographs of human faces. Comput. Aided Des. **45**(3), 671–682 (2013)
4. Arpa, S., Süsstrunk, S., Hersch, R.: High relief from 3D scenes. Comput. Graph. Forum **34**(2), 253–263 (2015)
5. Wang, M., Sun, Y., Zhang, H., Qian, K., Chang, J., He, D.: Digital relief generation from 3D models. Chin. J. Mech. Eng. **29**(6), 1128–1133 (2016)
6. Liu, S., Xu, X.: LI, B., Zhang, L.: An algorithm for generating line-engraving relief. J. Chin Comput. Syst. **32**(10), 2088–2091 (2011)
7. Wang, M., Kerber, J., Chang, J., Zhang, J.: Relief stylization from 3D models using featured lines. In: Spring Conference on Computer Graphics, pp. 37–42. ACM (2011)
8. Wang, M., Chang, J., Kerber, J., Zhang, J.: A framework for digital sunken relief generation based on 3D geometric models. Vis. Comput. **28**(11), 1127–1137 (2012)
9. Zhang, Y., Zhou, Y., Li, X., Zhang, L.: Line-based sunken relief generation from a 3D mesh. Graph. Models **75**(6), 297–304 (2013)
10. Wang, M., Chang, J., Pan, J., Zhang, J.: Image-based bas-relief generation with gradient operation. In: Proceedings of the 11th IASTED International Conference Computer Graphics and Imaging, Innsbruck, Austria, pp. 33–38. Acta Press (2010)
11. Zeng, Q., Martin, R., Wang, L., Quinn, J., Sun, Y., Tu, C.: Region-based bas-relief generation from a single image. Graph. Models **76**(3), 140–151 (2014)
12. Koenderink, J.: What does the occluding contour tell us about solid shape? Perception **13**(3), 321 (1984)
13. Raskar, R.: Hardware support for non-photorealistic rendering. In: ACM SIGGRAPH, eurographics Workshop on Graphics Hardware, pp. 41–46. Association for Computing Machinery (2001)
14. Decarlo, D., Finkelstein, A., Rusinkiewicz, S., Santella, A.: Suggestive contours for conveying shape. ACM Trans. Graph. **22**(3), 848–855 (2003)
15. Zhang, L., He, Y., Xie, X., Chen, W.: Laplacian lines for real-time shape illustration. In: 2009 ACM SIGGRAPH Symposium on Interactive 3D Graphics and Games, Boston, MA, United states, pp. 129–136. Association for Computing Machinery (2009)
16. Lee, Y., Markosian, L., Lee, S., Hughes, J.: Line drawings via abstracted shading. ACM Trans. Graph. **26**(3), 18 (2007)
17. Saito, T., Takahashi, T.: Comprehensible rendering of 3-D shapes. ACM Siggraph Comput. Graph. **24**(4), 197–206 (1990)
18. Liang, J., Gong, L.: An improved method of USM processing on color image. In: 2nd China Academic Conference on Printing and Packaging, Beijing, China, pp. 168–171. Trans Tech Publications (2012)

19. Mitra, S., Li, H., Lin, I., Yu, T.: A new class of nonlinear filters for image enhancement. In: Proceeding of the 1991 International Conference on Acoustics, Speech, and Signal, Toronto, Ontario, Canada, pp. 2525–2528. IEEE (1991)
20. Ramponi, G.: A cubic unsharp masking technique for contrast enhancement. Sig. Process. **67**(2), 211–222 (1998)
21. Lee, Y., Park, S.: A study of convex/concave edges and edge-enhancing operators based on the Laplacian. IEEE Trans. Circ. Syst. **37**(7), 940–946 (1990)
22. Deng, G.: A generalized unsharp masking algorithm. IEEE Trans. Image Process. **20**(5), 1249–1261 (2011)

Computer Animation Systems and Virtual Reality Based Applications

Prototype of Intelligent Data Management System for Computer Animation (iMCA)

Hui Liang[1], Fenglong Wu[1], Jian Chang[2], and Meili Wang[3(✉)]

[1] Zhengzhou University of Light Industry, Zhengzhou, China
[2] Bournemouth University, Poole, UK
[3] Northwest Agricultural and Forestry University, Xianyang, China
wml@nwsuaf.edu.cn

Abstract. In recent years, one of the most noticeable issues of current animation production is the challenge from the exponential growth of animation data known as an increasingly data-intensive process. There are obvious gaps between the animation production needs and research development, which call for novel design and new technology to tackle the emerging challenge of handling huge amounts of data. "iMCA" is designed to develop intelligent data management solution with the capability to handle massive and hyper type animation asset and analyze/summarize information for reuse of data to facilitate human creativity providing innovative interaction to allow the manipulation of massive animation data.

Keywords: Prototype · Intelligent data management · Animation data asset

1 Introduction

Computer animation has been booming and prospering for decades. Now, computer animation production is an increasingly data intensive process. One of the significant changes faced by animation industry is the evolution of computer animation data [1]. The animation data management strategy of an animation company revolves around the creation, presentation, storage, retrieval and reuse of its valuable animation data assets, which is playing an important role in CG production and video game industry. The demands for modern technologies to boost the data processing are urgent.

However, even though advanced theories, methods, and tools help a lot for managing animation data, the process of animation asset to be maintained, retrieved and reused is still a tedious work and can also be labor-intensive. Its inherent features of complexity throw out challenges to current animation producers: how can we develop intelligent solutions with the capability to handle huge amounts of data and analyze/summarize information to facilitate human creativity?

Targeting this "hot issue" to current animation practitioners and researchers, a prototype of intelligent animation data management (iMCA) is proposed in this paper for the purpose of facilitating the storage, organization, retrieval, utilization and reuse of digital animation data assets. Semantic and ontological analysis is leveraged to understand and describe the complexity of animation data. Domain-specific ontology and an ontology-based animation data retrieval system is developed in the context of

J. Chang et al. (Eds.): AniNex 2017, LNCS 10582, pp. 189–206, 2017.
https://doi.org/10.1007/978-3-319-69487-0_14

Chinese traditional shadow play art, which is used as a usage example to provide guidance in semantic animation data representation and retrieval. To provide seamless and scalable access to distributed resources of this data system, mobile app is designed to link the mobile clients to distributed servers, which allows access to animation data to remove the geographical constraints.

The rest of the paper is structured in four parts: Sect. 2 briefly reviews the related research works. Section 3 proposes a semantic model using ontological method to describe animation data asset. Section 4 presents the prototype of intelligent data management solution "iMCA" and Sect. 5 concludes this paper.

2 Related Work

Given the booming of the global computer animation industry in decades, more challenges arise in the extant animation production, especially the way we manage the data. There is no doubt that the animation industry is currently experiencing an accelerating increase of the constant and speedy generation of hybrid animation data. According to Desai's study, the animation data generated during the last few years has exceeded the total of the past [2]. Also, the animation data exists at almost all stages of the animation production in a wide variety of forms - text files, audio files, video files, texture files, graphic files, 3D model files, motion files, scene files, and many other types. And furthermore, within each of these types, the animation file may even be in different format. Taking the 3D model of a cartoon character for example, the 3D model file could be the format of *.ma or *.mb for MAYA, or *.max for 3DMax. The digital assets are expected to be stored and indexed in a fashion to be easily maintained, retrieved and reused.

A number of applications attempt to address some of the challenges of managing the animation data for the purpose of promoting animation production. Shotgun [3], Alienbrain [4] and TACTIC [5] are used by professional companies, which facilitates the monitoring of the pipeline and the management of data asset. However, the ability of current solutions is less than satisfactory: Alienbrain is similar to a kind of file storing and sharing system which lacks the functions of efficient information extracting and data reusing. Shotgun and TACTIC are commercial CG production toolsets, which mainly focus on production tracking rather than intelligent data managing.

To promote the reusability and accessibility of vast animation assets, text-based data retrieval is commonly used in current animation data management, which indexes the metadata such as keywords and tags associated with the annotated animation files [6]. However, the input of keywords or metadata can be labor-intensive and time consuming, and even the entered information may not describe the desired animation data properly, which is still a grand challenging and interesting problem in the field of multimedia information retrieval [7]. Contrastively, the content-based retrieval facilitates the searching of the animation data in a higher efficient and more user-friendly way, which analyzes and matches the content of the animation files rather than the metadata, e.g., the colors, contour profile, textures, or any other content information derived from the animation files [8]. But, both the traditional text-based and the content-based media data retrieval only depend on similarity matching of the textual or physical information [9]. The internal semantic information of the animation data is ignored. If the text or matching content does not exist, the retrieval cannot be executed. It has been proved that the semantic gap between the low level description and the high level semantic interpretation of multimedia objects does exist in the field of data management [10].

In recent years, being able to reflect users' query intent and consider the semantic information, semantics and ontology have begun to be used to describe the semantics of animation assets and data retrieval, which could reduce the semantic gap between low-level features and high-level semantics to achieve a better retrieval and to promote reusability [11].

Originated in philosophy, the term of ontology is an explicit formal specification of conceptualization that is used as an effective tool to describe general concepts of entities, as well as their properties, relationships and constraints [12, 13]. Taking the advantage of the establishment of common vocabulary and semantic term interpretation, the concept of ontology entered information science as a formal system for representing domain knowledge and their related linguistic realizations required by different applications that cover various fields, from knowledge engineering to software engineering [14, 15].

By defining semantic concepts, inferring usage rules and combining the semantic concepts and relations, we can leverage semantic and ontological analysis to understand and describe the complexity of animation data assets. Previous research on semantic data representation and retrieval provides us appealing solutions to construct a systematic and standardized model to describe animation data assets at a highly abstract and semantic level. Researchers in the AIM@SHAPE Network of Excellence project firstly use the semantic approach to interpret multimedia object for the purpose of facilitating animation file retrieval and reuse [16]. 3D model Search Engine [17] and Google 3D Warehouse [18] are also well-known semantic search engines for providing 3D content accessing. Ontology for Media Resources [19] and the Core Ontology for Multimedia (COMM) [20] are two specified ontologies developed to describe media data (e.g., images, 3D models, audio and video files) based on the standard models for data interchange (e.g., RDF, RDFS and OWL).

The concept of semantic and ontology is also incorporated into the description of complex animation content, for example, the virtual environment and games. The concept of annotated environment is proposed by Thalmann et al., which is modeled by ontology description at a high semantic level including the environment structures, entities' behavior and domain knowledge [21]. Some studies, for example, NiMMiT (Notation for MultiModal interaction Techniques) [22] and SCM (Semantic Content Model) [23] mainly focuses on the high-level description of 3D scenes. There are also some ontological applications in the domain of augmented reality and computer games. In Ruminski's research, a contextual augmented reality environment is provided to describe the virtual world using three kinds of elements: the trackables, content objects and interface [24]. Ontology is also used to describe games characteristics, properties and design process, to set rules to represent game logics and to construct ontological framework to develop and employ game-based training etc. [25–27].

Ontology-based semantic animation data description and management acts as an appropriate way to represent structured animation asset knowledge bases and advances in bridging the semantic gap, which provides us suitable technique on the animation assets management to facilitate data storage, organization, retrieval, reuse and repurposing. We consider leveraging semantic and ontological analysis to model animation data in a systematic and standardized way and then develop prototype of intelligent data management solution with the capability to handle huge amounts of data and to analyze information for reuse of data to facilitate human creativity.

3 Semantic and Ontological Analysis of Animation Data

3.1 Semantic Model of Animation Assets

Targeting different animation topics and depending on the specific application fields, the contents of the generated digital assets also vary. During the process of animation production, the digital assets are arranged in data repositories, which are multimodal and include a variety of data types - audio, video, 2D image/textual, 3D models, motion files, scene files etc. From a semantic perspective, the repository could be abstracted and analyzed in a systematic and standard way. In this session, a semantic model is proposed first to describe the animation data assets to provide a clear understanding of animation data, which is abstracted and analyzed with several sub-layers.

As illustrated in Fig. 1, the semantic model could be decomposed into four layers in the context of 3D animation production: Geometry, Structure, Appearance and Logic, from the basic geometry shape as the start to the logic meaning in the end. Geometry layer is the presentation of basic graphic elements. 2D content consists of simple metadata, such as points, lines, text, which further contributes to 3D content. 3D content provides low-level description of single model's geometric information and physical features, such as spheres, cones and other simple separated 3D objects. Structure layer is the combination of separated objects. Within this layer, single objects are combined into a complex one, for example, a table, which could be decomposed into simple objects, such as boxes etc. And the compounded object could also be integrated into other complex object to form a more complex model or as a part of a virtual scene. Appearance layer targets the appearance information including lighting, texture, color and transparency etc., which transforms the art design into working reality. Logic layer describes the contents' functions and properties from the aspect of logic, including the story plot, culture background and personality etc.

Figure 2 presents a usage example of the proposed semantic model, which describes the 3D model of a famous character - "Qin Shi Huang" in Chinese shadow play, who is the king of Qin Dynasty and China's first emperor. Mapped to the Geometry layer in the semantic model, the shape of the character is a composition of basic description of graphic elements, which provides low-level description of single model's geometric information and physical features, such as spheres, cones and other simple separated 3D objects. In the context of traditional Chinese shadow play,

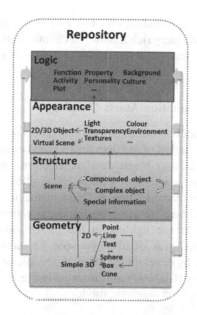

Fig. 1. Semantic model to describe the animation data assets

Chinese shadow puppet is mainly made of donkey's hide. A shadow puppet consists of several parts and its joints are connected by threads. When playing, puppeteers use their hands to manipulate the movement of the character through sticks attached on the different parts of the puppet. These different parts of the puppet are mapped to the Structure layer. Added with the appearance information mapped to the Appearance layer, such as color, pattern or accessories, a complete shadow play character is created.

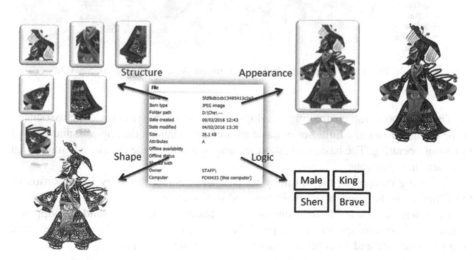

Fig. 2. Usage example of semantic model-"Qin Shi Huang", the king of Qin Dynasty in China

Further, provided with the information about story plot, culture background and personality, this character could carry rich traditional culture contents - the Logic layer. As a higher level of expressiveness, it represents a most famous Emperor in Chinese history.

3.2   Chinese Shadow Animation Assets Ontology

The proposed semantic model describes the animation data from the abstract high level, which guides the implementation of the domain specified ontology further. As a usage example, we used this ontology-based data management method in animating the performance of a Chinese traditional shadow play titled "The Emperor and the Assassin": a brave fighter named "Jing Ke" attempted to assassinate the king of Kingdom Qin -"Qin Shi Huang" to avert the imminent conquest of his home country by Kingdom Qin. After intense fighting in the palace, however, the assassination attempt failed, and "Jing Ke" was killed on the spot. The animation data asset used in this animation is presented by developing a domain-specific ontology: Chinese Shadow Animation Assets Ontology (CSAAO) as illustrated in Fig. 3, which is the ontological implementation of the proposed semantic model.

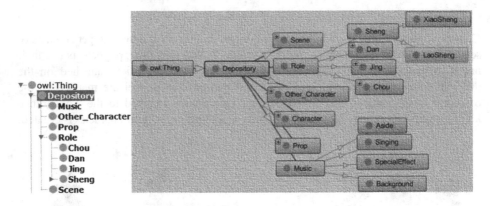

Fig. 3. Diagram of Chinese Shadow Animation Assets Ontology (CSAAO)

The main point in constructing ontology is to define a basis knowledge associated to the applied domain, a finite set of basic elementary relations description, and a set of functions operating. The basic variables then are used to label the type of an entity or an argument in a predicate.

Following composing the ontology basis is to construct ontology for a portion of the Chinese shadow play art domain covered in CSAAO:

R. Roles, defines the human characters of traditional Chinese shadow puppetry, which falls into four specific sub-types: *Sheng* (main male role), *Dan* (female role), *Jing* (painted-face and forceful male role), *Chou* (clown male role).

M. Music, defines melodies played by the accompaniment, which have standard melodies to indicate different art atmosphere. For instance, *manban* represents a slow tempo, *yuanban* represents standard or medium-fast tempo etc.

P. Props. On stage, characters interact with different objects to serve different purposes. For example, a piece of dark cloth is hung up to indicate a city wall.

S. Scene. Normally, a full-length shadow play consists with several key scenes. Each scene is a unit of action and follows the pattern of emotional progression. In a major scene, the beginning and end are often marked by a change of characters onstage or changing the stage set.

For instance, let us have the following predicates:

has_Prop_of (Roles: R, Props: P)
has_Music_of (Roles: R, Music: M)
has_Role_of (Scene: S, Roles: R)

Note that predicates **has_Prop_of, has_Music_of and has_Role_of** keep explicit polymorphism with respect to Roles. Using these predicates we are able to code, for instance, the information from the text "retrieval the props and music data asset used in the scene of the 'The Emperor and the Assassin'" as:

solution *search* **has_Role_of** (Scene: S, Roles: R)
-> **has_Music_of** (Roles: R, Music: M)
and
-> **has_Prop_of** (Roles: R, Props: P)

If we set S = "*The Emperor and the Assassin*", then all the roles involved in this scene are returned according to the predicates of **has_Role_of**, and after that, all the props and music related with the retrieved roles are searched by referring the predicates of **has_Music_of** and **has_Prop_of.**

We also propose data properties which provide attribute descriptions for classes in the CSAAO. Taking the class of **Role** for example, the data properties of a character include "name", "age", "rank" and "personality" etc. Figure 4 shows a usage example of the **Role** class defined in the ontology.

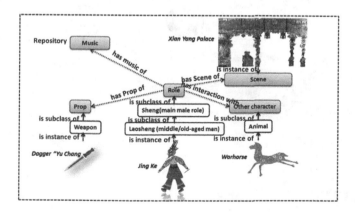

Fig. 4. Usage example of CSAAO-"*Jing Ke*"

4 Prototype of Intelligent Animation Data Management Solution "IMCA"

A prototype of intelligent animation data management system is built upon a central repository developed on the base of the proposed ontology CSAAO that facilitates the storage, organization, retrieval, utilization and reuse of animation assets. The system architecture is shown in Fig. 5.

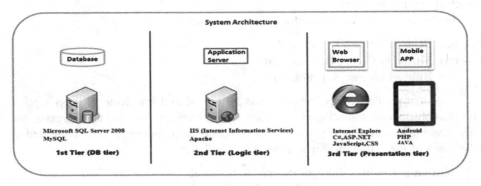

Fig. 5. System architecture of "iMCA"

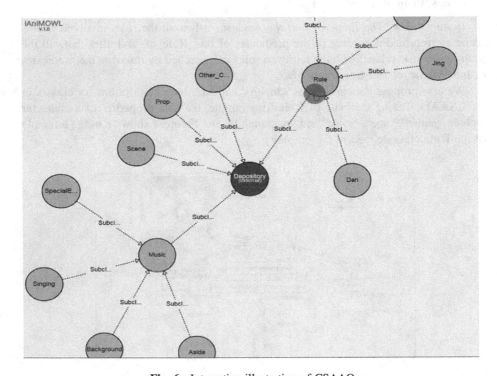

Fig. 6. Interactive illustration of CSAAO

4.1 Ontology-Based Animation Assets Retrieval

As shown in Fig. 6, we developed a visualization tool to demonstrate the concept of proposed ontology CSAAO, which leverages ontology to construct a systematic and standardized model to describe at a highly abstract and semantic level to provide a full view and understanding of the complex domain knowledge. Using structured terminology, ontological analysis could capture the core logic of complex system with natural language descriptions. This tool provides researchers with user-friendly and dynamic interaction: each colored circle encloses a subclass that fall under its superclass; users can click on any of the circles to zoom in or drag and drop them for interaction and check the entities' properties, relationships and constraints between them.

The ontology based "smart" digital assets management prototype provides seamless and scalable access to distributed animation resources. Animation data set interpret/display the information in a user-friendly manner. Assets Repository is a mixed-type animation database involving domain specified knowledge of traditional Chinese shadow play art using domain-specific information extraction, inference and rules to exploit the semantic metadata. This repository supports ontology-based retrieval, which improves searching performance by recognizing the animator's intent and contextual meaning of the digital assets in the context of Chinese traditional shadow play.

Through this ontology-based retrieval system which maps artist's intention on the data stored in the digital assets ontology, we can handle domain related query and provide more reasonable and relevant feedback to meet the artist's needs and to facilitate data reuse (Fig. 7).

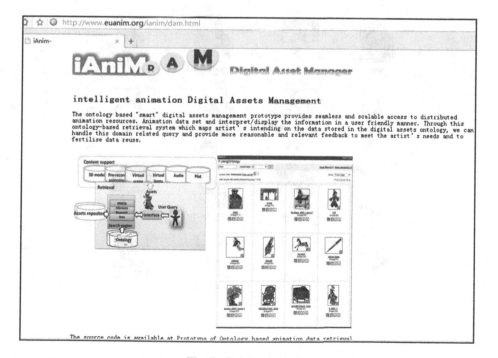

Fig. 7. Retrieval system

As illustrated in Fig. 8(a), when inputting the name of the character "Jing Ke", using traditional keywords matching, only the asset of character "Jing Ke" was retrieved. However, the best possibility is that there is still other animation asset may exist relating to "Jing Ke", such as his personalized weapon and his warhorse etc. This kind of asset is expected to provide more reasonable and relevant feedback to animators

(a)

(b)

Fig. 8. Interface of ontology based retrieval system

using ontological reasoning and referring through SPARQL queries. The result of ontological retrieval in Fig. 8(b) shows that not only the digital character "Jing Ke" is retrieved, but also other assets related to the searching target are also retrieved from the knowledge base.

The following SPARQL Query Language is used as inputs: *"SELECT ?property ? object WHERE {base: Jing_Ke? property ?object}"*.

The query will return a result that contains the set of all properties and objects that is related to the character *"Jing Ke"*.

Pseudocode of using a Java framework for building Semantic Web - Jena API [46] for querying from database is described as in Table 1 below:

Table 1. Pseudocode for querying from database

```
// create a connection to animation asset database
DBConnection conn=new DBConnection(URL,  USER,  PASSWORD);

//use connection to construct model (MODEL_NAME) in the database:
ModelRDB m = ModelRDB.open(conn, MODEL_NAME);

//create shadow puppet assets ontology model spOntology
OntModel spOntology = ModelFactory.createOntologyModel();

//create OWLReasoner, and bind with spOntology
Reasoner owlReasoner=ReasonerRegistry.getOWLReasoner();
Reasoner spReasoner=owlReasoner.bindSchema(spOntology);

//create inferring model
IModel iModel=ModelFactory. createIModel(spReasoner, imodel);

//When Query is ready; it will be passed to QueryEngine to execute querying

String queryStr="...";
Query q=new Query(queryStr);
q.setSource(iModel);
QueryExc qexec=new QueryExc (q);
QueryRs=qexec.exc();
```

4.2   Mobile App

Taking the advantage of the more economical and accessible technology tools, digital media production has evolved to be a highly collaborative activity that involves teams of people working with digital resources in different locations. The concept of collaborative production can be seen through the four core ideas: Opening, Peering, Sharing and Acting globally.

For the purpose of exchanging information and knowledge among animation studios and collaborators, a novel mobile app is developed which allows a great dynamism in the creative process and speeds up production. The mobile App makes it simple to search, browse, and view media cross all projects from one place in the cloud – then share them with anyone on the project, anywhere in the world.

App lets the artist access, review, and gives feedback on all the versions (media) they track in the shadow play animation asset, which provides artists with the following functions:

- Browse media, play back animation clips, movies and playlists in all the animation projects, whether at desktop or on-the-go. As long as having an internet connection, users can review from anywhere on the mobile device. App makes review easy. Screenshots of the data asset list and reviewing 3D model are shown in Figs. 9 and 10.

Fig. 9. Screen shot of the asset list

- Give feedback with comments, annotated frames, or camera images, add comments and draw right on top of media to pinpoint exactly where to find feedbacks. Artists receive a note with the annotated images detailing exactly what to do. Screen shots of providing annotation are illustrated in Fig. 11.

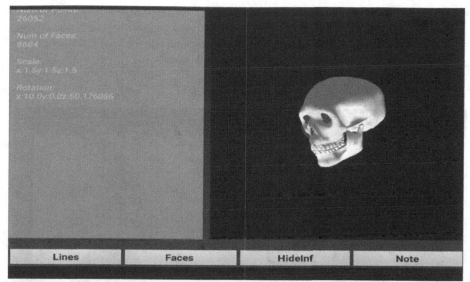

(a) Check detail by rotating and scaling

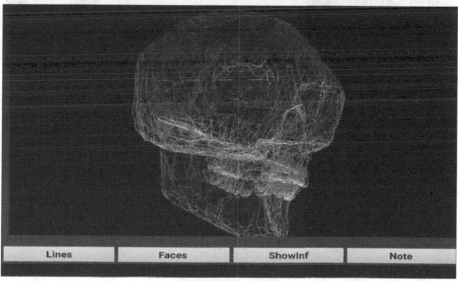

(b) Review wireframe model

Fig. 10. Screen shot of reviewing asset

- See history on related versions and their notes. Every note and annotation is tied to the central repository as shown in Fig. 12. Feedback and creative direction coming out of a review session is stored in one place and all the involved people are notified, so everyone is on the same page at all times.

(a)   Give cartoon design feedback

Fig. 11. Screen shots of providing annotation for hyper type animation data

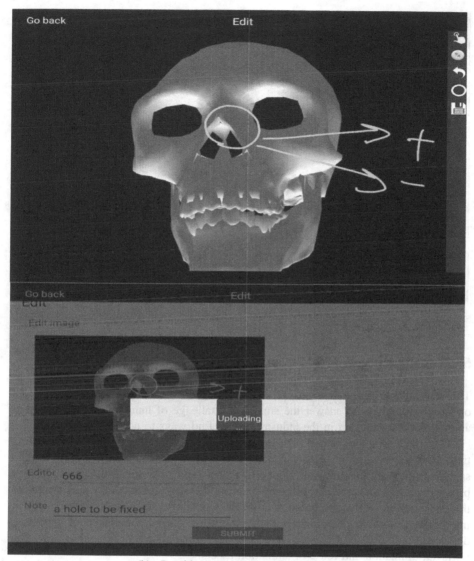

(b) Provide comments on 3D modeling

Fig. 11. (*continued*)

We built this App in Java for Android, which has been successfully tested and ran on Samsung Galaxy S2 tablet. We visited leading visual effects company Double Negative [28] and Picasso Pictures (one of London's top animation studios [29]) to conduct a questionnaire survey of industry experts. They provided positive feedback after preliminary trial.

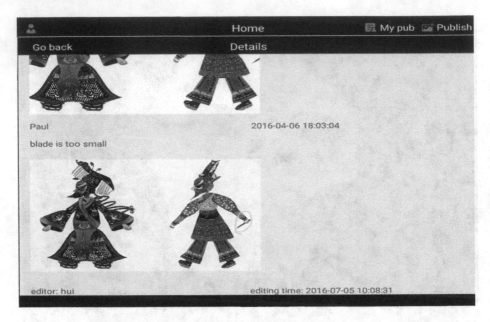

Fig. 12. List of related asset versions and their notes

5   Conclusion

The stage of our research is still proof-of-concept. We attempt to use semantic and oncological analysis to answer the emerging challenge of handling huge amounts of animation data produced in the industry and to find ways to address them.

Constructed on an abstract high-level, the semantic model is proposed for animation asset to provide a systematic and standardized semantic description. Domain specified ontology has been developed in the context of traditional Chinese shadow puppetry play as the implementation of the proposed semantic model, which formalizes the construction of the animation data assets repository. And finally, a prototype of intelligent animation data management system is built upon a central repository developed on the base of the proposed ontology to facilitate the storage, organization, retrieval, utilization and reuse of animation assets.

Our main goal is to utilize semantic/ontology concept to improve the reusability, extensibility of the animation data assets and facilitate collaborative production. We hope this appealing semantic method may provide guidance for other researchers to define various domain specified ontologies and construct animation asset repositories depending on the context and application.

At the next step, the usability of the system will be examined carefully in our test. Animation artists and designers from the industry will be invited to participate. The evaluation of the semantic retrieval system will be also carried out to illustrate the benefit of this data management approach.

Acknowledgment. The research leading to these results has been partially supported by the People Programme (Marie Curie Actions) of the European Union's Seventh Framework Programme FP7/2007-2013/under REA grant agreement n° [612627].

References

1. Liang, H., Sit, J., Chang, J., Zhang, J.J.: Computer animation data management: Review of evolution phases and emerging issues. Int. J. Inform. Manage. **36**(6), 1089–1100 (2016)
2. Desai, B.C.: The state of data. In: Proceedings of the 18th International Database Engineering & Applications Symposium, IDEAS 2014, pp. 77–86 (2014)
3. Shotgunsoftware Homepage. http://www.shotgunsoftware.com. Accessed 21 May 2017
4. Alienbrain Homepage. http://www.alienbrain.com. Accessed 21 May 2017
5. Tactic Homepage. http://www.tactic.net. Accessed 21 May 2017
6. Fisher, M., Hanrahan, P.: Context-based search for 3D models. ACM Trans. Graph. (TOG) **29**(6), 182 (2010)
7. Mei, T., Rui, Y., Li, S., Tian, Q.: Multimedia search reranking: a literature survey. ACM Comput. Surv. (CSUR) **46**(3), 38 (2014)
8. Eitz, M., Richter, R., Boubekeur, T., Hildebrand, K., Alexa, M.: Sketch-based shape retrieval. ACM Trans. Graph. **31**(4), 1–10 (2012)
9. Tangelder, J.W.H., Veltkamp, R.C.: A survey of content based 3d shape retrieval methods. Multimedia Tools Appl. **39**(3), 441 (2008)
10. Li, Z., Ramani, K.: Ontology-based design information extraction and retrieval. Artif. Intell. Eng. Des. Anal. Manuf. **21**(2), 137–154 (2007)
11. Kassimi, M.A., Elbeqqali, O.: Semantic based 3D model retrieval. In: International Conference on Multimedia Computing and Systems, pp. 195–199. IEEE (2012)
12. Gruber, T.R.: A translation approach to portable ontology specifications. Knowl. Acquisition **5**(2), 199–220 (1993)
13. Grüninger, M., Fox, M.S.: Methodology for the Design and Evaluation of Ontologies (1995)
14. Borst, W.N.: Construction of engineering ontologies for knowledge sharing and reuse, Universiteit Twente (1997)
15. Studer, R., Benjamins, V.R., Fensel, D.: Knowledge engineering: principles and methods. Data Knowl. Eng. **25**(1), 161–197 (1998)
16. Falcidieno, B.: Aim@ shape project presentation. In: Proceedings of the Shape Modeling Applications, p. 329. IEEE (2004)
17. Funkhouser, T., Min, P., Kazhdan, M., Chen, J., Halderman, A., Dobkin, D.: A search engine for 3D models. ACM Trans. Graph. (TOG) **22**(1), 83–105 (2003)
18. Google 3D Warehouse. https://3dwarehouse.sketchup.com
19. Ontology for Media Resources 1.0. http://www.w3.org/TR/mediaont-10
20. Arndt, R., Troncy, R., Staab, S., Hardman, L.: Comm: a core ontology for multimediaannotation. In: Staab, S., Studer, R. (eds.) Handbook on Ontologies, pp. 403–421. Springer, Heidelberg (2009)
21. Thalmann, D., Farenc, N., Boulic, R.: Virtual human life simulation and database: why and how. In: Proceedings of the 1999 International Symposium on Database Applications in Non-Traditional Environments (DANTE 1999), pp. 471–479. IEEE (1999)
22. De Boeck, J., Raymaekers, C., Coninx, K.: Comparing NiMMiT and data-driven notations for describing multimodal interaction. In: Coninx, K., Luyten, K., Schneider, Kevin A. (eds.) TAMODIA 2006. LNCS, vol. 4385, pp. 217–229. Springer, Heidelberg (2007). doi:10.1007/978-3-540-70816-2_16

23. Flotyński, J., Walczak, K.: Conceptual semantic representation of 3D content. In: Abramowicz, W. (ed.) BIS 2013. LNBIP, vol. 160, pp. 244–257. Springer, Heidelberg (2013). doi:10.1007/978-3-642-41687-3_23
24. Ruminski, D., Walczak, K.: Semantic contextual augmented reality environments. In: 2014 IEEE International Symposium on Mixed and Augmented Reality (ISMAR), pp. 401–404. IEEE (2014)
25. Teixeira, J.S.F., Sá, E.D.J.V., Fernandes, C.T.: A taxonomy of educational games compatible with the LOM-IEEE data model. In: Proceedings of Interdisciplinary Studies in Computer Science SCIENTIA, pp. 44–59 (2008)
26. Dubin, D., Jett, J.: An ontological framework for describing games. In: Proceedings of the 15th ACM/IEEE-CE on Joint Conference on Digital Libraries, pp. 165–168. ACM (2015)
27. BinSubaih, A., Maddock, S., Romano, D.: Game logic portability. In: Proceedings of the 2005 ACM SIGCHI International Conference on Advances in Computer Entertainment Technology, pp. 458–461. ACM (2005)
28. Double Negative Homepage. http://www.dneg.com/. Accessed 21 May 2017
29. Picasso Pictures Homepage. http://www.picassopictures.com. Accessed 21 May 2017

A VR-Based Crane Training System for Railway Accident Rescues

Jianxi Xu[1], Zhao Tang[1(✉)], Xihui Wei[1], Yinyu Nie[2], Xiaolin Yuan[1],
Zong Ma[1], and Jian J. Zhang[1,2]

[1] State Key Laboratory of Traction Power, Southwest Jiaotong University, Chengdu, China
tangzhao@swjtu.edu.cn
[2] National Centre for Computer Animation, Bournemouth University, Poole, UK

Abstract. The railway crane is frequently used in railway accident rescues. However, it is generally impractical to train crane operators widely in real accident sites considering the costs and human safety. A VR-based crane training system for railway accident rescues is proposed in this paper. The training system reconstructs the railway accident scenes by integrating geographical environments, head-on collision scenarios between two high-speed trains and the railway crane kinematics models. Crane operators can interact with the virtual accident environment through some VR devices and gain the valuable experience of railway accident rescues. Results of a field test show that the VR-based crane training system for railway accident rescues can provide a safe, low-cost, efficient and user-friendly platform for crane operators.

Keywords: Railway crane · Training system · Accident rescue · Head-on collision · VR devices

1 Introduction

When a railway accident occurs, rescuers must deal with the accident efficiently to restore the railway traffic to mostly minimize the economic loss. As a railway accident rescue equipment, the railway crane plays a significant role in quickly handling railway traffic accidents to avoid further destruction. And the proficiency of railway crane operators is crucial to the rescue efficiency, so enhancing the proficiency of operators is significant and urgent. Training operators in actual accidents is the best way to improve their rescue ability. However, considering the economic costs and the potential security risks, it is not practical for trainees to experience the real railway accidents.

Virtual reality training uses VR technology to generate the virtual environment for trainees to practice and improve their skills. With the help of VR, a large number of trainees can be trained within a virtual environment without spending vast amounts of money. On the contrary, the traditional approaches have many limitations. For example, it has to train one person at a time on a particular piece of equipment, which is often costly and time-consuming. Hence, VR training is now used in many industries like education [1–3], medicine [4, 5], architecture [6, 7] and the military practice [8, 9]. Benefitting from the VR technology, trainees can immerse themselves in the virtual scenes. They can interact with the virtual environment and conduct training. The VR

© Springer International Publishing AG 2017
J. Chang et al. (Eds.): AniNex 2017, LNCS 10582, pp. 207–219, 2017.
https://doi.org/10.1007/978-3-319-69487-0_15

technology has also been applied in the crane training. Dong et al. [10] have developed a virtual bridge crane in order to train and test the skills of operators safely and efficiently. Lin et al. [11] have constructed a VR simulation based on Multigen-Vega, and the railway crane model is established to help operators to control movement states of cranes. A kind of interactive truck crane simulation platform based on the VR technology is developed by Sang et al. [12], which can complete the simulation experiment of the crane's movement. Wang et al. [13] have studied on some key technologies of VR application on the tower crane operating simulation system.

A VR-based crane training system for railway accident rescues is developed in this paper, which provides a safe, low-cost and efficient virtual training platform for crane operators. In this training system, we reconstruct the accident scenes using Unity. The train crash simulation performed by the built-in PhysX engine can provide different railway accident scenes for crane operators. Several VR devices, including two wireless controllers, one HMD, two lighthouse base stations, are utilized to interact with the virtual environment. With these devices, crane operators can enter the virtual training scenes, evaluate the situation of the railway accident, and conduct the rescue training.

2   System Architecture

As shown in Fig. 1, the developed VR-based crane training system consists of the software system and the hardware system. In this VR training system, most VR simulations, such as collision detection, railway crane simulation, and the head-on collision between

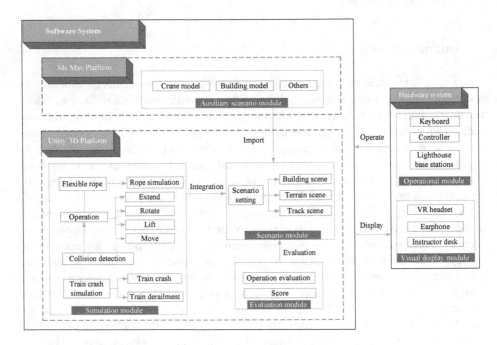

Fig. 1. System architecture

two high speed trains, are implemented in Unity. Unity is a professional game engine which supports Android, iOS and VR platform. It can also provide the high-level functions of controlling and interacting with real-time simulations, so the Unity is selected as a platform to build our system. Most of 3D models in the system, which are created by 3ds Max, are imported into Unity directly.

The software system is composed of four modules: simulation module, scenario module, model module and evaluation module. The software system is utilized to generate a variety of virtual railway accident scenes, which include buildings, rivers, trees, terrains, etc. The virtual scenes can be changed in order to meet needs of users at any time. The hardware system is composed of the operation module and the visual display module. The hardware system is used to provide a better sense of immersion for operators, then to make the training process as similar as a real railway crane process. The detailed description of the six modules is given in the following section.

2.1 Scenario Module

The virtual environment generation is the first step to develop the VR-based crane training system. The virtual environment construction is simplified as the following steps:

1. The number of the patches of 3D models should be simplified as few as possible
2. The pixel number of the texture is processed into even number, and the texture data of 3D models is compressed.
3. Complex 3D models consist of thousands of components. The hierarchical model method is developed to reduce the time cost of each multiplication in the process of frame rendering, and speed up the rendering to improve the ability of real-time response.

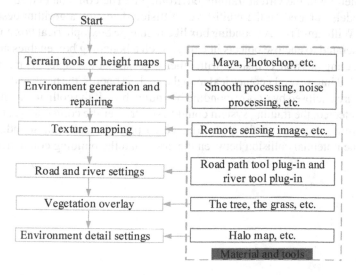

Fig. 2. Virtual environment construction method based on Unity

The virtual scene that we construct includes the 3D models and the virtual environment. We use the 3ds Max modeling software to build the 3D model of railway cranes, buildings and other objects. The virtual environment includes the visualization of the real terrain, which is the prerequisite for building VR-based training system. The process of the virtual scene is shown in Fig. 2 and the whole final virtual scene is shown in Fig. 3.

Fig. 3. Virtual railway accident scene

2.2 Simulation Module

Collision Detection. In the railway accident rescues, the boom and the rotating platform is possible to collide with the lifting load. The existence of catenary could also lead to the collision. The collision during the rescue operation could reduce rescue efficiency and even lead to casualties. Hence collision detection is proposed to efficiently detect the potential spatial conflicts between the crane and the obstacles, accident vehicles and catenary in the virtual training environment. The collision detection between two 3D models is based on the multi-level collision detection algorithm described by Moore and Wilhelms [14]. A bounding box like rectangle box, spherical box and capsule box are generated to enclose objects in Unity. Such a bounding box enables an efficient test for detecting possible collisions with other objects. For example, the railway crane can be divided into several geometrical models, such as booms, the hook and outriggers, etc., which are enclosed by a corresponding bounding box. If the collision in the training system is detected, the training system could firstly trigger the collision event, and then send a warning message to the audio device to play the collision sound. Figure 4 describes the potential collision between the crane and the building components.

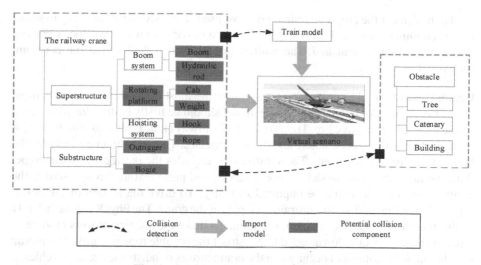

Fig. 4. Collision detection between objects

Trains Crash Simulation. To enable crane operators to experience the real railway accident scenes, it is important to retrieve the position of accident vehicles after collisions between two high speed trains. It is easy to perform the head-on collision between two high-speed trains in Unity platform. Developers can use the built-in PhysX engine to realistically simulate the rigid body collision, vehicle travelling, gravity and other physic kinematics. In Unity, rigid body components allow the object to move under the control of the physical system. To perform the train crash, a 3D kinematic model of single-car should be firstly built in Unity. A high-speed train is composed of multiple rigid bodies and connections. The Unity provides four basic constraint joints for developers, including fixed joint, configurable joint, hinge joint and spring joint. The relative motion between two rigid bodies, like the bogie and car body, are connected by the constraint joints.

Fig. 5. Crash between two high-speed trains

To implement the proposed train model, we use the PhysX engine in Unity to simulate its continuous motion [15]. The process that a moving train at any velocity crashes into a static train is simulated. The positions of accident vehicles after the crash are shown in Fig. 5.

Crane simulation. The railway crane is one of the most important rescue equipment in railway recues. A reasonable 3D crane model should be firstly built in 3ds Max based on the practical crane structure. The 3D model of railway crane is divided into two major parts, including the superstructure and the substructure. The superstructure includes the boom, the rope, the hook, etc. The substructure includes the outrigger and the bogie. After building the crane model, it should render and paste texture through setting the entity color. Then it should be imported in Unity. To drive the motion of the crane, physical joints are utilized to constrain each part of the crane. The PhysX engine in Unity is also used to simulate its continuous motion. To make the hoisting process more realistic, the rope plug-in is downloaded to construct the flexible rope in Unity. The inertia oscillation of the cable will occur when the crane moves or hoists the accident vehicles.

2.3   Evaluation Module

The evaluation module is developed to evaluate the performance of the crane operators. There are two operation contents for the crane operators in the evaluation process.

Firstly, the operators should lift the accident vehicles from the original location to the target location. Generally, the railway accident rescue is about placing the derailed accident vehicle on or outside the track by the railway crane, as shown in Fig. 6. When the railway accident occurs, operators are asked to arrive at the accident site, and put down the hook on the center of the vehicles to avoid vehicles vibration during the hoisting process, then place accident vehicles at the target location. Scores will be deducted if accident vehicles deviate from the target location or the hook deviates from the center of the vehicles.

Secondly, to increase the difficulty of training, the cable is designed to be flexible. The inertia oscillation of the cable will occur when the boom moves, and further lead to the hoisting load vibration. It is difficult to control the orientation of the load and may interfere with the building components. The score will be deducted if the collision happens.

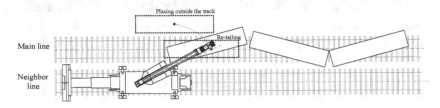

Fig. 6. Crane operation scene (top view)

3   VR Devices

The HTC Vive [16] launched by HTC Co. and Valve Co is utilized to provide users with immersive experience by the following effective human interaction devices, a head mounted display (HMD), two wireless controllers and two lighthouse base stations. It has more than 70 sensors, including MEMS gyroscopes, acceleration sensors and so on, and the refresh rate of screen could reach 90 Hz. The details of the three parts described above are given in the following section.

3.1   Wireless Controller

The wireless controller is a plastic handle with some buttons, tracking sensors and an open loop on top of each one, and it is an important part of the I/O device for the crane training system (see Fig. 7). There are just two separated wireless interactive controllers in the system. One of the two controllers controls the movement of the railway crane. There are some buttons and indicator lights programed to control lift process, including extending the crane boom, lifting the hook, steering the wheel, rotating the platform and braking, etc. In addition, there are a menu button and a system button on this controller, which are designed to provide the virtual interface for the crane operators to choose the suitable crane and auxiliary tools (like the support beam, re-railing device, etc.). Operators can also change views when they are operating through pushing the button for camera switch.

The other controller is mainly used to interact with the railway accident scenes. The larger circular button enables operators to navigate in the virtual world. Operators can reach any place where they want to go in the VR environment. There are various accident scenarios that are designed for operators to conduct the rescue training. According to

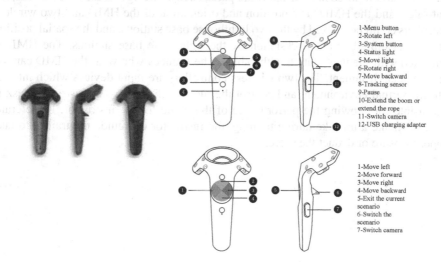

1-Menu button
2-Rotate left
3-System button
4-Status light
5-Move light
6-Rotate right
7-Move backward
8-Tracking sensor
9-Pause
10-Extend the boom or extend the rope
11-Switch camera
12-USB charging adapter

1-Move left
2-Move forward
3-Move right
4-Move backward
5-Exit the current scenario
6-Switch the scenario
7-Switch camera

Fig. 7. Interaction controllers

the different requirements of operators, the training system could switch scenarios via pushing the button for scenario switch.

3.2 HMD

The head mounted display (HMD) is a window to the VR environment. As the name implies, it is worn on the head, and it ensures that no matter which direction the user's head may turn to, the display is positioned right in front of the user's eyes. It allows users to have a 360° view of the virtual environment. Earphone is included as an accessory of HMD in order that users can receive the warning message from the system.

3.3 Spatial Tracking System

The spatial tracking system is mainly used to track the position and orientation of operators. In this system, the HTC Vive lighthouse base stations are used to track sensors from the headset and controllers and determine the location of operators. Thus developers can achieve extremely high positioning accuracy in the 3D space. Users are able to relieve discomfort of the vertigo because they can move freely in the large VR environment.

3.4 System Hardware Configuration

Figure 8 shows that the developed VR-based crane training for railway rescue system consists of three parts including a workstation, an instructor desk and the VR equipment. The workstation is responsible for model rendering, performing the simulation of the high-speed crane and the railway crane, the collision detection warning and the performance analysis. It also transmits the 3D scenario to the HMD continuously. The VR equipment is composed of three hardware parts, such as the lighthouse base stations, the controllers and the HMD. The position and orientation of the HMD and two wireless controllers could be tracked by the two lighthouse base stations, and the spatial position data is transmitted to the workstation by the lighthouse base stations. The HMD is connected with the workstation with cables. The trainees who wear the HMD can see the virtual environment. The two wireless controllers are input devices which interact with the virtual environment and control the motion of cranes. The instructor desk is responsible for showing the performance of the crane for the instructor. If the crane operators make a mistake during training, the instructor can guide the trainee to take proper measure or deduct the score.

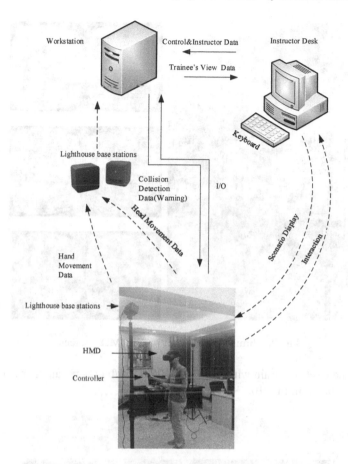

Fig. 8. Structure of VR-based crane training system

4   Application of the Training System

For the entire crane training, the crane drivers should put on the HMD and hold two wireless controllers with their hands. When operators push the system button on the controllers, the virtual environment is displayed on the HMD's screen, as shown in Fig. 9, and then operators can start the training. The instructor can supervise the crane operators' performance through the instructor desk. The training is performed step by step according to the actual work procedure.

Fig. 9. Virtual environment in the HMD's screen

Firstly, the case of a train with a speed of 27.5 km/h crashes another static train is simulated as shown in Fig. 10.

Fig. 10. Head-on crash between two high-speed trains

Secondly, when railway accident occurs, rescuers should arrive at the accident site as soon as possible and formulate rescue schemes. Figure 11 shows rescuers are ready for the railway accident rescues.

Fig. 11. The preparation for the accident rescue

Thirdly, for the head car of the train, it should be lifted outside the track timely. The railway crane should move close to the head car and put down the hook to the support beam. Figure 12(a) describes that the railway crane is ready to lift the head car from

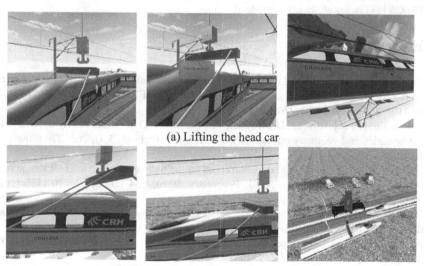

(a) Lifting the head car

(b) Placing the head car to the target location

Fig. 12. Railway accident rescue operation (Color figure online)

the track. When the head car crashes with other objects during the hoisting process, the warning message is sent to the headphone of the HMD, operators must adjust the angle of boom to avoid the collision. In Fig. 12(b), the crane operator must lift the head car to the target place outside the track. The yellow area represents the target place. Then the first round rescue training is completed. The operator can continuously choose the second derailed single-car to carry on the hoisting training.

5 Conclusions

This paper presents an immersive virtual system that is used to train railway crane operators. The system enables operators to have more field adaptability through interacting with the VR environment. The train crash is simulated by the built-in PhysX engine in Unity, which provides different railway accident scenes for crane operators. The combination of the immersive VR hardware and 3D graphic engine makes them experience the realistic railway accident scenes and finish the whole railway accident recues training safely without getting injured. Even though operators could not feel the movement sense of their bodies with the developed training system, the immersion provided by VR devices can significantly enhance the efficiency of the crane rescue training. The system is powerful and easy to operate. In future study, the training system will be further updated by taking the rescue schemes, the crane location, and the motion planning into account.

Acknowledgements. We would like to thank Shujie Deng for proofreading this manuscript. The financial support of the National Science Foundation of China (No. 51405402, NO. 51475394), the Independent Research Project of the State Key Laboratory of Traction Power (No. 2015TPL_T06), and the Fundamental Research Funds for the Central Universities (No. 2682016CX128) is gratefully acknowledged.

References

1. Jin, G., Nakayama, S.: Virtual reality game for safety education. In: International Conference on Audio, Language and Image Processing, pp. 95–100. IEEE Press, Shanghai (2014). doi: 10.1109/ICALIP.2014.7009764
2. Kaufmann, H., Schmalstieg, D., Wagner, M.: Construct3D: a virtual reality application for mathematics and geometry education. Educ. Inform. Technol. **5**(4), 263–276 (2000). doi: 10.1023/A:1012049406877
3. Yellowlees, P.M., Cook, J.N.: Education about hallucinations using an internet virtual reality system: a qualitative survey. Acad. Psychiatry **30**(6), 534 (2006). doi:10.1176/appi.ap. 30.6.534
4. Robb, R.: Virtual reality in medicine: a personal perspective. J. Vis. **5**(4), 317–326 (2002). doi:10.1007/BF03182346
5. Akay, M., Marsh, A.: Virtual reality in medicine and biology. Medicine **319**(12), 1–31 (2001). https://doi.org/10.1016/S0167-739X(98)00023-5

6. Reitmayr, G., Schmalstieg, D.: An open software architecture for virtual reality interaction. In: Proceedings of the ACM Symposium on Virtual Reality Software and Technology, pp. 47–54 (2001). doi:10.1145/505008.505018
7. Steinicke, F., Ropinski, T., Hinrichs, K.: A generic virtual reality software system's architecture and application. In: International Conference on Augmented Tele-Existence, pp. 220–227. ACM, New York (2005). doi:10.1145/1152399.1152440
8. Moshell, M.: Three views of virtual reality: virtual environments in the US military. Computer **26**(2), 81–82 (1993). doi:10.1109/2.192003
9. Lele, A.: Virtual reality and its military utility. J. Ambient Intell. Humaniz. Comput. **4**(1), 17–26 (2013). doi:10.1007/s12652-011-0052-4
10. Dong, H., Xu, G.: An expert system for bridge crane training system based on virtual reality. In: International Conference on Artificial Intelligence and Computational Intelligence, pp. 30–33. IEEE Press, Sanya (2010). doi:10.1109/AICI.2010.247
11. Lin, S., Li, T., Zhang, R.: Research on motion simulation of railway rescue crane based virtual reality technology. In: International Conference on Automatic Control and Artificial Intelligence, pp. 30–33. IEEE Press, Sanya (2012). doi:10.1049/cp.2012.1325
12. Sang, Y., Zhu, Y., Zhao, H., Tang, M.: Study on an interactive truck crane simulation platform based on virtual reality technology. Int. J. Distance Educ. Technol. **14**(2), 64–78 (2016). doi: 10.1109/CAR.2010.5456842
13. Wang, Y., Chen, D., Dong, H., Wang, B.: Research on operating simulation system for tower crane based on virtual reality. In: Zu, Q., Vargas-Vera, M., Hu, B. (eds.) ICPCA/SWS 2013. LNCS, vol. 8351, pp. 593–601. Springer, Cham (2014). doi:10.1007/978-3-319-09265-2_60
14. Moore, M., Wilhelms, J.: Collision detected and response for computer animation. In: Proceedings of the 15th Annual Conference on Computer Graphics, pp. 289–298. ACM, New York (1988). http://doi.acm.org/10.1145/378456.378528
15. Hung, W.H., Kang, S.C.: Configurable model for real-time crane erection visualization. Adv. Eng. Softw. **65**(11), 1–11 (2013). https://doi.org/10.1016/j.advengsoft.2013.04.013
16. Dempsey, P.: The teardown: HTC Vive VR headset. Eng. Technol. **11**(7), 80–81 (2016). doi: 10.1049/et.2016.0731

Virtual Reality Surgery Simulation: A Survey on Patient Specific Solution

Jinglu Zhang, Jian Chang, Xiaosong Yang, and Jian J. Zhang(✉)

National Centre for Computer Animation, Bournemouth University, Poole, UK
{zhangj,jchang,xyang,jzhang}@bournemouth.ac.uk

Abstract. For surgeons, the precise anatomy structure and its dynamics are important in the surgery interaction, which is critical for generating the immersive experience in VR based surgical training applications. Presently, a normal therapeutic scheme might not be able to be straightforwardly applied to a specific patient, because the diagnostic results are based on averages, which result in a rough solution. Patient Specific Modeling (PSM), using patient-specific medical image data (e.g. CT, MRI, or Ultrasound), could deliver a computational anatomical model. It provides the potential for surgeons to practice the operation procedures for a particular patient, which will improve the accuracy of diagnosis and treatment, thus enhance the prophetic ability of VR simulation framework and raise the patient care. This paper presents a general review based on existing literature of patient specific surgical simulation on data acquisition, medical image segmentation, computational mesh generation, and soft tissue real time simulation.

Keywords: Patient Specific Modeling · Surgery simulation · Virtual reality

1 Introduction

Approximately 200,000-injury or death cases come from preventable human medical errors in hospitals annually [15]. Undesirable effects caused by human technique errors during surgeries and the fast development of new approaches (such as minimally invasive surgery), which requires more complex technical proficiency, have significantly emphasized the importance of surgical skills training in a secure and reusable environment. With the rapid explosion of Virtual Reality (VR) technology, the VR based surgery simulator provides the solution of teaching and assessing training skills outside the operation room with high efficiency and low risks [11]. Examples of commercial high-fidelity VR simulators, including Neuro Touch, LapSim [16], and Lap Mentor [58], are inclusive training systems consisting of laparoscopic and endoscopic surgery, general surgery, and bariatric surgery.

Usually, a treatment might not be able to directly applied to a specific patient due to the fact that the diagnostic results are based on averages, which result in a

© Springer International Publishing AG 2017
J. Chang et al. (Eds.): AniNex 2017, LNCS 10582, pp. 220–233, 2017.
https://doi.org/10.1007/978-3-319-69487-0_16

rough solution [32,52]. PSM could handle medical image data (e.g. CT, MRI, or Ultrasound), geometry, and material properties by anatomically accurate means. It presents the potential for surgeons to practice the surgical procedure preoperatively using VR simulator with the precise anatomy structure and its dynamics for an individual patient [46]. This concept would improve the accuracy of diagnosis and treatment, enhance the predictability of VR based surgery simulation framework, and raise the patient care [4,40,44]. In recent years, several surgical systems in laparoscopic nephrectomy [38], wrist joint [18,19], hepatectomy and pancreatectomy [17] have combined the patient specific characteristics into the simulator.

However, it is still challenging for the state of the art algorithms in computer graphics and computer vision fields to bring patient specific modeling into standard clinical usage concerning too many manual steps involved from data acquisition, segmentation, 3D mesh generation to final surgery simulation [22,28,47]. The nonlinearity and complexity of their biomechanical models also cause extreme challenges to give haptic feedbacks in real-time. Automating existing manual steps in the workflow (such as soft-tissue segmentation, labelling, and geometric corrections), identifying the complicated patient-specific material properties, and creating a reusable and extendable pre-modeled prototype database are indispensable for the future clinical approval. A general patient-specific workflow is shown in Fig. 1. This survey focuses on comparing and discussing current progress in medical image segmentation, mesh generation, and soft tissue simulation.

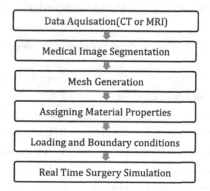

Fig. 1. General workflow of patient-specific modelling

2   Geometry and Material Properties Acquisition

Patient-specific modeling takes the advantage of personal geometry and material properties to generate the accurate computational mesh. There are primarily two techniques to obtain the necessary parameters for a tissue or an organ. The first way is directly extracting the information from 3D medical images, namely

Computed tomography (CT), Magnetic Resonance (MR), three-dimensional ultrasound (3D-US), positron emission tomography (PET) and rotational angiography (RA) scanners. These kinds of medical images could provide anatomical information represented as a 3D array of grey scale intensities in Digital Imaging and Communications in Medicine (DICOM) format [3]. Meshes are first generated from the image preprocessing and then assigned the material properties to create the computational model.

3D image segmentation could also be conducted in a top-down fashion by forming, training, and matching statistic models with shape and appearance variations. The approach of concentrating on landmark-based shape representation and variants of Active Shape [14] and Active Appearance [13] models are known as Statistic shape models (SSM) [26]. Comparing with the first method, SSM could prevent the risks correlated with CT scans [6], largely save the computational cost for the sake of fewer image preprocessing steps involved, and the final output model could be put into the pre-model database for the future application. However, studies in SSM field are still immature and need further validation, so this review mainly discusses the patient-specific modeling through the medical image processing.

Although there are different modalities of medical images, this review focuses on CT and MRI based methods considering they are the most widely accepted non-invasive radiographic techniques. Comparing with MRI, CT is well suited for bone injuries, cancer detection, and lung and chest diagnose. Whereas MRI could produce clearer differences between normal and abnormal tissues, it is more suitable for soft tissue evolution studies such as brain tumors and spinal cord injury. Table 1 compares the difference of characteristics between CT and MRI.

Table 1. Comparison between CT and MRI

Image types	Characteristics	Appropriate study areas
CT	1. Time and cost efficient	1. Bone injuries
	2. Painless	2. Cancer detection
	3. Shows up the acute bleed	3. Lung and chest diagnose
MRI	1. No radiation exposure	1. Brian tumors
	2. Good resolution	2. Ligament and tendon injuries
	3. Clearer differences between normal and abnormal tissues	3. Spinal cord injury

3   Segmentation

Segmentation, a process of dividing medical images into regions with similar properties such as color, texture, contrast, and gray level that specifically display different tissue structures, organs, or pathologies, is critical for 3D anatomical reconstruction in PSM pipeline [23]. Segmentation has been regarded as the most tedious step for the reason that human anatomical structures are naturally complicated and rarely own any linear features. Even the segmentation of bone, the tissue that is considered as physically and geometrically linear, faces obstacles like the similar intensity with adjacent soft tissues and different grey values for different bone regions [33]. While various algorithms have been proposed in recent years, to achieve complete, accurate, and efficient automatic segmentation is still a tough problem. Medical image segmentation algorithms could be roughly divided into three categories: edge based segmentation, region based segmentation, and clustering and classification based segmentation.

3.1 Edge Based Segmentation

Edge based segmentation generally applies the derivative operator to search and identify gradient fields in images. This conventional method separates the objects boundaries by locating sharp discontinuities in different color or gray level information. Prewitt [51] provides the first order derivative edge-detecting operator to approximate the magnitude and orientation of an image limited in the 3×3 district for eight directions. Second order derivative edge detective introduced by Marr and Hildreth in 1980 [39] who suggest applying Gaussian smoothing before Laplacian. Edge based segmentation methods are noise-sensitive. Sometimes the fake edge and weak edge could not be detected so that they always need to be combined with the region based segmentation algorithms.

3.2 Region Based Segmentation

Compared with the edge-based segmentation that segments images depending on sharp changes between edges, region-based segmentation partitions images into homogeneous regions according to predefined rules. They are rather simple and noise immune.

Region Growing. Starting with a seed region and the stop condition (gray level intensity, shape, color, texture or model), regions growing by appending pixels that share similar properties to the seed region, and finally, stop when no more pixel meets the predefined growing criteria [1].

Region Splitting and Merging. Region splitting and merging [29] the conjunction of splitting and merging algorithms. The former algorithm sets an initial region includes the whole image, then iteratively splits regions into sub-regions referring to similarity criteria, and stops when no more splitting is possible. Merging algorithm complies with a contrast rule with splitting techniques by repeatedly merging similar region with similarity criteria. Region-based approaches hugely rely on seed regions according to the selection and the similarity principles, consequently, it might have the chance to over or under segment and waste computational costs both on time and memory.

3.3   Clustering and Classification

Supervised Learning. In 1993, Pal and Pal [49] predicted that Artificial Neural Network (ANN) based algorithms would be widely used in image segmentation. ANN, a self-learning model consists of large number of connected simple units called Artificial Neurons, could offer real-time automatic medical image segmentation by training classifier using training set (extracting features) in advance. Latterly, various supervised, semi-supervised, and unsupervised learning algorithms are developed. Recently, Havaei et al. [25] propose an automatic brain tumor segmentation method based on deep neural networks which achieve very fast segmentation between 25 s to 3 min, the sample result is shown in Fig. 2. The biggest problem for all machine learning methods is that the learning methods are not able to formulate the model far outside the data collected during the training stage, so this made the data capture the crucial part of the supervised methods.

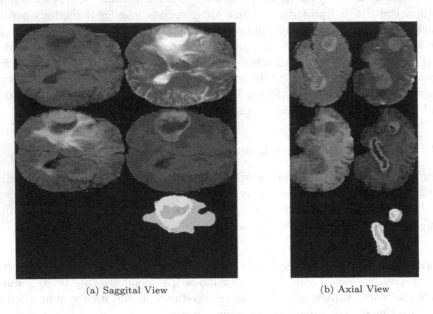

(a) Saggital View   (b) Axial View

Fig. 2. Brain tumor segmentation based on deep neural network [25]

Unsupervised Learning. Unsupervised learning algorithms often target on building decision boundaries towards unlabeled training set. Clusters are then formed in the multidimensional feature vectors. K-means Clustering Methods [24] implement the hard segmentation for a certain number of K clusters while Fuzzy C-means [35] algorithms produce soft segmentations. It works by assigning the membership to pixels of the corresponding cluster in which they have maximum membership coefficients. Despite the advantages such as accuracy, efficiency and more image information presented, the final outcomes of unsupervised algorithms are constrained to the initial cluster matrix and feature extraction.

There is no unique standard segmentation algorithm could be applied to all the circumstances for all the organs, tissues or tumors. Some hybrid techniques could achieve better results. For instance, Unsupervised algorithm GA(Genetic Algorithm) derived from ANN are combined with Self-Organizing Maps (SOM) to detect the main features in medical images [27]. Table 2 compares the lists of current open-source tools for medical image segmentation.

Table 2. Segmentation software comparison

Name	Characteristics	Reference
ITK-SNAP	1. Easy to learn and use software	[12]
	2. Rely on well-defined boundaries and homogeneous structure	
MITK	1. General and Extensible	[45]
	2. Less suitable for complicated anatomy structure	
3D Slicer	1. Extensible	[20]
	2. Not time efficient	
	3. Not appropriate for tissue with ill-boundaries and inhomogeneous structure	
Seg 3D	1. Flexible	[31]
	2. Difficult to learn for non-professional user	

4 Mesh Generation

In patient-specific modeling, computational mesh representation of anatomical structure is considered as the most crucial step, which contains discretization of multidimensional problems into fundamental geometry elements, such as tetrahedron or hexahedron [42]. Despite numerous automating algorithms have been developed, most of them target at engineering design and application, thus, are normally not suitable for anatomic modeling representation. Generating high quality three-dimensional computational finite element mesh from the segmented output for surgical simulation is facing many challenges. A good mesh should be accurately embodied for multi-material intersection mesh features: corners (none intersection), edges (1 intersection), and surfaces (2 intersections) [8]. As Vicecontl et al. [56] identified, four general rules should be followed for segmentation and mesh generation:

- **Automation:** Algorithms should be as automatic as possible to serve the patient-specific pipeline for any input patient data
- **Geometrically Accuracy:** Computational mesh simulation outcomes would be applied for the virtual surgery training, so that mesh generation must be geometric accurate

- **Robustness:** Image information from CT or MRI and segmented output might be inadequate, complicated, or difficult to process. The mesh generation algorithm need to be robust enough to deal with these kinds of circumstances
- **Generality:** Quality mesh should be generated regardless of their geometric complexity

4.1   Mesh Types

Hexahedral Mesh. One hexahedral mesh needs to be represented by at least five tetrahedral meshes. The geometry structure of hexahedral mesh is more accurate, and volumetric locking free. However, it often requires a huge amount of time and operators even for a single mesh, consequently, by far, there are no automatic hexahedral mesh generation algorithms for the complicated human tissue modeling.

Meshless Methods. Finite element methods suffer from several technical limitations, for instance, huge computational cost of soft tissue deformation and accuracy of calculation relying on the generated mesh quality. Meshless methods are regarded as one possible solution to solve these technical difficulties. But in current stage, there is still a long gap before meshless algorithms are transferred to clinical practice.

Tetrahedral Mesh. Tetrahedral meshes are well accepted for patient-specific mesh generation because they are relatively easier to express complex geometry of organs and tissues like brain, heart, blood vessels, bones etc. If given the human organs or tissues geometric information in a surface manner, the tetrahedral meshes could be generated automatically. Unfortunately, tetrahedral elements present artificial stiffness known as volume locking when coping with incompressible materials, especially for brain [41] and soft tissues. Bonet and Burton proposed the average node pressure (ANP) tetrahedral mesh to achieve better results for nearly incompressible materials [9]. More recently, Leea et al. [34] present a robust and efficient form of the smoothed finite element method (SFEM) to prevent this issue.

4.2   Tetrahedral Mesh Generation Strategy

Tetrahedral elements are still the mainstream for the state of the art patient subject mesh expression. Mesh Generation strategies could be approximately divided into three groups: *Advancing Front, Octree-based, and Delaunay Triangulations*. Basic idea behind *Advancing Front* is to subdivide element by element iteratively to reduce the domain with an initial boundary mesh [54]. Mesh quality hugely relies on surface remeshing, and poor quality meshes are always produced along boundaries. *Octree-based algorithms* partition geometric cubes iteratively until touching the anticipated resolution [59] where multi-material junction consistency problem could be resolved. Tetrahedral meshes are produced from both the irregular cells, which is formed along with boundary and internal regular cells. However, orientation of the meshes changes with the octree cell. Quality improvements, namely local refinement, local remeshing, and Laplacian smoothing are often needed in the post-processing step.

Among three mesh generation strategies, only Delaunay based techniques offer the quality control and able to deal with arbitrary complexity anatomic tissue or organ structures Table 3 compares the properties of three mesh generation algorithms. Delaunay triangulation strategies could be further divided into three types: *Boundary Constrained, Delaunay Refinement, and Voronoi-Delaunay:* (Table 3).

Table 3. Three types of mesh generation algorithms applied in medical image

	Surface mesh preserved	Quality control	Arbitrary complexity input
Advancing front	✓	✗	✗
Octree-based	✗	✗	✗
Delaunay refinement	✓	✓	✓

Boundary Constrained. The goal of boundary constrained is to keep the input boundary mesh unchanged [57]. In patient-specific solutions, this characteristic would be typically useful as it could maintain the intrinsic geometry attributes and save the operations like flips and vertex insertion. However, the complexity of human anatomy made the boundary-constrained algorithm hard to implement and can not guarantee the mesh quality.

Voronoi-Delaunay method creates a convex mesh-dependent energy function to ensure the local or global minimum exists [2]. High quality tetrahedral meshes with uniform distribution are produced and optimized at the same time, while the input boundary meshes must be changed, and implementation process is not computationally and timely efficient.

Delaunay Refinement aims at ensuring the mesh quality that leads the requirement of input boundary mesh modification. One way to achieve this goal is to keep the boundary elements while meshing the input domain after meshing or remeshing the input surface boundary. An alternative way is to operate the surface and volume mesh instantaneously by getting new boundary mesh through restricted Delaunay triangulation [53], which is a preferred solution for computational mesh generation.

There are several advantages of this technique. Firstly, instead of conventional mesh generation process who needs to go through a few tedious steps: isosurface extraction (usually done by marching cubes [37]), simplification, surface remeshing, merging and volume mesh generation, Delaunay refinement is an integrated process. Moreover, it gives the size and quality control for the tetra-hedral mesh and approximation of surfaces and sharp features. Whereas two inevitable problems are also raised: small (dihedral) angles might destroy the refinement process, and ill-shaped tetrahedral (quasi-degenerate tetrahedral of special kind named Sliver) might be included in the final outcomes. Figure 3 is a 3D computational model generated from segmented image by CGAL [30]. From the review of current progress in mesh generation, it can be concluded that gen-erating the high quality computational mesh and handling the boundary domain in a reasonable time frame is still very challenging.

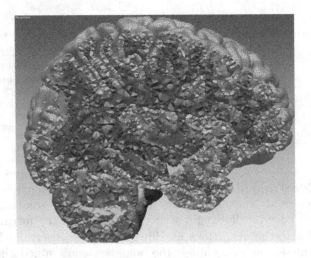

Fig. 3. Mesh generation by Delaunay refinement [30]

5   Surgery Simulation

Besides from precise anatomical modeling for a specific patient, real time soft tissue simulation is also a crucial part of the fast surgery simulation system [50]. Due to the fact that most of anatomical parts are soft tissue within the surgery, the accuracy of soft tissue deformation would enormously influence the perfor-mance of the whole framework [21]. There are mainly four types of simulation approaches have been widely used nowadays.

5.1   Force Based Approach

Mass-spring [5,10,36], a simple and inexpensive scheme takes Newtons second law of motion as the theory basis to first compute the velocity from accelerations and then the positions from velocities, which is hard to tune the spring constants to get desired behavior and leads to overshooting problem.

5.2 Structural Based Approaches

Finite element method (FEM) [60] takes the continuum mechanics as the theory basis, which could produce accurate physical behaviors for different types of elastic material. However the model complexity makes the technique high computational cost, and the sparsity patterns from FEM are highly unstructured in 2D+, thus it could be difficult to efficiently parallelize a FEM code [55].

5.3 Position Based Dynamics

Position Based Dynamics (PBD) [43] is a method works on positions directly in each simulation step. It is fast, stable, and controllable which makes the simulation process highly efficient, easier, and best suited for the interaction environment [7]. Even though the behavior of deformable objects can be modeled using PBD with additional constraints such as shape matching. It cannot accurately simulate the realistic behavior of soft tissues. The real-world human soft tissues produce non-linear and anisotropic behaviors or heterogeneous properties that hugely limits the results for surgery simulation. Although designing the complicated non-linearly constitutive model might solve these kinds of problems, this could also lead to high computational cost and difficult parameters. Data driven methods could be a possible solution.

5.4 Data Driven Methods

Geometric Data Driven Simulation [7]. captures the deformation example and decomposes the large scale geometry (the overall shape of the tissue) and the fine scale geometric (the details such as wrinkles). They can be represented as different resolutions, modeled separately, and connected by the subdivision schemes. Finally, high-resolution output with details is the synthesis of these two scales geometry, which could follow the position based dynamics method.

Mechanical Data Driven Simulation [48]. Unlike the geometric data driven methods where the parameter data could be directly measured from the training sets, mechanical data driven methods require both the deformation and forces data from the data captured stage, and parameter data are estimated through the numerical optimization based on physics mechanics (for example, FEM method).

6 Future Challenges and Conclusion

This paper takes a survey for current progress in virtual reality surgery simulation, particularly, concentrates on patient-specific modeling and real time soft tissue simulation. The complexity of human anatomical representation and the uniqueness for an individual patient and their ailments yield many challenges yet. Further works in these fields are desired, including accurately analyzing the geometric and anatomic structures from medical images, transferring the information to high quality computation models, and solving technical difficulties related to realistic soft tissue simulation and high fidelity natural human computer interactions, to present the trainee an immersive surgery environment with realistic visual and haptic feedback.

Acknowledgements. We would also like to thank the People Program (Marie Curie Actions) of the European Union's Seventh Framework Program FP7/2007-2013/ under REA grant agreement n° [612627] for their support.

References

1. Adams, R., Bischof, L.: Seeded region growing. IEEE Trans. Pattern Anal. Mach. Intell. **16**(6), 641–647 (1994)
2. Alliez, P., Cohen-Steiner, D., Yvinec, M., Desbrun, M.: Variational tetrahedral meshing. ACM Trans. Graph. (TOG) **24**, 617–625 (2005). ACM
3. Antiga, L., Piccinelli, M., Botti, L., Ene-Iordache, B., Remuzzi, A., Steinman, D.A.: An image-based modeling framework for patient-specific computational hemodynamics. Med. Biol. Eng. Comput. **46**(11), 1097 (2008)
4. Badash, I., Burtt, K., Solorzano, C.A., Carey, J.N.: Innovations in surgery simulation: a review of past, current and future techniques. Ann. Transl. Med. **4**(23), 453 (2016)
5. Baraff, D., Witkin, A.: Large steps in cloth simulation. In: Proceedings of the 25th Annual Conference on Computer Graphics and Interactive Techniques, pp. 43–54. ACM (1998)
6. Barratt, D.C., Chan, C.S., Edwards, P.J., Penney, G.P., Slomczykowski, M., Carter, T.J., Hawkes, D.J.: Instantiation and registration of statistical shape models of the femur and pelvis using 3d ultrasound imaging. Med. Image Anal. **12**(3), 358–374 (2008)
7. Bender, J., Koschier, D., Charrier, P., Weber, D.: Position-based simulation of continuous materials. Comput. Graph. **44**, 1–10 (2014)
8. Boltcheva, D., Yvinec, M., Boissonnat, J.D.: Mesh generation from 3d multi-material images. In: Medical Image Computing and Computer-Assisted Intervention MICCAI 2009, pp. 283–290 (2009)
9. Bonet, J., Burton, A.: A simple average nodal pressure tetrahedral element for incompressible and nearly incompressible dynamic explicit applications. Int. J. Numer. Meth. Biomed. Eng. **14**(5), 437–449 (1998)
10. Bouaziz, S., Martin, S., Liu, T., Kavan, L., Pauly, M.: Projective dynamics: fusing constraint projections for fast simulation. ACM Trans. Graph. (TOG) **33**(4), 154 (2014)
11. Bryson, S.: Virtual reality in scientific visualization. Commun. ACM **39**(5), 62–71 (1996)
12. Cevidanes, L.H., Tucker, S., Styner, M., Kim, H., Chapuis, J., Reyes, M., Proffit, W., Turvey, T., Jaskolka, M.: Three-dimensional surgical simulation. Am. J. Orthod. Dentofac. Orthop. **138**(3), 361–371 (2010)
13. Cootes, T.F., Edwards, G.J., Taylor, C.J.: Active appearance models. In: Burkhardt, H., Neumann, B. (eds.) ECCV 1998. LNCS, vol. 1407, pp. 484–498. Springer, Heidelberg (1998). doi:10.1007/BFb0054760
14. Cootes, T.F., Taylor, C.J.: Active shape models-'smart snakes'. In: Hogg, D., Boyle, R. (eds.) BMVC 1992, pp. 266–275. Springer, London (1992)

15. Davis, J.E.: The use of simulation in causal analysis of sentinel events in healthcare. Ph.D. thesis, University of Pennsylvania (2016)
16. Duffy, A., Hogle, N., McCarthy, H., Lew, J., Egan, A., Christos, P., Fowler, D.: Construct validity for the LapSim laparoscopic surgical simulator. Surg. Endosc. Interv. Tech. **19**(3), 401–405 (2005)
17. Endo, K., Sata, N., Ishiguro, Y., Miki, A., Sasanuma, H., Sakuma, Y., Shimizu, A., Hyodo, M., Lefor, A., Yasuda, Y.: A patient-specific surgical simulator using pre-operative imaging data: an interactive simulator using a three-dimensional tactile mouse. J. Comput. Surg. **1**(1), 10 (2014)
18. Eschweiler, J., Stromps, J.P., Fischer, M., Schick, F., Rath, B., Pallua, N., Radermacher, K.: A biomechanical model of the wrist joint for patient-specific model guided surgical therapy: part 2. Proc. Inst. Mech. Eng. Part H J. Eng. Med. **230**(4), 326–334 (2016)
19. Eschweiler, J., Stromps, J.P., Fischer, M., Schick, F., Rath, B., Pallua, N., Radermacher, K.: Development of a biomechanical model of the wrist joint for patient-specific model guided surgical therapy planning: part 1. Proc. Inst. Mech. Eng. Part H J. Eng. Med. **230**(4), 310–325 (2016)
20. Fedorov, A., Beichel, R., Kalpathy-Cramer, J., Finet, J., Fillion-Robin, J.C., Pujol, S., Bauer, C., Jennings, D., Fennessy, F., Sonka, M., et al.: 3d slicer as an image computing platform for the quantitative imaging network. Magn. Reson. Imag. **30**(9), 1323–1341 (2012)
21. Gallagher, A.G., Ritter, E.M., Champion, H., Higgins, G., Fried, M.P., Moses, G., Smith, C.D., Satava, R.M.: Virtual reality simulation for the operating room: proficiency-based training as a paradigm shift in surgical skills training. Ann. Surg. **241**(2), 364–372 (2005)
22. Goel, V.R., Greenberg, R.K., Greenberg, D.P.: Mathematical analysis of DICOM CT datasets: can endograft sizing be automated for complex anatomy? J. Vasc. Surg. **47**(6), 1306–1312 (2008)
23. Gonzalez, R., Wintz, P.: Digital Image Processing. Prentice-Hall, Englewood Cliffs (1977)
24. Hartigan, J.A., Wong, M.A.: Algorithm as 136: a k-means clustering algorithm. J. Royal Stat. Soc. Ser. C (Applied Statistics) **28**(1), 100–108 (1979)
25. Havaei, M., Davy, A., Warde-Farley, D., Biard, A., Courville, A., Bengio, Y., Pal, C., Jodoin, P.M., Larochelle, H.: Brain tumor segmentation with deep neural networks. Med. Image Anal. **35**, 18–31 (2017)
26. Heimann, T., Meinzer, H.P.: Statistical shape models for 3d medical image segmentation: a review. Med. Image Anal. **13**(4), 543–563 (2009)
27. Indira, S., Ramesh, A.: Image segmentation using artificial neural network and genetic algorithm: a comparative analysis. In: 2011 International Conference on Process Automation, Control and Computing (PACC), pp. 1–6. IEEE (2011)
28. Iwamoto, N., Shum, H.P., Yang, L., Morishima, S.: Multi-layer lattice model for real-time dynamic character deformation. Comput. Graph. Forum **34**, 99–109 (2015). Wiley Online Library
29. Jain, R., Kasturi, R., Schunck, B.G.: Machine Vision, vol. 5. McGraw-Hill, New York (1995)
30. Jamin, C., Alliez, P., Yvinec, M., Boissonnat, J.D.: CGALmesh: a generic framework for delaunay mesh generation. ACM Trans. Math. Softw. (TOMS) **41**(4), 23 (2015)
31. Johnson, C.: Biomedical visual computing: case studies and challenges. Comput. Sci. Eng. **14**(1), 12–21 (2012)

32. Kent, D.M., Hayward, R.A.: Limitations of applying summary results of clinical trials to individual patients: the need for risk stratification. JAMA **298**(10), 1209–1212 (2007)

33. Lai, J.Y., Essomba, T., Lee, P.Y., et al.: Algorithm for segmentation and reduction of fractured bones in computer-aided preoperative surgery. In: Proceedings of the 3rd International Conference on Biomedical and Bioinformatics Engineering, pp. 12–18. ACM (2016)

34. Leea, C.K., Mihaib, L.A., Halec, J.S., Kerfridena, P., Bordasc, S.P.: Strain smoothing for compressible and nearly-incompressible finite elasticity. Comput. Struct. **182**, 540–555 (2016)

35. Lei, T., Sewchand, W.: Statistical approach to X-ray CT imaging and its applications in image analysis. II. A new stochastic model-based image segmentation technique for X-ray CT image. IEEE Trans. Med. Imag. **11**(1), 62–69 (1992)

36. Liu, T., Bargteil, A.W., O'Brien, J.F., Kavan, L.: Fast simulation of mass-spring systems. ACM Trans. Graph. (TOG) **32**(6), 214 (2013)

37. Lorensen, W.E., Cline, H.E.: Marching cubes: a high resolution 3d surface construction algorithm. ACM SIGGRAPH Comput. Graph. **21**, 163–169 (1987). ACM

38. Makiyama, K., Nagasaka, M., Inuiya, T., Takanami, K., Ogata, M., Kubota, Y.: Development of a patient-specific simulator for laparoscopic renal surgery. Int. J. Urol. **19**(9), 829–835 (2012)

39. Marr, D., Hildreth, E.: Theory of edge detection. Proc. Royal Soc. Lond. B Biol. Sci. **207**(1167), 187–217 (1980)

40. Mihalef, V., Ionasec, R.I., Sharma, P., Georgescu, B., Voigt, I., Suehling, M., Comaniciu, D.: Patient-specific modelling of whole heart anatomy, dynamics and haemodynamics from four-dimensional cardiac CT images. Interface Focus **1**(3), 286–296 (2011)

41. Miller, K.: Biomechanics of Brain for Computer Integrated Surgery. Warsaw University of Technology Publishing House, Warsaw (2002)

42. Mohamed, A., Davatzikos, C.: Finite element mesh generation and remeshing from segmented medical images. In: 2004 IEEE International Symposium on Biomedical Imaging: Nano to Macro, pp. 420–423. IEEE (2004)

43. Müller, M., Heidelberger, B., Hennix, M., Ratcliff, J.: Position based dynamics. J. Vis. Commun. Image Represent. **18**(2), 109–118 (2007)

44. Neal, M.L., Kerckhoffs, R.: Current progress in patient-specific modeling. Briefings Bioinform. **11**(1), 111–126 (2010)

45. Nolden, M., Zelzer, S., Seitel, A., Wald, D., Müller, M., Franz, A.M., Maleike, D., Fangerau, M., Baumhauer, M., Maier-Hein, L., et al.: The medical imaging interaction toolkit: challenges and advances. Int. J. Comput. Assist. Radiol. Surg. **8**(4), 607–620 (2013)

46. de Oliveira, J.E., Giessler, P., Deserno, T.M.: Patient-specific anatomical modelling. In: E-Health and Bioengineering Conference (EHB), pp. 1–4. IEEE (2015)

47. O'Reilly, M.A., Whyne, C.M.: Comparison of computed tomography based parametric and patient-specific finite element models of the healthy and metastatic spine using a mesh-morphing algorithm. Spine **33**(17), 1876–1881 (2008)

48. Otaduy, M.A., Bickel, B., Bradley, D., Wang, H.: Data-driven simulation methods in computer graphics: cloth, tissue and faces. In: ACM SIGGRAPH 2012 Courses, p. 12. ACM (2012)

49. Pal, N.R., Pal, S.K.: A review on image segmentation techniques. Pattern Recognit. **26**(9), 1277–1294 (1993)

50. Pan, J.J., Chang, J., Yang, X., Liang, H., Zhang, J.J., Qureshi, T., Howell, R., Hickish, T.: Virtual reality training and assessment in laparoscopic rectum surgery. Int. J. Med. Rob. Comput. Assist. Surg. **11**(2), 194–209 (2015)
51. Prewitt, J.M.: Object enhancement and extraction. Picture Process. Psychopictorics **10**(1), 15–19 (1970)
52. Ricotta, J.J., Pagan, J., Xenos, M., Alemu, Y., Einav, S., Bluestein, D.: Cardiovascular disease management: the need for better diagnostics. Med. Biol. Eng. Comput. **46**(11), 1059–1068 (2008)
53. Rineau, L., Yvinec, M.: Meshing 3d domains bounded by piecewise smooth surfaces. In: Brewer, M.L., Marcum, D. (eds.) Proceedings of the 16th International Meshing Roundtable, pp. 443–460. Springer, Heidelberg (2008)
54. Schöberl, J.: Netgen an advancing front 2d/3d-mesh generator based on abstract rules. Comput. Vis. Sci. **1**(1), 41–52 (1997)
55. Sifakis, E., Barbic, J.: FEM simulation of 3d deformable solids: a practitioner's guide to theory, discretization and model reduction. In: ACM SIGGRAPH 2012 Courses, p. 20. ACM (2012)
56. Viceconti, M., Davinelli, M., Taddei, F., Cappello, A.: Automatic generation of accurate subject-specific bone finite element models to be used in clinical studies. J. Biomech. **37**(10), 1597–1605 (2004)
57. Weatherill, N.P., Hassan, O.: Efficient three-dimensional delaunay triangulation with automatic point creation and imposed boundary constraints. Int. J. Numer. Meth. Eng. **37**(12), 2005–2039 (1994)
58. Zhang, A., Hünerbein, M., Dai, Y., Schlag, P.M., Beller, S.: Construct validity testing of a laparoscopic surgery simulator (lap mentor®). Surg. Endosc. **22**(6), 1440–1444 (2008)
59. Zhang, Y., Hughes, T.J., Bajaj, C.L.: An automatic 3d mesh generation method for domains with multiple materials. Comput. Meth. Appl. Mech. Eng. **199**(5), 405–415 (2010)
60. Zienkiewicz, O.C., Taylor, R.L.: The Finite Element Method for Solid and Structural Mechanics. Butterworth-Heinemann, Oxford (2005)

Virtual Reality Based Immersive Telepresence System for Remote Conversation and Collaboration

Zhipeng Tan[1], Yuning Hu[2], and Kun Xu[1(✉)]

[1] Department of Computer Science and Technology, Tsinghua University, Beijing, China
xukun@tsinghua.edu.cn
[2] City College, Zhejiang University, Hangzhou, China

Abstract. We developed a Virtual Reality (VR) based telepresence system providing novel immersive experience for remote conversation and collaboration. By wearing VR headsets, all the participants can be gathered into a same virtual space, with 3D cartoon Avatars representing them. The 3D VR Avatars can realistically emulate the head postures, facial expressions and hand motions of the participants, enabling them to conduct enjoyable group-to-group conversations with people spatially isolated from them. Moreover, our VR telepresence system offers conspicuously new manners for remote collaboration. For example, users can play PPT slides or watch videos together, or they can cooperate on solving a math problem by calculating on a virtual blackboard, all of which can be hardly achieved using conventional video-based telepresence system. Experiments show that our system can provide unprecedented immersive experience for tele-conversation and new possibilities for remote collaboration.

Keywords: Virtual reality · Telepresence system · VR avatar · Remote collaboration · Teleconferencing

1 Introduction

Enabling people to naturally communicate, interact and cooperate with those spatially apart from each other has been a hot research topic these years. Literally speaking, it is a considerably nontrivial task to create hallucination for isolated users to feel like they are just seating face-to-face in a room.

Conventional teleconferencing systems mainly rely on Internet video chat, only allowing users to talk with flat images on the screens. Such video conferencing systems are far from enough to create an immersive communicating experience, and it is scarcely possible for users to remotely collaborate with each other with such systems. To cope with such problems, these years, 3D rendering techniques have been utilized by researchers to create immersive telepresence systems ([1–3] etc.). Virtual 3D spaces are constructed to accommodate the avatars representing the participants, then frames viewing from the first person's perspective are generated by advanced rendering techniques to be shown on the screen in front of the users. Though such systems may remarkably ameliorate the teleconferencing experiences, it is still considerably unnatural for users to view 3D scenes through 2D flat screens.

J. Chang et al. (Eds.): AniNex 2017, LNCS 10582, pp. 234–247, 2017.
https://doi.org/10.1007/978-3-319-69487-0_17

Recently, emerging VR/AR/MR techniques offer new possibilities for highly immersive telepresence experiences that differ greatly from conventional ones. These state-of-the-art techniques can directly immerse people into an elaborately designed virtual space, creating the illusion that they have been transmitted to a new world, where they can communicate and interact with other people in novel manners.

This paper aims at exploring the potential of Virtual Reality techniques for telepresence and proposes a VR-based telepresence system for remote conversation and collaboration. Figure 1 shows a demonstration of our system when two users are using VR telepresence system to conduct a remote conversation with a PPT shown beside them. Our system has the following features.

Fig. 1. Demonstration of our VR telepresence system, two users are conducting a remote conversation with a PPT shown beside them. the image on the left is rendered from third person's perspective, with photos of two users at this moment shown at the corners. actual views in users' VR HMDs are shown on the right.

Firstly, inside our virtual spaces, users will automatically be arranged to stand within a circle according to the number of the participants. Although currently we only allow two users in our telepresence system due to the lack of VR facilities in our laboratory, it can be easily extended to support a flexible number of participants. So two people can use our system to communicate face-to-face with each other while a group of people can hold a small conference with our system.

Secondly, users will turn into virtual cartoon avatars picked by themselves to communicate with the avatars of the other users. Their head motions and body gestures will be emulated by their avatars to deliver eye contacts and body languages that are essential for effective communications.

Additionally, with the help of advanced motion capture techniques, users also have the ability to interact with the virtual world just with their hands using handheld controllers or motion capture gloves, which is literally the most natural and spontaneous interaction mode for people. Thus, users can play PPT slides or watch videos on virtual screens, or they may cooperate on solving a math problem by calculating on a virtual blackboard, or they can observe, manipulate and even design 3D models together, etc. We envisage that our VR-based immersive telepresence system offers various new possibilities for remote collaboration.

2   Related Work

2.1   Telepresence System

Building telepresence system to virtually gather together people spatially separated has always been a hot research topic for computer science researchers.

Video-based telepresence systems, though seriously lack of immersion, have been widely used due to its simplicity. Therefore, many novel systems have been proposed to improve the experience. A video-based telepresence system in [1] has made the use of Kinect display avatars to simulate face-to-face teleconferencing with eye gazing. To overcome the limitation of the video-based systems, these years have witnessed more and more occurrence of rendering-based immersive teleconferencing systems. For instance, [2] is the forerunner to utilize RGB-D cameras to dynamically reconstruct the models for users, which is then been rendered to the screen of the remote users. As an improvement, the Viewport system in [3] has used sparse 3D representations from point clouds and enabled virtual seating to better simulate face-to-face communication. An improved videoconferencing system with Kinect 3D modeling and motion parallax has been proposed in [4]. Recently, Mixed Reality based telepresence system has been proposed in [5], which has opened up a new way to do teleconferencing. However, most of these telepresence systems require users to view 3D images from 2D flat screens, and users have to imagine that they are one of the people in the 3D scenes, thus they cannot have satisfying immersive telepresence experiences with such systems.

2.2   Remote Collaboration System

Besides enabling remote conversations, researchers have been trying to realize remote collaboration for people spatially separated.

The stereo-vision system demonstrated in [6] implements real-time 3D reconstruction of users to immerse them into a virtual space where they can conduct interactions with virtual objects, thus creating the novel teleimmersive collaboration experience. However, the real-time 3D reconstruction cannot provide high-quality rendering results. [7] proposed an ImmerseBoard system that realistically creates an immersive experience of writing side-by-side on board for users at two different locations, which utilizes state-of-the-art real-time rendering and visualization techniques for depth cameras. The limitation of the ImmerseBoard lies in the fact that they only support very limited ways of remote collaboration, and can only support two users at the same time. The Mixed Reality telepresence system proposed in [5] provides a novel way of collaborative space exploration. However, they only support very limited ways of man-machine interaction, and users are still viewing from 2D flat screens, thus they cannot provide as immersive experience as our VR telepresence system can provide.

2.3   3D Avatars

Generation and manipulation of 3D Avatars are of great importance to provide immersive telepresence experiences.

Many researchers have proposed various algorithms for the generation of 3D avatars. Some systems mentioned above ([2], [3] and [6] etc.) use depth cameras to dynamically generate 3D models of users by stitching together 3D point clouds from multiple Kinects placed around the users, which, unfortunately, consumes massive computational resources and the 3D reconstruction from point clouds still have many perceptible artifacts due to the low resolution of depth cameras. Image-Based Reconstruction (IBR) can generate high-quality 3D avatars from images taken around users, some offline algorithms have the advantage of creating photorealistic 3D face models. For instance, [8] puts forward a method of creating a dynamic 3D facial avatar from video input that captures the different angles of the users' faces. However, such methods can only generate 3D facial models, it cannot produce full body rigged avatars, and reconstructing photorealistic facial avatars is still an extraordinarily nontrivial work. Therefore, in our VR telepresence system, we compromise to use premade cartoon avatars and let users choose the avatars according to their own preference.

Given 3D avatars, facial expression tracking and motion capture emerge to become important research fields. Many computer vision algorithms have been proposed to deal with real-time facial animation tracking. [9] utilizes a 3D shape regression algorithm to locate facial landmarks for real-time facial animation tracking, given the prerequisite of users performing specific predefined facial poses and expressions. Except for using computer vision method, voice-based expressive lip synchronization is another alternative of driving the facial animation of avatars. Recently, [10] proposed an advanced lip-sync algorithm that is capable of generating an expressive lower-face animation with authentic lip and jaw movements, given predefined speech transcripts along with the sound. As for motion capture, Kinect-based motion capture techniques are popular these years, and [11] put forward a full body motion capture algorithm leveraging two Kinect sensors. However, it still cannot provide detailed movements of fingers. Besides, there also exist some motion capture data gloves capable of accurately tracking users' arm and finger movements. For instance, a motion capture glove with 18 inertial and magnetic measurement units (IMMUs) is presented in [12].

3 System and Implementation

3.1 System Overview

Our client-server procedure modules are demonstrated in Fig. 2. Concisely speaking, the clients mainly handle the processing of the media and sensor data collected locally and transmitted from the server side to generate accurate body animations and facial blendshape parameters for the avatars, before sending them along with other scene objects to the rendering pipeline; while the server mainly deals with receiving and synchronizing media and sensor data from clients, arranging virtual seating for avatars, and synchronizing motions and commands from all clients to determine the states of the scene objects that would be sent to the clients.

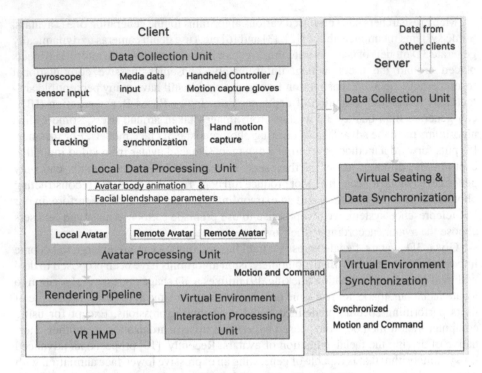

Fig. 2. System structure overview of the clients and the servers.

More explicitly, the clients' local data processing unit is composed of head motion tracking part, facial animation synchronization part and hand motion capture part, which manages the gyroscope sensor data from the VR head mounted device (HMD), the media input from media devices, and the data from either handheld controller or motion capture glove respectively. The output can then be used to constantly drive the rigged cartoon avatars to imitate users' actions. Based on these features, users can mutually conduct a remote conversation using their avatars with eye contact, facial expressions and body gestures in virtual space.

The virtual environment interaction processing unit is the foundation for remote collaboration of our telepresence system. It continually detects the collision between avatars and virtual scene objects to make proper responses by modifying the state of the scenes according to different occasions. Besides, certain commands would be generated by using handheld controller's command keys or pressing virtual buttons in the scenes. Because motions and commands of different clients might run into contradictions, and different clients may end up with different states without necessary synchronization, the clients will first send their motions and commands to the server before receiving the synchronized data from it.

The following sections will elaborate more on the implementation details.

3.2 Facial Animation Synchronization

Facial Feature Tracking. Computer vision methods are the most common ways to perform facial feature tracking to generate facial animations for avatars, which is the first way we tried in our telepresence system to handle facial animation synchronization of the avatars.

We firstly apply face detector from OpenCV [13] open source library on the input images taken by the web cameras to mark out the location of the face. Then, using the output of OpenCV as the initial rough estimates of the facial feature points, we make use of the supervised descent method (SDM) described in [14] to optimize the positions of the facial feature points. However, further experiments show the limitations of using computer vision methods for facial animation synchronization. Since nowadays most VR HMDs are still considerably huge, more than half of the face will inevitably be occluded by the VR headsets. And faces may be completely under shadows when users are even slightly looking down, making it hard to use computer vision methods to track the feature points of the lower half of the face.

Considering the dilemma using computer vision methods to accomplish the synchronization of facial animations, we did not use this method in our final system and instead turned our focus on algorithms that use voice to synchronize the lip movements for avatars.

Voice to Lip Synchronization. Sound-based lip synchronization algorithms aim to directly generate natural and plausible lip movements from audio input streams without the necessity of face capture. Besides, the algorithms are efficient enough so that lame-accurate lip synchronization with the voice can be achieved. These features make it the best candidate to generate facial animation for our telepresence system when facial expression capture is hard to implement as mentioned in the previous sections.

Over the years, researchers have been constantly making progress to propose much more effective real-time lip synchronization algorithms. Although methods proposed in [10] can generate an expressive lower-face animation with authentic lip and jaw movements. However, it requires predefined speech transcripts along with the sound input, which is impractical for our system. After comparing between several other state-of-the-art lip synchronization methods, we finally chose the DCT-based lip-sync animation generation algorithm [15] for its outstanding rapidity and satisfied performance.

Phoneme and veseme are two basic concepts for lip-sync algorithms [16]. Phonemes are the most basic constitutional sound units in a language to form the words, and different phonemes are pronounced by certain kind of lip movements. Each phoneme corresponds to a certain lip movement pattern, which is academically called veseme [10]. The DCT-based lip-sync algorithm [15] uses the Discrete Cosine Transform (DCT) to automatically pick out the phonemes from the audio input streams based on the fact that different phonemes correspond to distinguishable spectral peaks in the frequency domain. Based on their work, we extract the basic phonemes of [a], [e], [i], [o], [u], [s] from input audio. Noticing that the above phonemes are mainly vowels, it is because most consonants correspond to visually unobvious subtle lip movements. We then map these phonemes to the corresponding predefined facial blendshapes of the avatars that represent the visual lip patterns. It is common for a word to contain a sequence of phonemes that match to different lip patterns, so interpolation techniques are applied to smoothly transit between different lip patterns to generate natural and fluent lip animations.

3.3   Motion Tracking

Apart from generating facial animations for the avatars, it is also quite important to accurately manipulate their head and body motions in accordance with the users.

Head Motion Tracking. The sensitive gyroscopes inside the VR HMDs significantly simplify the head motion capture task, which would still be a computationally costly task using visual-based head posture tracking method like the SDM algorithm afore-mentioned. The gyroscope will constantly output quaternions, indicating the rotating trajectory of the VR HMD. On account of the fact that we expect our users to sit or stand toward a relatively fixed orientation using our telepresence system, it is legitimate for us to regard the difference of the quaternions from gyroscope between consecutive frames as the head rotating orientation of the users, which will be applied to manipulate the head rotation of the avatars.

Hand Motion Tracking Using Handheld Controller. It is no doubt that there exist many advanced motion capture techniques capable of accurately tracking the motions of the users, whereas they are generally quite heavy-weight and deadly expensive, contradicting with our original intention of building a light-weighted and user-friendly VR telepresence system. Additionally, we expect our users to use our telepresence system sedentarily, hence it can already provide immersive VR experience with hand motion capture.

Currently, the most common commercial VR HMDs, including HTC VR, Oculus VR, and PS VR, all incorporate their specially-made handheld controllers equipped with advanced indoor positioning techniques. For instance, the HTC VR equipment that we use in our telepresence system owns the innovative "Lighthouse" indoor tracking system that is capable of instantly providing the precise positions and orientations of the headset and its two handheld controllers. Making use of these features, we can generate plausible hand motions for avatars with the inverse kinematic algorithm with high-efficiency.

We use the state-of-the-art forward and backward reaching inverse kinematics (FABRIK), a fast inverse kinematic solver proposed in [17] to instantly update the positions and rotating angles of the arm joints using the input locations of the two handheld controllers as the targets for the avatars' hands. The FABRIK algorithm updates the positions and rotations of the rigid bones iteratively. To put it simply, in each iteration, it first moves the endpoint to the target, then places its other bone point in the line formed by the target and the endpoint of its parent bone, continually applies the algorithm to reach the root joint, after which a second pass will be applied backward from root to the target in a similar way. Besides, further constraints are imposed on the placing strategy to ensure that only biomechanically plausible results are achieved by the authors, since people cannot conduct some actions that are mathematically valid like reversely rotating their arm to the back. The FABRIK algorithm can quickly converge to a plausible placement of the joints in little iterations so that the endpoint can get as close as possible to the target.

Hand Motion Tracking Using Motion Capture Gloves. Although we can already animate the VR avatars using algorithms described above, the produced animation is only at the coarse level without details of finger movements, which may be inadequate if we consider incorporating hand gesture manipulation into our system.

As stated in the section of related work, motion capture gloves may have its advantage of capturing users' motions at fine-grained level including finger movements over Kinect-based motion capture techniques. After comparing several motion capture gloves, we chose the light-weight Noitom motion capture glove, which comprises several sensitive inertial and magnetic measurement units called perception neurons. Experiments show that the Noitom gloves can achieve desired performance, and can generate accurate animation to drive our VR avatars.

It is worth noticing that, the Noitom motion capture glove is optional for our system, we tried it for the purpose of achieving better VR immersive telepresence experience by using gestures to manipulate. Using the handheld controller to drive the avatar still has its advantage of better convenience for users.

3.4 Virtual Interaction and Collaboration

With facial animation synchronization and motion tracking applied on VR Avatars, users can already conduct an immersive conversation with remote users inside a virtual environment with the assistance of an intermediate server. Furthermore, we aim to explore the full potential of VR by supporting natural remote interaction and collaboration.

Since the most straightforward and instinct way for us to interact within VR is directly using their hands to touch. Hence, we mainly rely on real-time collision detection to allow users to conduct virtual interaction and collaboration by directly touching the virtual objects in VR.

When simply touching is not enough for some considerably complex operation, control buttons on the handheld controller will be used to allow users to launch some commands. To ensure that scene states on different clients keep the same, the clients will response to the motions and commands transmitted from the server, which is responsible for merging and synchronizing the operations from all clients.

4 Experiments and Applications

4.1 Hardware

The VR HMD that we use is the HTC Vive VR system, incorporating a VR HMD, two handheld controllers, and two infrared localization devices. The motion capture glove that we use is the Noitom perception neuron glove with 32 Neurons. The computers that run our program comprise Intel® Xeon® CPU E5-2620 of 2.00 GHz with dual core, and NVIDIA Quadro M4000 GPU, running Windows 8.1 operating system.

4.2 System Performance

The Accuracy of Lip Synchronization. Figure 3 shows some lip synchronization results of 6 typical phonemes including [a], [e], [i], [o], [u], and [s], which resemble the common mouth movements people will generate phonating these sounds. We conducted several experiments using recordings of different people and got satisfactory results, which show that our system can perform real-time lip synchronization and produce reasonable and life-like mouth movements that match well with the input sound streams. And since we perform lip synchronization by extracting phonemes from the sound input, which is language independent, our system can hence achieve satisfactory synchronization results with different input languages, and we tested on English and Chinese.

Fig. 3. Lip synchronization results for typical phonemes of [a], [e], [i], [o], [u], and [s]

The Accuracy of Head and Upper Body Motion Tracking. Head motion tracking is accurate since the VR HMD can instantly provide precise quaternions indicating head orientation, so we focus on testing the accuracy of upper body motion tracking respectively using HTC handheld controller and Noitom perception neuron motion capture gloves.

Figure 4 shows the motion tracking results using Noitom perception neuron gloves. These results show that Noitom glove is capable of accurately tracking the movements of arms and hands on real-time, and it can also provide considerably accurate tracking of fingers, enabling users to perform body languages to efficiently communicate with each other. During the experiments, however, we found that the perception neuron gloves may run into chaos after using for a while, then calibrations were needed to put them back on the right track again. This may derive from magnetic field interference.

Fig. 4. Motion tracking results using noitom perception neuron gloves

Figure 5 shows the motion tracking results using handheld controllers with inverse kinematic. Given the two positions of the hands, the inverse kinematic algorithm can figure out the plausible hand movement. The method can provide relatively accurate

Fig. 5. Motion tracking results using handheld controller with inverse kinematic

hand animations when conducting small-scale hand movements, but it cannot guarantee the accuracy when performing gross movements. Additionally, it is unable to provide tracking of fingers. Nevertheless, the method can generate reasonable hand and arm animation in most cases, and it is much more convenient for users to use handheld controller compared with wearing motion tracking gloves.

Network Latency. The data we need to transmit through the network are users' audio stream, the motion parameters and the data used to synchronize the scenes. The users' mouth blendshape parameters are calculated directly from audio streams to guarantee the synchronization of mouth movements with the sound input. We tested the network latency of our VR telepresence system, the average latency is around 100 ms – 150 ms under our local area network. The latency is considerably low to provide well telepresence experience for users.

4.3   Application Demo: Remote Conversation and Collaboration

We have implemented an application to demonstrate the versatility of our VR telepresence system. Although our system can actually support a flexible number of users, due to the insufficiency of the VR facilities, we temporarily only developed a two-user application, yet most of the features of our VR telepresence system can still be shown.

Inside our VR telepresence system, users are transformed to become cartoon avatars standing around each other. We developed two scenes for our application. Figures 1 and 6 are the demonstrations of our first scene. Users were virtually sent to a grassland, where they can conduct face-to-face conversations, play PPT slides or watch videos together. Figure 7 demonstrates our second scene, where they are transferred into a classroom placed with desks, blackboards, platforms, and they are standing side-by-side with a writable board before them. Since we only have one suit of Noitom perception neuron

Fig. 6. Users are watching videos together on grassland within our VR telepresence system (rendering from third person's perspective).

glove, so we equip one user with motion capture glove and another user holds the hand-held controller. As depicted in the above sections, the avatars' head and body motion will be driven by the gyroscope inside the HTC Vive HMD and the Noitom gloves or HTC handheld controllers, while the avatars' facial blendshapes will be driven by the sound input. Each person will see from the first person's perspective, so they can see their virtual hands and the avatars performing the actions of the other users.

Fig. 7. Demonstration of the second scene of our application, where users are transferred to a classroom with a writable board in front of them and they can write down whatever they want to each other. The first image is rendered from a third person's perspective and the following images are the actual views that the users see in VR.

Besides allowing users to conduct a remote conversation, we add many collaborative features into our telepresence system. First, users can play PPT slides or watch videos on a virtual screen placed beside them, with which users can conveniently share opinions with each other using images or videos. Second, a board is placed in front of the users in the virtual classroom, upon which they can write down whatever they wish to show to the other users. Therefore, they can easily collaborate on to solve some problems by sharing sketches with each other.

From this application we can draw the conclusion that our system can provide unprecedented immersive experience for tele-conversation and new possibilities for remote collaboration.

5   Discussion and Future Work

A VR telepresence system is proposed in this paper which can provide novel immersive experience for remote conversation and collaboration. We use 3D cartoon avatars with facial blendshapes and body skeleton system as our VR avatars, of which the facial animations are generated from real-time lip synchronization algorithm from sound input; the head gestures are tracked using quaternions provided from gyroscope sensors of VR headsets and the body gestures are either generated using handheld controllers of HTC Vive by inverse kinematic algorithm or tracked utilizing Noitom perception neuron motion capture gloves. Experiments show that our VR avatars are capable of realistically emulating user's motions, making it possible for users to conduct remote conversations. Besides, we allow users to virtually interact with objects in the scenes, thus enabling users to conduct remote collaboration. We developed an application demonstrating the ability of our system, users can discuss PPT slides or watch videos together on a grassland, or they can go to a classroom with a writable board before them. This application shows the unlimited potential of our VR telepresence system.

There is no doubt that our system still has many limitations and many works are needed to improve our current system. Firstly, in our system, we use 3D cartoon models as our VR avatars, which though can provide enjoyable VR experiences, are insufficient to create realistic telepresence experiences. So, more advanced techniques can be applied to generate specific photorealistic VR avatars of users. Secondly, we only use sounds to generate mouth movements for avatars, which can be improved if a back camera is available to make it possible for visual facial tracking method, and if eye-tracking techniques are supported inside the VR HMDs in the future, VR avatars could have more realistic and complex facial expressions. Thirdly, although Noitom motion capture gloves can provide fine-grained real-time motion tracking, it is still inconvenient for users to wear. So, more advanced motion capture system could be used in the further development.

Acknowledgements. This work was supported by Research Grant of Beijing Higher Institution Engineering Research Center and the People Programme (Marie Curie Actions) of the European Union's Seventh Framework Programme (MC-IRSES, grant No. 612627).

References

1. Otsuka, K.: MMSpace: kinetically-augmented telepresence for small group-to-group conversations. In: Virtual Reality (VR) 2016 IEEE, pp. 19–28. IEEE (2016)
2. Maimone, A., Fuchs, H.: Encumbrance-free telepresence system with real-time 3D capture and display using commodity depth cameras. In: International symposium on mixed and augmented reality (2011)
3. Zhang, C., Cai, Q., Chou, P.A., Zhang, Z., Martin-Brualla, R.: Viewport: a distributed, immersive teleconferencing system with infrared dot pattern. IEEE Multimedia **20**(1), 17–27 (2013)
4. Zhu, Z., Martin, R.R., Pepperell, R., Burleigh, A.: 3D modeling and motion parallax for improved videoconferencing. Comput. Visual Media **2**(2), 131–142 (2016)
5. Fairchild, A.J., Campion, S.P., García, A.S., Wolff, R., Fernando, T., Roberts, D.J.: A mixed reality telepresence system for collaborative space operation. IEEE Trans. Circuits Syst. Video Technol. **27**(4), 814–827 (2017)

6. Vasudevan, R., Zhou, Z., Kurillo, G., Lobaton, E., Bajcsy, R., Nahrstedt, K.: Real-time stereo-vision system for 3D teleimmersive collaboration. In: International Conference on Multimedia and Expo (2010)
7. Higuchi, K., Chen, Y., Chou, P. A., Zhang, Z., Liu, Z.: Immerseboard: immersive telepresence experience using a digital whiteboard. In: Proceedings of the 33rd Annual ACM Conference on Human Factors in Computing Systems, pp. 2383–2392. ACM (2015)
8. Ichim, A., Bouaziz, S., Pauly, M.: Dynamic 3D avatar creation from hand-held video input. Int. Conf. Comput. Graph. Interact. Tech. **34**(4), 45:1–45:14 (2015)
9. Cao, C., Weng, Y., Lin, S., Zhou, K.: 3D shape regression for real-time facial animation. ACM Trans. Graph. **32**(4), 41:1–41:10 (2013)
10. Edwards, P., Landreth, C., Fiume, E., Singh, K.: JALI: an animator-centric viseme model for expressive lip synchronization. ACM Trans. Graph. (TOG) **35**(4), 127 (2016)
11. Gao, Z., Yu, Y., Zhou, Y., Du, S.: Leveraging two kinect sensors for accurate full-body motion capture. Sensors **15**(9), 24297–24317 (2015)
12. Fang, B., Sun, F., Liu, H., Guo, D.: A novel data glove using inertial and magnetic sensors for motion capture and robotic arm-hand teleoperation. Ind. Robot Int. J. **44**(2), 155–165 (2017)
13. Bradski, G.: Opencv Libr. Doct. Dobbs J. **25**(11), 120–126 (2000)
14. Xiong, X., De la Torre, F.: Supervised descent method and its applications to face alignment. In: Proceedings of the IEEE conference on computer vision and pattern recognition, pp. 532–539 (2013)
15. Xie, N., Yuan, T., Chen, N., Zhou, X., Wang, Y., Zhang, X.: Rapid DCT-based LipSync generation algorithm for game making. In: SIGGRAPH ASIA 2016 Posters, p. 2. ACM (2016)
16. Hoon, L., Chai, W., Rahman, K.: Development of real-time lip sync animation framework based on viseme human speech. Arch. Des. Res. **27**(4), 19–29 (2014)
17. Aristidou, A., Lasenby, J.: FABRIK: a fast, iterative solver for the inverse kinematics problem. Graph. Models **73**(5), 243–260 (2011)

Author Index

Printed in the United States
By Bookmasters

Printed in the United States
By Bookmasters